There's No Crying
in Newsrooms

There's No Crying in Newsrooms

What Women Have Learned about What It Takes to Lead

Kristin Grady Gilger
and Julia Wallace

ROWMAN & LITTLEFIELD
Lanham · Boulder · New York · London

Published by Rowman & Littlefield
An imprint of The Rowman & Littlefield Publishing Group, Inc.
4501 Forbes Boulevard, Suite 200, Lanham, Maryland 20706
www.rowman.com

6 Tinworth Street, London SE11 5AL, United Kingdom

British Library Cataloguing in Publication Information Available

Library of Congress Cataloging-in-Publication Data

Names: Gilger, Kristin, 1952– author. | Wallace, Julia, 1956- author.
Title: There's no crying in newsrooms : what women have learned about what it takes to lead / Kristin Gilger and Julia Wallace.
Description: Lanham : Rowman & Littlefield, 2019. | Includes bibliographical references and index.
Identifiers: LCCN 2018060886 (print) | LCCN 2019009012 (ebook) | ISBN 9781538121504 (ebook) | ISBN 9781538121498 (cloth : alk. paper)
Subjects: LCSH: Women journalists—United States—Biography. | Women in journalism—United States—History—20th century.
Classification: LCC PN4872 (ebook) | LCC PN4872 .G55 2019 (print) | DDC 070.4082—dc23
LC record available at https://lccn.loc.gov/2018060886

For our daughters—Dana and Lauren, and Emmaline and Eden—who bear the burdens and hold the promise of the next generation of women leaders

Contents

Foreword: We Learn from Each Other's Experiences,
 and We Have Lots to Learn   ix
 Campbell Brown

Acknowledgments   xiii

Introduction: Finishing the Job We Started   1

1   Too Wimpy or Too Bitchy? Finding an Effective Way to Lead   7
2   From Getting Coffee to Running the Place   23
3   Dealing with the Lechers among Us   37
4   The Dollars and Sense of Diversity   55
5   A Short History of the First Female Editor of the *New York Times*   71
6   Changing the News: How Women Shape Culture and Coverage   89
7   What Could Possibly Go Wrong? Balancing Work and Family   105
8   The Unfulfilled Promise of Digital Media   123
9   The Next Generation: What Has Changed and What Has Not   139

List of Interviews   155
Notes   159
Index   171

Foreword

We Learn from Each Other's Experiences, and We Have Lots to Learn

CAMPBELL BROWN

I have a vivid memory of trying to secure my first job in television. I was earning six dollars an hour as a reporter at KSNT in Topeka, Kansas. Back then my hair was big, my wardrobe was uniformly red, and my lipstick matched. One day early on, I remember completely freezing up on camera. Calmly, the female news director slid behind the cameraman, smiled at me, and whispered, "Relax. You're fine."

Years later I would have some male bosses who were more effective at grinding me down. Not her. She felt her job was the opposite.

Every woman I know in the news business has at least one story to tell about another woman who helped show her the way. Sometimes these women supported you and sometimes they gave you a kick in the pants. They may have led in very different ways, but their mere presence, the fact that they—women—were in charge, proved that leadership had more than one gender. They somehow survived, and that meant you could, too.

Over the past four decades, scores of women have walked into newsrooms only to find they were unwanted and unsupported and, still, they worked their way to the top. Until now, their stories have gone largely unreported. *There's No Crying in Newsrooms* captures the voices of these funny, strong, and brash women who learned—often the hard way—exactly what it takes for women to lead, not just in the news business but in any business.

My own story echoes many of their experiences. After Topeka I went to Richmond, then to Baltimore, and then to Washington, DC. But the break that vaulted me to national news came in 2000, when I joined the campaign trail for NBC covering George W. Bush in his presidential race against Al Gore. It's customary that the reporters who cover the winning candidates follow them to Washington. Since Bush won, that set me up for my dream: the

White House beat. I was offered the job, but it wasn't the one I expected: I would be the junior correspondent, filing stories to the morning shows, while my counterpart had the senior White House correspondent role and filed for *Nightly News*.

I wasn't thrilled about this division, but I also wasn't about to let it stand between me and the White House beat. That night I went out with some women reporters I knew from the campaign trail and told them about the offer. Their response was universal: I shouldn't play a subservient role to my male counterpart. The next day, my agent took my demand to NBC and, after some jousting, the network agreed to a co-equal split.

I learned that if I was going to succeed within the male power structure that sustains most newsrooms, it would take *some* nerve. Men, then as now, make most of the decisions felt through the ranks. They drive most news coverage and determine who occupy the prime jobs. It shouldn't surprise anyone that men thrive more easily in this environment. It was built with them in mind.

Challenging institutional habits means pushing back, willfully so. Too often women are subtly coaxed toward "female" roles and steered clear of those that aren't. Politics is masculine; lifestyle news is feminine. Aggressive questioning? Masculine. Engaging smiles? Feminine. In broadcasting it can be even worse because the audience has grown accustomed to these stereotypes and reinforces them.

I remember at times feeling derailed by other people's ambitions for me. Once I was assigned a coach to help sand my edges so I would come off as less combative. The idea was to mold me into morning show material. Turns out this wasn't such a good idea. One day during my "training," a young boy was my guest on *Today*, and I proceeded to grill him like he was under indictment. I soon returned to hard news.

I was back in my natural habitat, but still, hard news is no cakewalk. In 2008, I was a moderator for the Democratic presidential debate between Hillary Clinton and Barack Obama. I had had my first son, Eli, just eight weeks earlier. I was breastfeeding, and while the baby was home with my husband, I still needed to pump. Since the debate was three hours long and I couldn't exactly dash off in the middle, I needed to do it in the minutes right before the debate began. The only private space I could find was a closet off the make-up room. So, while my co-moderators were doing their last-minute prep, I was sitting on a closet floor pumping milk—truly an experience unique to the working mom.

Often the obstacles women face are subtle. No man shut me in a closet right before the debate. It's just one of the realities that women deal with, especially women in demanding fields like journalism. Staying home with a sick child, taking maternity leave, asking to return with limited work travel—the repercussions rarely announce themselves. Their impact on your career might at first be inscrutable, only becoming visible much later on.

If there is one lesson that I can add to the many profound lessons this book offers, it is this: Focus on what's best for you and then throw yourself at it. And remember that the cause of women in newsrooms will take on urgency only if we make it happen—together.

*   *   *

Campbell Brown is head of global news partnerships at Facebook and formerly was a reporter and anchor at CNN and NBC.

Acknowledgments

This book would not have been possible without all of the brave and brilliant women who have made journalism a better profession. Nearly one hundred of them spoke to us for this book, willingly sharing both their successes and their mistakes and talking movingly about what it's like to lead as a woman. They, as well as the more than a dozen men we interviewed, are listed at the end of this book, and we are forever grateful to them for their generosity.

A special thanks to Jill Abramson, Monika Bauerlein, Melissa Bell, Clara Jeffery, Wanda Lloyd, Marcy McGinnis, Mi-Ai Parrish, and Sandy Rowe for spending hours and hours with us and welcoming us into their workplaces, their homes, and their lives.

We want to thank our amazing colleagues at the Walter Cronkite School of Journalism and Mass Communication at Arizona State University. Dean Christopher Callahan has been supportive every step of the way, encouraging us to pursue this idea, giving us the time to do it, reading chapters, and helping in numerous other ways. He is an inspirational leader, and we feel fortunate that he is in our lives. Many other Cronkite colleagues contributed editing, brainstorming, encouragement, and their creative talents. They include Rebecca Blatt, Monica Chadha, Sarah Cohen, Linda Davis, Leonard Downie Jr., Christia Gibbons, Venita Hawthorne James, Mi-Ai Parrish, Fernanda Santos, Jean Sheeley, Amy Silverman, Terry Green Sterling, and John West.

We also are grateful to friends and family members who connected us to key people and who provided support and editing help throughout the process. Thanks especially to Dana and Brandon Bauer, Brenda Campbell, Caroline Campbell Rogers, Don Campbell, Eden Campbell, Emmaline

xiv   *Acknowledgments*

Campbell, Gary Gilger, Patrick Gilger, Karen Kurtz, Alex Novet, Lauren and Jesse Teer, Charles Wallace, and Rob Yarin.

As we worked, we kept in mind the many wonderful students at the Cronkite School and how women of our generation might help them as they begin to craft their futures. We asked several students and recent alumni for their feedback and their help with fact-checking and copy editing. Grace Clark, Yael Grauer, Ashley Mackey, Adrienne St. Clair, and Rebekah Zemansky all give us hope for the future.

This book would not have been possible without the support of Elizabeth Swayze at Rowman & Littlefield. From the beginning, she understood our vision and believed in it. Her guidance, and that of Megan Manzano, made writing a book almost fun.

Both of us have benefited from strong female leaders who have guided our careers. For Julia, those mentors include Sandy Rowe, her first female editor; Amy Eisman, who encouraged her to think beyond her wildest dreams; Nancy Monaghan, who gave her a much-needed kick in the pants when it counted; Karen Jurgensen, who taught her about servant leadership; Sara Bentley, who gave her a chance when she most needed it; and Pam Johnson, who was a visionary leader decades ahead of her time.

It was Sister John Marie who first convinced Kristin, back in the sixth grade, that a girl could lead. Years later, at the University of Nebraska, Wilma Crumley proved it through her own quiet example. Joanne Heisler showed Kristin that kindness and leadership are not opposites, and Mary Schier taught her that words matter. And then there was Julia, who walked into the *Statesman Journal* newspaper in Oregon and turned the place upside down—in a good way—and later brought her to Phoenix so they could work together again.

There are men who have made a difference to us as well. Sometimes they acted as linemen, blocking the worst blows, and sometimes they offered quiet support that boosted our confidence.

For Julia, they include Ron Martin, who always gave great advice that she didn't listen to often enough; Mark Nadler, who guided her through her first big job as an editor; John Oppedahl, who taught her the importance of bravery; Doug Franklin and Jay Smith, who supported her through difficult times; James Mallory, who was an amazing partner and ally; Jim Kennedy, who defended her work at the *Atlanta Journal-Constitution* in ways she wasn't even aware of at the time; and Alex Taylor, who demonstrated the incredible power of humility.

Kristin has had the great gift of working for two of journalism's most inspirational leaders: Jim Amoss, who led the *Times-Picayune*, in New Orleans, through the paper's most formative and most trying years; and Christopher

Callahan, who truly possesses superhuman powers of energy and understanding that have buoyed her for the past fifteen years.

We also want to thank our husbands for their support during the writing of this book. They barely complained about the late nights, lost weekends, and endless conversations about the perfect title.

To Don: Ever since that fried chicken picnic, you have been that rock of support, that voice in my head. On this project, as on every one before, you gave me room to be me but knew when to step in when "me" needed a bit of moderating and editing.

To Gary: You are the one person I know who never equivocates, who never holds back. Even when you don't understand what I'm doing or why, you're all in. That's what makes a marriage work, and it's not a bad foundation for a career either.

Introduction

Finishing the Job We Started

*W*hen we began thinking about writing on women and leadership, we made a list of all the female news leaders we wanted to interview. It was a very long list, and it had some pretty big names: Jill Abramson, the first and only female editor of the *New York Times*; CNN correspondent Christiane Amanpour; television executive Kate O'Brian; digital mogul Arianna Huffington; Vox publisher Melissa Bell; and dozens more. We wanted to hear their stories. We wanted to know how they had managed to make it to the top in a media industry that has been resistant if not downright hostile to women from the start. Did they have to act like men to get ahead? Were they sexually harassed? Did their marriages fall apart? Did their children resent them? Did they make a difference?

These are not the kinds of questions you typically pose to people with whom you have only a passing acquaintance—or no acquaintance at all—and we were not at all sure anyone would want to answer them. But we have spent our careers as journalists and journalism educators and we're used to asking uncomfortable questions, so we began sending emails and making phone calls.

To our surprise, nearly every single one of the women leaders we contacted not only agreed to talk to us but they couldn't wait to talk to us. And once they started talking, it was difficult to get them to stop. Our interviews, conducted in person and on the phone, often stretched into hours and sometimes days and more often than not ended with suggestions of yet other women who had something important to say—women we shouldn't overlook. In the end, we conducted nearly one hundred interviews with women who have changed American journalism over the past forty years and who continue to shape news as we know it.

1

For the most part, we focused on the women behind the scenes rather than those in front of the camera: women who run control rooms, newsrooms, and boardrooms of established and emerging media powerhouses. They are the ones responsible for managing the machinery that is the American news business, and their decisions help shape what millions of Americans watch and read every day.

Power—how to get it, use it, and hold onto it—is a fascinating subject in any industry, but it is especially so in the rambunctious world of news media, in which personalities are large, the stakes are high, and mistakes are all too visible. The women who set out to make this world their own found themselves in the cultural crosshairs of an America still exceedingly ambivalent about how much authority, if any, should be ceded to them. And what they learned, often the hard way, holds powerful lessons for women not just in journalism but in any profession in which they are still regarded as sexual prey, they still make less than men, and the tone of their voices and their looks still matter.

In journalism, as in other professions, women appear to be slipping. The number of women heading Fortune 500 companies peaked at thirty-two in 2017 and then slid to twenty-four in 2018, according to *Fortune* magazine, largely the result of women leaving (or being ousted from) their positions. The female CEOs who no longer occupied corner offices in 2018 included Meg Whitman of Hewlett Packard, Denise Morrison of Campbell Soup, and Marissa Mayer of Yahoo.[1]

At newspapers, women seemed to hit a peak in the late 1990s and early 2000s. In 2004, seven women held the top editor jobs at the twenty-five largest circulation daily newspapers in the U.S.[2] In 2017, the latest year for which figures are available, there were five, and only one of those, Deborah Henley, editor and vice president at *Newsday*, headed a top ten newspaper.[3] (The number of women leading a top ten circulation newspaper increased to two in 2018, when Nicole Carroll was appointed editor in chief of *USA Today*.)

Nor are many women poised to move into top news jobs. The number of women in newspaper leadership positions has barely budged in twenty years. Women accounted for 38.9 percent of all newsroom supervisors in 2017, according to the American Society of News Editors' annual newspaper diversity survey.[4] The number in 1998, the first year ASNE began tracking women, was 33.8 percent.[5]

Women aren't doing much better in television and radio. According to a 2018 Radio Television Digital News Association report, women made up just 22 percent of general managers at the nation's radio stations, 34 percent of TV news directors, and fewer than 20 percent of general managers, the top broadcast management jobs.[6] And only one woman—Judy Woodruff at PBS—regularly anchored a network newscast.

When women began entering journalism in significant numbers fifty years ago, the hope was that progress would be much faster. At least that was the hope of some. A fair number of men had a different view, especially as women began to demand equal pay and equal work. Tom Collins of *Newsday*, who wrote a widely syndicated column about media, spoke for these men in the 1975 bulletin of the almost all male American Society of Newspaper Editors. "It is my solemn and onerous duty to report that it looks as if the good times are over," Collins wrote. "The day is coming, if it's not already here, when it may be impossible for a hiring editor to look at a chick just out of journalism school and only see a pair of boobs."[7]

In fact, ASNE, now known as the American Society of News Editors as a nod to the rise of digital news products, was where the tensions between the sexes played out in subtle and not so subtle ways. In 1973, hundreds of editors gathered at the Shoreham Hotel in Washington, DC, for what may be one of the most colorful debates in the annals of journalism. The theme of the conference was "Problems in Journalism," and an entire morning was devoted to the particular problem of women in newsrooms. The women spoke first and in a fury about being thrown out, felt up, passed over, ignored, and humiliated, and they illustrated their points with a skit that was alternately hilarious and devastating. In one exchange, a male city editor tells a woman she isn't management material because she has periods. The woman, referred to as a "newshen" in the script, replies: "Yes, Nick, yes. Women have periods. They have commas; they have semicolons; some of them even have complete sentences."

Afterward, the men of ASNE, clearly rattled, debated the women on everything from hiring and promotion to the wisdom of sending female reporters out after dark. When nationally syndicated columnist Ellen Goodman argued that restricting women's assignments to daytime hours was a ploy to keep them out of the business, Tom Eastham, then executive editor of the *San Francisco Examiner*, shot back, "You mean you don't mind getting raped on the way to work?"[8]

Goodman went on to win a Pulitzer Prize in Commentary, and Eastham, in true ironic fashion, became press secretary to San Francisco's first female mayor, Dianne Feinstein, now a U.S. senator and one of Congress's most outspoken feminists.[9]

Goodman began her career as a researcher at *Newsweek* magazine in 1963, part of a pool of low-paid women who clipped newspaper stories, checked facts, and backgrounded stories for the male reporters. She wanted to be a writer but, with one exception, there were no women writers at *Newsweek*, so she left, along with other such talented women as Nora Ephron and Jane Bryant Quinn.[10]

A few years later, in 1970, the women of *Newsweek* sued over gender discrimination and won. The landmark case triggered a string of similar lawsuits at other news organizations, including the *New York Times*, the *Detroit News*, and the Associated Press. It was a heady time for women in journalism. Newsrooms that had been closed to women or that hired women in only the lowliest jobs were forced open, and, for the first time, women in large numbers saw the possibility of advancement, of building real careers as reporters and editors and producers—and perhaps even as executives.

And advance they did. Women now can be found at almost every size and every level of news organization. They edit national publications like *National Geographic* and influential media start-ups like Vox; they're senior managers at TV networks; and they run dozens of local television stations and hundreds of small- and medium-sized newspapers. But they are still the exception.

In 2010, three young women working at *Newsweek* discovered the history of their own magazine when they stumbled on a story about the 1970 lawsuit that challenged the notion that women couldn't be writers. They were fascinated, not just because these women, who could have been their grandmothers, had paved the way for them but because they recognized so much that seemed vaguely familiar. "In countless small ways, each of us has felt frustrated over the years, as if something was amiss," they wrote in an article for *Newsweek*.[11] Men still dominated the masthead, were assigned the vast majority of cover stories, and got promoted more quickly than women.

But as part of a generation that had grown up believing the gender wars had been won, "we had neither the language to describe it nor the confidence to call it what it was," they wrote.[12] Instead, like many women, they seemed to blame themselves for their lack of progress. Maybe they just weren't good enough. Maybe what they suspected to be sexism wasn't sexist at all. Maybe they were just plain crazy.

If the #MeToo movement has accomplished anything, it is to explode this narrative of self-doubt. Women in the media increasingly are speaking up about sexual harassment in the workplace, with the result that such men as Roger Ailes and Charlie Rose and Matt Lauer and Mark Halperin and Michael Oreskes and Leslie Moonves and Roy Price have been toppled like so many bowling pins. (In another satisfyingly ironic twist, Price, the former head of Amazon Studios who was forced out of Amazon in the wake of sexual harassment charges, is the same man who reportedly killed the television series *Good Girls Revolt* about the historic struggle for equity at *Newsweek*.[13])

No matter how many more men are exposed, the avalanche of these cases is evidence both of how much has changed and how much has not. Navigating the workplace, perhaps especially in media, is in many ways more confusing and more challenging for women than ever before. Which is where we come in.

We were part of a wave of young people who flooded journalism schools in the post-Watergate, post-Vietnam, post–civil rights era. We had the backing of new laws that prohibited discrimination and, as baby boomers, we had the certitude that comes with numbers. We entered the workforce with the Enjoli perfume ad ringing in our heads: "I can bring home the bacon, fry it up in a pan, and never, never, never let you forget you're a man, 'cause I'm a woman." We knew it was a silly jingle, but it seeped into our heads along with all the other assurances that we could be and do whatever we wanted.

Several decades and many frying pans later, it occurred to us that even if we didn't accomplish everything we had planned to do, we did learn an awful lot we hadn't planned on that could be helpful to women coming up in the news business today. And we were pretty sure there were a lot of other women who felt the same way. Maybe, we thought, someone should ask them about it.

There are several other reasons we wanted to explore the ways gender and leadership play out in news organizations. We love newsrooms and we care about what happens to them, and we're convinced that journalism (and consequently our country) will be stronger if women share power and influence in equal measure with men. We teach journalism in a school filled with smart, ambitious young women who inspire us every day. We wish for them a world in which they really can be everything they want to be.

And, finally, more than anything, we love our daughters, who are just beginning to understand how tenuous and troubling the workplace can be. We want to spare them the same old battles and speed them on their way. We want them to finish the job we started.

Too Wimpy or Too Bitchy?

Finding an Effective Way to Lead

One of the things I've learned the hard way is that you actually have to lead by being who you really are. And you can't fake who you are.

—Margaret Low

Cynthia Hudson, the head of CNN en Español, describes herself as having "Cuban passion in my bloodstream." She realized that when she got excited about something, she could come across as loud and angry. Hudson learned to temper her delivery to her audience. "I'm not abrasive," she said, "but sometimes my style comes across as dominant, so I pull back."

*

During her long career, Susan Lyne ran the entertainment division of ABC, managed Martha Stewart's empire while Stewart was in prison, and served as CEO of the company that spawned Gilt, an enormously popular online shopping website. She learned to navigate all-male corporate hierarchies by being the best-prepared person in the room. She not only mastered whatever issue was up for discussion but she also became a student of those around her. "You have to understand who could cause trouble for you, who your natural allies are, and how you can get what you need," she said.

*

Jessica Lessin founded a technology news company, The Information, after a successful career covering technology at the Wall Street Journal. *Leading her own staff, she discovered, meant that she was visible in a way she never had been before. If she was having a bad day in the office, everyone else ended up having a bad day too. She now tries to be careful about the impression she makes. "I tend to show how I'm feeling, and that's not a great trait in a manager," she said. "I want to make sure that I'm communicating what I want deliberately rather than just reacting to the moment."*

*

Kim Guthrie, president of Cox Media Group, can drink, swear, and go toe-to-toe with almost anyone. She's blunt and outgoing, and she effortlessly dominates a room. "I'm authentic," she said. "But sometimes my big mouth gets me into trouble." While she was comfortable with her style, Guthrie knew she wasn't exactly winning people over, so she decided to make a deliberate effort to "lead from the back of the boat." Leadership, she said, is a little like running for office—you have to focus on your people and win them over one by one.

*   *   *

*E*very one of these women rose to top leadership positions in a news organization before they had really figured out what kind of leader they were—or what kind of leader they wanted to be. Some, by instinct or personality, were collegial, accommodating, bossy, motherly, outgoing, reserved, or a mix of comparable traits. They quickly learned that they could be some of these things some of the time but none of these things all of the time. They found themselves running up against their company's and society's expectations of what a female leader looks like and acts like.

Perhaps nothing captures that dilemma better than an old riddle, which goes something like this: A father and son have a car accident. The father is killed and the boy is badly hurt. When the boy is wheeled into the operating room, the surgeon says, "I can't do this surgery because this boy is my son." How is this possible?

This brainteaser is surprisingly difficult for most people to solve. In one study, children came up with exceptionally creative answers: Maybe the surgeon was a robot or a ghost, they suggested, or perhaps the father didn't really die (and presumably was ready to operate shortly after being in an accident). Respondents were three times more likely to say the boy had gay parents than to come up with the correct answer: The surgeon is the boy's mother.[1]

The riddle illustrates what researchers and organizational psychologists have repeatedly documented: When people picture a leader, they picture a man. And if they are asked to actually draw a picture of a leader, they almost invariably draw a man.[2]

Men, to revisit familiar stereotypes, are supposed to be tough, analytical, confident, and competent, the common characteristics ascribed to leaders. Women, on the other hand, are expected to be compassionate, helpful, collegial, and enthusiastic, which may be attributes of leadership but not the ones that make it to the top of the list.[3]

Women who violate those norms—adopting "male" styles in order to get ahead—end up in a double bind. If they're good at their jobs—if they're competent and decisive and tough—they may get promoted, but they will be judged harshly. Their colleagues and employees will think them less likable, and their bosses will evaluate them more severely. Even when they do rack up accomplishments, their successes are likely to be attributed to luck rather than competence.[4]

New York University's Madeline Heilman put it this way in an article for the *Journal of Social Issues*: "Women, quite simply, are not supposed to excel at jobs and tasks that are designated as male in our culture. [If they do,] they are personally derogated, and they are disliked."[5]

In 2007, women who held high-level positions in the public, private, and nonprofit sectors came together to discuss their work experiences as part of a leadership project conducted by Leadership in Action at New York University's Robert F. Wagner Graduate School of Public Service and The White House Project, a nonprofit organization that promoted women's leadership. The women spoke about how impossible it was to get leadership "right," no matter what kind of style they employed. They said they felt confined to a "narrow band" of actions—somewhere between being "too wimpy or too bitchy."[6]

Behavioral psychologists caution that there is no one management style inherent to men or women. Some men are more feminine and some women more masculine in their styles. But they note that while men don't often see a need to change how they act, many women soften their approaches, knowing how poorly people respond to "bossy" women. The women who don't pay a price.[7]

* * *

In her seminal book about the history of women in news, Kay Mills tells the story of Agnes Underwood, who in 1947 became one of the first female city editors of a major American newspaper. Aggie, as she was called, cut her teeth as a crime reporter for the *Los Angeles Herald-Express*, writing about prostitution, kidnappings, murders, and mayhem of all sorts. Later, as city editor, she reportedly kept a baseball bat on top of her desk and a gun loaded with blanks in a drawer. If things got too quiet in the newsroom, she would pull out the gun and fire it at the ceiling. After retiring, Underwood told an interviewer, "I had to be tough and hard or those men would have taken advantage of me and I would never have gotten any work out of them."[8]

Underwood may have been unusual for the baseball bat and gun, but journalism is filled with women who made their mark in newsrooms by being as tough, if not tougher, than the guys.

Newsrooms in Underwood's day were dingy, smoky places populated by male reporters who were scruffy and profane and male editors who were loud and possibly a little drunk. Women who braved such places either hid in the features department or learned to smoke, drink, and swear.

By the 1970s, newspaper newsrooms had become somewhat more sanitized (if you don't take into account the profanity and smoking), and women were infiltrating departments beyond features. Business and sports remained largely male enclaves, but women were covering cops, courts, and city hall and were being promoted to midlevel editing positions on city desks and copy desks at small- and medium-sized newspapers all over the country. At local television stations, they were co-anchoring newscasts and delivering the weather.

To a large extent, the women entering newsrooms in the 1970s and 1980s adopted the management styles that worked for the men around them. They were intent on "fitting in and getting along," observed Vivian Schiller, who served as president and CEO of NPR and also was an executive at NBC News and the head of the *New York Times* website at various times in her career. She said women like her who were coming up in the news business in the 1980s won their seats at the table the hard way, and they weren't about to risk standing out. "Most women of our generation didn't consider themselves 'feminists,' and the notion of calling out 'the patriarchy' would have been a professional death sentence," she said.

Charlotte Hall was often the only woman at the table when she took over as managing editor of *Newsday* in 1981. "It was management by argument," she said. "It was very difficult to get a word in edgewise. You had to interrupt, and you had to yell and scream." She remembers a supervisor once pulling her aside and telling her, "You know, you have a sort of schoolmarmish way of acting," so she learned to interrupt and talk over people (although she never quite got the hang of yelling). "That's what we all thought—that we had to play like a man to succeed," she said.

But for these women, playing like a man also meant losing—or hiding—an authentic part of themselves—the part that wanted to be both strong and nice. Janet Coats, who was top editor at both the *Sarasota Herald-Tribune* and the *Tampa Tribune* in Florida, said women, especially Southern women like her, have two options: They can be either the willful and formidable Scarlett O'Hara or the dutiful and saccharine Melanie Wilkes of *Gone with the Wind* fame. As Coats put it, "You're either a stone-cold bitch or you're waiting for Ashley to come home from the war. The perception of me was more in the Melanie category, but I'm secretly Scarlett."

Christiane Amanpour thinks it's about time women stop apologizing for their Scarlett-like tendencies. "Look, I think that women have been playing nice for an awfully long time, playing the game, climbing the ladder, being patient, accepting the tidbits and morsels that are handed out," she said. "I think that we have to start kicking the door down."

Amanpour is easily one of the most recognizable women in journalism and possibly the most formidable. She started as a desk assistant at CNN in 1983 and by 1990 had become one of a handful of female foreign correspondents working in television. One of her first assignments was covering Saddam Hussein's invasion of Kuwait. CNN had planned to send an all-male crew to cover the conflict, but when the crew couldn't get there in time, Amanpour, who was based in London and had been begging for the assignment, went instead. She has since covered wars and conflicts around the world, earning a reputation as fearless, outspoken, and uncompromising both as a journalist and as a woman doing the kind of news coverage that is still largely the domain of white men.

"I cannot tell you the number of times people have either called me a bitch, thought I was a bitch, or called me bossy or thought I was bossy or called me a control freak or thought I was a control freak just because I was good at my job," she said. "And I didn't shut up."

Samuel Burke, who was a field producer for Amanpour and traveled with her to cover stories in the Mideast, said people often are intimidated by her, at least initially. He remembers the first time he met her in the CNN newsroom. "She comes in with her big British accent and starts on about whatever she saw in the *New York Times* or someplace else that morning, and she makes her proclamation about the day's news, for better or worse. Then she's down to business. She doesn't mess around."

Burke, who went on to be a business and technology news correspondent for CNN and anchors programs on both CNN International and CNN en Español, said Amanpour can be loud, demanding, and intense—exactly like her male counterparts. "I've watched a male anchor or a male correspondent do the same exact thing and get no flak for it," he said. "I think they call her a bitch just because they've never seen a woman like that before, a woman who acts like a man in the workplace. And you know, there's no male equivalent for that word. There is no single word that could crystallize more the difference between how women and men are treated in the workplace."

Burke said he once observed Amanpour tell another female anchor to cover up her cleavage. She told the woman, "You're setting back all of us who don't want to be judged that way." The woman started telling Amanpour that she was only doing what she had to do to keep her contract, to feed her family, and then she added, "I'm not as tough as you are or as strong as you are." Amanpour didn't flinch, according to Burke. She replied, "Well, you have to be, or you're the weakest link in the chain for all of the women around you."

Burke said Amanpour has paved the way for many women, especially foreign correspondents, at CNN. She'll tell women who are working their way up the ladder, "Do not let a man tell you that you cannot do that."

After PBS canceled distribution of Charlie Rose's public affairs program in the wake of multiple sexual harassment accusations, the network named Amanpour to take his place—a development that Burke calls a "karma moment" for television if there ever was one. The irony is not lost on Amanpour. Rose, she said, allegedly tried to take advantage of young women who were trying to do exactly what she has long urged them to do and what she herself has done—"climb the ladder, knock the doors down, work hard, and get into positions of power."

Once there, she doesn't think women have to act tough. That's the wrong word, she said. "*Tough* is like bossy. It's a crap word. But you do have to act confident, convincing, competent. You have to be competent and convinced of your abilities." She also believes in being polite, convivial, and collegial. "I do believe in trying to work together," she said. "And only when it doesn't work, then you have to knock some heads together."

*   *   *

Diane McFarlin has knocked many heads together during her forty-year career as an editor, publisher, and now dean of the University of Florida College of Journalism and Communications. But it's possible that the people whose heads were being knocked together were not entirely aware it was happening.

McFarlin is a fifth-generation Floridian whose father ran a vintage hotel in Lake Wales, a tiny town smack in the center of the Florida peninsula. Her mother was very much a Southern lady, soft-spoken and gracious but with a will of cast iron, and she made sure her only child understood the value of manners. She also made sure McFarlin knew she could aspire to be or do anything she wanted.

One summer, a friend of her father's, who was the publisher of the *Lake Wales Daily Highlander*, showed the teenaged McFarlin around his newsroom. When she seemed interested, he handed her a press release and said, "Rewrite it." Finally, satisfied with her effort, he asked if she wanted to cover a meeting at city hall. McFarlin could hardly believe her luck.

After getting her journalism degree from the University of Florida, she began reporting for Florida's *Sarasota Journal,* the afternoon "sister" paper to the *Sarasota Herald-Tribune.* She would spend most of her career at the latter paper, rising to become executive editor and then president and publisher.

McFarlin was only twenty-four when she was put in charge of the city desk at the *Journal,* and, while she wasn't exactly sure how to go about leading a newsroom, she did her best to look the part—business suits, shoulder pads, pumps, high necklines, and "hair like a helmet." She also worked hard to lose her Southern accent because she thought she would sound smarter without it.

Janet Coats, who worked as McFarlin's number two at the *Sarasota Herald-Tribune,* described her former boss as someone who spoke in perfect paragraphs, never had a hair out of place, and never, ever, raised her voice. "Diane didn't need to yell," Coats said. "Diane has an eyebrow arch." Her staff called it the "scary eyebrow."

"One time she came into my office with something circled in blue pen and that arched eyebrow," Coats said. "She said something like, 'I'm disappointed this happened on your watch.' . . . I went and sat in my car and cried. She was someone you didn't want to disappoint."

McFarlin said she has worked with women who think the only way to succeed is to act as masculine as possible. That made sense for earlier generations of women who blazed trails in newsrooms, she said, but she doesn't think the "tough broad routine" works any longer, and she is certain it would never have worked for her.

By the time she was running a newspaper, employees were beginning to demand a different kind of management—one that was less about barking orders and more about nurturing individual talent. That kind of style comes more naturally to women, she said, but it's not the only way to lead.

As women, she said, "we have to know ourselves and be true to ourselves and not try to adapt our natural instincts or strengths just because we think there's some kind of mold we have to fit into."

* * *

Susan Goldberg was a girl in a hurry.

Between her junior and senior years of college, she landed a reporting internship at the *Seattle Post-Intelligencer.* As far as Goldberg was concerned, it was eight weeks of pure fun, and she must have done well enough because at the end of the summer her editor came up to her and said, "Kid, why don't you stay?" Goldberg decided that college could wait.

One day she was covering a visit to Seattle by Coleman Young, the first African-American mayor of Detroit. This was in the pre-internet days, and Young made some comments about his home city that he probably wouldn't have made had he thought they would get into the Detroit papers. Goldberg saw an opportunity. She pitched the story to the *Detroit Free Press*, and after it ran on the front page, she called the editor and said, "Why don't you hire me?'

"I was very pushy about it," Goldberg said. She was pushy about a lot of things early in her career, to the point that "I was maybe not as nice as I should have been," she said. It took time and personal tragedy for her to develop a leadership style that was softer without losing its edge.

In the space of three years, Goldberg lost the three people who mattered most to her—her mother, her father, and her husband. She was thirty-nine years old when her husband died of a cancer that had started years earlier as a melanoma behind his eye. She took a leave from her job as deputy managing editor at *USA Today* to care for him; he died five months later. She then did what everyone tells you not to do after the death of a loved one: She uprooted her life. She left her job, her house, and her friends in Washington, DC, and moved to San Jose, California, to take over as the managing editor of that city's newspaper.

Goldberg went on to become the first female editor of the *San Jose Mercury News*, the first female editor of the *Cleveland Plain Dealer*, and the first female editor in the 130-year history of *National Geographic* magazine, a position she assumed in 2014.

During more than thirty years in the news business, she has developed a persona that is part *Vogue* magazine and part *Detroit Free Press*—elegant on the outside and tough as nails on the inside. She wears her clothes like armor—silk blouses, tailored jackets, chunky jewelry, high heels, and the occasional leather skirt—and she manages her staff with equal parts steel and sympathy.

At *National Geographic*, she has earned a reputation as being fearless. She shepherded and vigorously defended a controversial 2017 edition about gender that featured a transgender girl on the cover, and another edition in 2018 that explored the subject of race. For the latter, Goldberg wrote an acknowledgment of the magazine's decades of coverage that largely ignored people of color who lived in the United States while "picturing 'natives' elsewhere as exotics, famously and frequently unclothed, happy hunters, noble savages—every type of cliché."[9]

Goldberg doesn't back down when she feels strongly about something, and she thinks her straightforward approach has generally served her well. "To have a reputation as a sort of no-bullshit person is a pretty good thing," she said, although she has learned to handle things—and people—more delicately over time.

She doesn't think she was ever "a terrible jerk" as a boss, but the loss of her husband made her more empathetic. "When something terrible happens to you, people come to you and tell you *their* terrible stories—about parents or children or spouses—and it just made me realize that I had not been paying as much attention as I maybe should have," she said. "I'm more attuned now, and I watch for it, if somebody is in trouble. I listen better. If someone isn't doing well in their job, I think maybe it's not about [incompetence or laziness]. Maybe there is another reason."

At *National Geographic*, Goldberg works hard to find the sweet spot between being too pushy and being too soft. All women, she said, have to be mindful of this limited band of behavior or risk almost certain failure.

"There are so many more ways for men to be a leader, so many more paths of acceptable behavior for men," she said. "And for women, there's a much narrower range, because if you're too nice you'll get run over, and certainly being too tough does not work at all because then you are the *b*-word, and that's a real show-stopper."

Although she has learned to operate within those margins, Goldberg still finds it infuriating that women are expected to be nice, but not too nice, that they're told to speak up, but not too loudly, and that to be successful they must take charge, but not in a bossy way.

It's altogether too easy, she said, "to fail leading while female."

*   *   *

Men who adopt feminine management styles seem to do just fine, giving them more latitude to lead in different ways depending upon the circumstance. Women, on the other hand, must strike a balance between assertiveness and cooperation, with less of a range in which to experiment, in order to be effective. But how to strike that balance?

Some research suggests that confidence is part of the answer. In an article in the *Harvard Business Review*, Leslie Pratch, a clinical psychologist and author of the book *Looks Good on Paper?*, writes that women who exhibit high self-esteem and high self-confidence are more likely to be seen as effective leaders. Her research indicates that to overcome the limitations on their leadership styles, women "must be more self-confident, task-focused and open to the perception of frustration and difficulty than their male counterparts." In other words, they have to be able to cope with difficult situations in an open and confident manner.[10]

Confidence alone, of course, is not enough. Women also have to excel at the task at hand and be "pro-social," acting in a way that communicates they care about others in the workplace.[11] But confidence, or at least the *appearance* of confidence, may be one way that women can gain influence.

Two broadcast journalists, Claire Shipman and Katty Kay, said they were surprised when researching their book, *The Confidence Code: The Science and Art of Self Assurance*, to discover how much accomplished women doubted themselves. In an article for the *Atlantic* magazine, they call it a "vast confidence gap that separates the sexes. Compared with men, women do not consider themselves ready for promotions, they predict they'll do worse on tests, and they generally underestimate their abilities." Men have doubts, too, they wrote, "but they don't let their doubts stop them as often as women do."[12]

When Jan Leach was being recruited for the managing editor post at the *Cincinnati Enquirer* back in 1993, her first thought was, "Really? They want me?" She had a similar reaction twenty-one years later when she won the distinguished teaching award at Kent State University, where she is now an associate professor of journalism. "The whole time I kept thinking, they're going to figure out it [the award] belongs to someone else," she said. "I still wonder when they're going to figure out I'm not as good as they think I am." Throughout her career, including a five-year stint as editor of the *Akron Beacon Journal* in Ohio, Leach often felt these kinds of doubts. She would think, "Maybe I'm not ready; maybe it shouldn't be me; maybe it should be someone who has done more."

Hudson, the head of CNN en Español, worries all the time about how she is perceived as a leader. "You don't want to look like a pushover, and you don't want to look like a bitch, and men don't have to worry about that," she said. "If a man has a bad day, he has a bad day and the next day no one cares about it. If a woman has a meltdown, well, we're more self-conscious about how people perceive us, and we need to be. You have to prove you're worthy of the position, that you're up to the task, that you're dedicated, and that nothing will get in the way."

Even Arianna Huffington, best known as a founder of the Huffington Post, has struggled with this kind of self-doubt. "We all live with that voice, but the times it comes out the most is when we're tired, stressed and run down," she said in an email interview. "That's when we're most likely to doubt ourselves, most likely to react emotionally, and when our perceptions are at their shakiest." She said women face far too many critics to add *self*-criticism to the mix. Her advice is to ignore the voice she calls "the obnoxious roommate living in our heads—that voice that feeds on putting us down and strengthening our insecurities and doubts."

Over and over in interviews, women news leaders voiced feelings of uncertainty. Despite their accomplishments, many felt they could never stop proving they were worthy of their positions. They described feeling as if they had never truly arrived, questioned whether someone else could do the job better, and mentally steeled themselves to the possibility of getting tossed at any moment. But they also pointed out that self-doubt isn't necessarily a bad thing in a leader, as long as it doesn't paralyze you. "I have self-doubts," said Schiller, the former president of NPR. "But I don't get intimidated."

Executives can either operate from a position of strength or a position of weakness, said Pat Fili-Krushel, who had leading roles at the NBCUniversal News Group, Time Warner Inc., and the ABC Television Network. She advises women to figure out their strengths and then act with confidence. She said she was once offered a promotion that would require her to negotiate company contracts, but she knew she would be a very different kind of negotiator than her boss, who was "a renowned yeller and screamer," so she told him she would take the job on one condition. "I said to him, 'I am not going to negotiate in your style, but that doesn't mean my style won't be effective.'" She always told herself, "So what if they get rid of me? I'll find something else. I'm not afraid."

For Margaret Low, vice president of the *Atlantic* and president of the company's event sector, "AtlanticLive," it all boils down to being authentic. "I think there are so many layers to leadership, and one of the myths is that one person can embody twelve things," she said. "It's just not the case. One of the things I've learned the hard way is that you actually have to lead by being who you really are. And you can't fake who you are.

"It's classic to think that women have all the soft skills, but we're as different from one another as men are. I know my leadership style is, in part, very female. It's empathetic at some level, but I had to make really hard decisions, and I had to make them all the time. That's not exclusive to women; it's exclusive to good leadership. And the qualities that make women great leaders are the qualities that make great leaders."

*   *   *

ADVICE FOR WOMEN LEADERS

Kristin Gilger

When I think about the culture of newsrooms, I think about the line in the movie *A League of Their Own*. Jimmy Duggan, the reluctant women's baseball coach played by Tom Hanks, calls over one of his players during a game and reams her out for a bad play. When she starts crying, he says, "Are you crying? Are you crying? There's no crying! *There's no crying in baseball!*"

I tell my students there's no crying in newsrooms, either, especially if they want to be seen as leaders or potential leaders. The same is true of any workplace where men have long prevailed. Janet Coats, who is quoted in this chapter, told me that when she was an intern in Knoxville, she worked for "an awful city editor who drank whiskey all day from a thermos." One day he tore into her about a story she had done, and Coats ran to the bathroom and burst into tears. A night cops reporter, a woman, followed her into the bathroom and locked the door. "She said, 'You can cry all you want in here, but don't you ever, ever cry out there. Don't do it.'" Coats never forgot that lesson.

Many of the women we interviewed find themselves carefully calibrating their behavior in the workplace. They worry about being too motherly, too brash, too opinionated, and not opinionated enough. They worry about being judged.

Audrey Cooper, the forty-year-old editor in chief of the *San Francisco Chronicle*, has struggled with a compulsion to cut cakes. At every office celebration, there would be a cake, and after the congratulations and speeches were over, the men would invariably walk away or stand aside, waiting for someone else to serve. With the instincts of a hostess, Cooper would step in and do the honors. "Then I thought, 'Why am I the one cutting the cake every single time?'" she said. To avoid temptation, she began positioning herself as far from the cake as she possibly could. She stuck with the strategy until she was named top editor and was less concerned about sending an overly domestic message to the staff.

I understand why Cooper avoided cakes, and I'm glad she no longer worries about picking up a knife. The women I admire most are confident enough to be exactly who they are, with or without knives. I laughed out loud when Paula Ellis, the former vice president of Knight Ridder newspapers, told me about a particularly contentious male colleague who shot down an idea she had raised in a meeting. Ellis turned to him and said, "I feel like you just raised your leg and peed all over a fire hydrant, and I'm the fire hydrant."

And I love the story Sara Just, executive producer for the *PBS NewsHour*, told me about a meeting she once attended with longtime NPR reporter and commentator Cokie Roberts. Roberts brought her knitting to the meeting and sat there knitting away while the men in the room pretended not to notice. Afterward, she told Just, "It makes them uncomfortable. Let's keep doing it."[13]

Here are some of the comfortable and not-so-comfortable conclusions that can be drawn from the experiences of these women leaders.

Embrace Your Scarlett and Your Melanie

While it's true that women have a more limited range of management options available to them than men have, they still have room to develop their own distinctive and effective styles. Diane McFarlin leads with a gentle touch and sublime manners. Christiane Amanpour is unapologetically commanding. Susan Goldberg has developed a style that falls somewhere in between. She is, as Janet Coats put it, part Scarlett O'Hara and part Melanie Wilkes. Moreover, the most successful women adapt their approach, depending on the circumstances and the people with whom they're dealing. Sometimes they speak out—loudly—and sometimes, like Kim Guthrie, they "lead from the back of the boat."

Be Your Authentic Self

Leadership styles are a little like clothes. You can try on different styles, but if the style doesn't suit you, it's going to look like a costume and people are going to know it. Many of the women we talked to made the point that leaders must be authentic to be believed and to be effective. Figuring out what works for you requires a high degree of self-awareness. Are you the kind of person who can confront a colleague in a meeting the way Paula Ellis did, or are you more comfortable talking about differences in private? When an employee starts crying, do you want to give her a hug or hand her a box of tissues? As Margaret Low says, there are some things you just can't fake.

Confidence Counts

We all have doubts about our abilities, and doubts can be useful when they prompt us to think more deeply about what we should do or how we should do it. Besides, who wants to work for someone who is always convinced she is absolutely right? The problem isn't so much doubt as it is allowing doubt to keep us from acting. Good leaders don't second-guess themselves to the point of paralysis; they make the tough decision and move on. They aren't intimidated by bullies or fear of the unknown—or even the prospect of failure. They're supremely confident sometimes and just confident enough to get things done the rest of the time.

You Don't Always Have to Be Liked

Sara Just said this best: "Women have a tendency to be people pleasers. They have to balance their desire to make people happy with the need to deliver bad news or impose tough deadlines or policies. We have to be willing to not be liked [even if] that's painful sometimes." Being a leader means doing what's best for the entire organization, and that is going to make some people unhappy at least some of the time. Live with it.

Dress and Act the Part

You're communicating all the time, even when you're not saying a word. Diane McFarlin, Christiane Amanpour, Susan Goldberg, and Cynthia Hudson all understand that what they wear, how they enter a room, and their tone of voice speak volumes about their expectations of themselves and others. This doesn't mean you have to always be perfect. (McFarlin says she now musses her hair every once in a while in an effort to dispel her Southern belle image, and Hudson still can get a little loud when she's animated.) But it does mean that if you want to be treated like a professional, you have to look and act like one.

Stand Up for Other Women

Some of the women we interviewed had worked with "queen bees," that is, women who resent other women's success and do their best to thwart them, but none of them aspired to be queen bees themselves. They see it as their responsibility to mentor, promote, and support other women, especially talented young women coming up behind them in their organizations.

Gail Evans, the author of two books on gender and leadership, including the best-selling *Play like a Man, Win like a Woman*, told us that the most important thing women can do is band together with other women. She doesn't believe workplaces will change until there is a critical mass of women who "come to understand that they are connected to each other and have to support each other, and they have to play like a team."

Find Your Tribe

As Audrey Cooper notes, workplaces can be lonely for women, especially for those at the top. Ann Marie Lipinski hit on one solution when she was editor of the *Chicago Tribune* in the early 2000s. She had agreed to be interviewed by a Japanese woman who was doing research for a book, and as the interview was wrapping up the woman asked Lipinski, "Do you know of any other 'large ladies'?"

Lipinski hesitated for a moment and then suggested Karen Jurgensen, the first female editor of *USA Today*. Lipinski had never actually met Jurgensen, but she figured that if she was a large lady so was the editor of the nation's largest circulation daily.

Afterward, Lipinski couldn't get the idea of "large ladies" out of her mind. The phrase tickled her so much she decided to make a call herself to Jurgensen. The two chatted for a while and then arranged to meet for dinner at the next gathering of the American Society of Newspaper Editors, where the top editors of U.S. newspapers gathered each year. ASNE was a sort of club for top dogs in journalism, and almost all the top dogs were men; Lipinski and Jurgensen thought it might be a relief to get away from the guys for a while.

"I'd been to lots and lots of editor meetings, but for the most part, the people there didn't look like us," Lipinski said. "It was kind of a comfort and calm being with her that night. It just felt really good to exchange perspectives and experiences. At the end of the night, we agreed we'd had a really nice time and it would be fun to continue and expand the group."

And so the "Large Ladies" club was born. Each year, the women who led newspapers—in Portland (Oregon), Atlanta, Cleveland, San Diego, and a half dozen other cities—would schedule one night just for themselves.

Think about finding your own group of "large ladies" with whom you can commiserate, compare notes, and network. It could be just the lifeline you need.

Create Your Own Narrative

Stories are powerful at work, just as they are in the rest of life. Help write the narrative of you as a colleague and a boss, especially when you first assume a position.

Shortly after I arrived at the *Chicago Sun-Times*, I assigned a story to a veteran reporter who assured me it could not be done. He may have meant it, or he just may have been challenging my authority, but I knew I had to do something or I would lose the respect of not just this reporter but others in the room. So, I spent several days researching the story, identifying sources, and outlining a strategy. The reporter was a little chagrined to be told in such detail how to do his job, but he did it, and I gained a reputation as an editor who knew what she was doing (and didn't lightly take "no" for an answer).

In her first few years at the *Times-Picayune* in New Orleans, Kristin was known as the "pregnant editor." She was pregnant when she arrived and pregnant again two years later. She also was the only female bureau chief for the newspaper and felt that she had to prove she was just as devoted, if not more devoted, to the job as her male counterparts.

The night before she was due to give birth to her second daughter, Kristin made the trek across the Mississippi River to cover a parish council meeting. Several council members took one look at her and politely inquired when she expected the baby. "Don't worry," she told them. "My due date isn't until tomorrow."

The council meeting ended late, well after the paper's final deadline, so she figured she would wait until morning to write the story. That night she went into labor. From about 3 a.m. to 8 a.m., she and her husband timed contractions from home while she waited for the first reporter to arrive in the bureau. When he did, she got him on the phone and said she needed to dictate a story to him. Every four to five minutes, she would put down the phone and breathe through a contraction, then pick it up again and say, "OK, where we were?" Story finally dictated, she headed to the hospital with a few hours to spare.

That story became *the* story people told about Kristin for the next decade. It defined her in a way nothing else could.

What are the stories people tell about you? And what do those stories say about you? The answers to those questions are powerful indicators of how people see you. And how people see you is absolutely critical to your success.

· 2 ·

From Getting Coffee to Running the Place

I want to be the best secretary you've ever had in your entire life.

—Marcy McGinnis

$\mathcal{T}$he news came across the wires at CBS headquarters in New York at 7:58 p.m. on Saturday, the first day of the long Labor Day weekend in 1997: "Diana injured in a car crash in Paris."[1]

It was supposed to be a slow news day, so CBS News had no anchor on duty and only a skeleton staff. Someone thought to call the head of newsgathering to tell him what was happening, but he was cautious and decided to see what developed before summoning a crew and anchor.

In London, it was 12:58 a.m. on Sunday when the news broke about the Princess of Wales. CBS Bureau Chief Marcy McGinnis was not inclined to wait. If this was anything more than a fender bender, McGinnis reasoned, it would be a major news story and she would need every resource she could muster. She called everyone she could reach into the office and dispatched a crew to Paris.

The decision not to immediately mobilize the New York staff turned out to be, by network standards, nothing less than a capital offense. While the other networks were reporting the story live, CBS was showing a wrestling match. For hours, the only original footage CBS had was what McGinnis provided.

Andrew Heyward, then the president of CBS News, was far from happy. He decided his cautious head of newsgathering had to go, and he had a pretty good idea who the replacement should be—McGinnis, the London bureau chief who had acted so quickly in the hours before Princess Diana's death was confirmed.

No woman had ever held the number-two position in the news division before. McGinnis would be in charge of a sprawling operation of hundreds of journalists, producers, and other staff members in New York and in bureaus around the world and would make decisions that determined what millions of Americans watched on the news each night.

McGinnis's rise was all the more remarkable because she had started out at CBS twenty-seven years earlier as a secretary.

Determined to escape her hometown of Allenhurst, New Jersey, McGinnis had taken a train to New York and started knocking on doors in Manhattan. At the CBS personnel office, she handed over her resume and took the typing and shorthand tests. She aced the tests and got the recruiter's attention when she mentioned that she had been a volunteer at the Democratic National Committee. That was a bit of a stretch. A guy she was dating worked there and she had typed his letters, but it was enough to land her an interview for a secretarial job in the special events department, which handled political conventions, elections, and other live events.

When department head Bob Wussler asked her about her career goals, McGinnis replied, "I want to be the best secretary you've ever had in your entire life." He laughed and asked what she wanted to do after that. "I don't know," she told him, "because I don't know how to do anything else. But I guess I'll learn, and I'll figure it out; then I'll let you know."

*   *   *

When McGinnis arrived at CBS in 1970, the vast majority of women working in television were either secretaries or researchers. There were a few exceptions. Pauline Frederick reported for both ABC and NBC through the 1950s and 1960s and was the first woman to moderate a presidential debate in 1976. Barbara Walters became the first female co-anchor of a network evening newscast when she joined Harry Reasoner on ABC in 1976.

Women also were making their way onto air in local television, but most station managers thought anything in excess of one or two female reporters was more than their audiences could handle. It was even harder for women to get behind-the-scenes jobs that would put them in charge of news decisions—and in charge of male employees. A woman simply wouldn't be able to manage the demands of a newsroom, they thought, and besides, how many men wanted to work for a woman?

For many women, there was only one way in—and that was at the bottom. Judy Woodruff, anchor and managing editor of the *PBS NewsHour*, started as a news secretary at an Atlanta television station after being turned down for a reporting job. The station, she was told, already had one female reporter. Woodruff would become one of a handful of women to ever anchor a national nightly news broadcast.

Pat Fili-Krushel was a secretary at ABC Sports when she got to know an up-and-coming executive by the name of Bob Iger, who was impressed by the speed with which she moved around the office. Even though she never reported directly to him, Iger recommended her for various promotions. He went on to serve as chair and chief executive officer of the Walt Disney Company, and Fili-Krushel rose to become one of the most powerful women in television, heading both the NBCUniversal News Group and the ABC Television Network. While at NBC, she appointed the first woman to head a network news operation: Deborah Turness.

Patti Dennis was buffing studio floors, emptying the trash, and painting sets at KOCO-TV in Oklahoma City, Oklahoma. When she wasn't waitressing at Steak and Ale, she would show up at the station and volunteer to do whatever job needed to be done. She learned enough to snare a producing position and eventually rose to vice president of talent and recruiting for TEGNA, one of the largest TV groups in the country.

All of these women parlayed their entry-level jobs into remarkable careers. They were a smart, funny, tough, and driven bunch who took on an industry that was often downright hostile to them, and they ended up running multimillion-dollar news operations that determine a large part of what Americans read, view, and think about the world.

* * *

The first wave of women to rise to the top of news organizations benefited from a national movement to win equal rights for women. The 1964 Civil Rights Act prohibited employment discrimination based on sex as well as race, religion, and national origin. It was followed in 1972 by Title IX, which guaranteed women equal access to educational programs, including athletics. A few years later, in 1978, a federal law banned discrimination based on pregnancy.[2]

With these newfound legal protections, women in news organizations began fighting back. In March 1970, the year McGinnis began working at CBS, forty-six women who worked at *Newsweek* sued the magazine for sexual discrimination.

"We were protesting a system in which all but one of the writers and editors were men and the women clipped newspaper stories, checked facts and did research—lower-paying jobs without much opportunity to move up," Lynn Povich, one of the women who sued, wrote in a 2012 op-ed column.[3] "In our job interviews, we were told, 'Women don't write at *Newsweek*. If you want to be a writer, go someplace else.'" While ultimately successful, the women were widely derided. The *New York Daily News* published a story about the women's action with this headline: "Newshens Sue Newsweek for 'Equal Rights.'"[4]

In August 1970, the American Civil Liberties Union filed a discrimination complaint saying that women at ABC News were relegated to low-level jobs. The case got little public attention, earning only a brief mention on page 33 of the *New York Times*.[5]

But the lawsuits kept coming. Over the next several years, women from the *New York Times*, the *Washington Post*, the *Detroit News*, and the Associated Press sued their employers, some of whom had to pay handsome sums to address systemic discrimination. In a lawsuit that went on for years, the Associated Press was ordered in 1983 to pay $2 million in back pay to women and minorities.[6]

Allen Neuharth, CEO of Gannett at the time and a well-known advocate for women and minorities, applauded the legal actions. A few years after the Associated Press was forced to pay out, he told author Kay Mills, "It took a hell of a lawsuit to convince those damned male chauvinists on that board and their management that they could no longer do this."[7]

Broadcast companies faced additional pressures. In December 1970, the National Organization for Women filed a petition with the Federal Communications Commission asking for equal employment opportunities for women working in television. NOW also wanted employment data to be made public and factor into a station's license renewal process. The FCC implemented the suggestions a year later.

In 1973, a group of dissatisfied female employees at CBS asked for a meeting with then president Arthur Taylor. They presented him with a litany of complaints, which prompted Taylor to form an advisory group to tell him what should change at the network. As a result, salaries were evaluated, maternity policies were created, and the "secretary's guide" was revised to remove some of the sexist language.[8]

Women like Marcy McGinnis found that the doors to TV news, while not wide open, were suddenly propped slightly ajar.

*   *   *

McGinnis didn't know she was about to become part of sweeping changes that would soon engulf newsrooms across the country. She was just a young woman from a small town who didn't want to go back home, get married, and have seven children like her mother.

McGinnis grew up on the Jersey shore, where her dad was a businessman who ran a small vending machine company and then a restaurant. She was petite—five feet tall and approximately ninety pounds—with a bubbly personality and a giant smile, all of which made her a natural for the high school cheerleading squad.

One of her early lessons in conformity came during Catholic elementary school when she asked her teacher, a nun, if she could leave class to go to the bathroom. The nun told her, "No," but McGinnis got up and went anyway, and when she returned the nun didn't say a word. "Something clicked in me about the ability to challenge authority," McGinnis said.

She was intent on going to college, in part because, as she had announced at the age of ten to her mother, the "mommy thing" didn't look like much fun. After high school, she enrolled at a Catholic all-women's school, Marymount College in suburban Washington, DC, where her parents figured she would pick up enough skills to get a secretarial job. McGinnis was thrilled to be in the capital, which was roiling with energy and war protests, but after two years, her parents told her money was tight and she should come home and look for work.

McGinnis had other plans. "If there was one thing I knew, it was that I was going to New York City to find a job," she said. "I wanted a place that people knew the name of it, and it was interesting and exciting to work there. That was my criteria." So she put on a red, white, and blue dirndl dress and got on the train.

McGinnis loved being at CBS, and she enjoyed the work, which consisted mainly of taking dictation, running errands, and getting coffee. Being part of the special events team meant she often was at the center of the action. During the Watergate scandal, she took shorthand and sat with producers as they went through tape and decided what to put on air. She answered phones at political conventions, but she also made sure to listen to what the producers were saying. She said she learned a lot "from watching, asking, being there, asking to do more, constantly asking to do more. 'Can I do this? Can I do that? Can I sit with you while you do that piece? Can I ask you a question?'"

In 1971, McGinnis helped coordinate CBS's coverage of the Apollo 14 launch at Cape Kennedy, Florida. "I thought it didn't get any better than this," she said. "I'm standing outside watching the Apollo launch and Walter Cronkite is inside the building doing the broadcast."

But after three years as a secretary, she was itching for a new challenge. She had her eye on a producing job, working with reporters, camera crews, and others to pull together news packages. She applied for an opening as an assistant producer only to have her boss tell her he was thinking of splitting the work among the three secretaries already on staff instead of filling the position. "I got myself all worked up. That was just wrong," McGinnis said. The next day, she suggested an alternative to her boss: He should eliminate her secretarial position and promote her to the producer's job. To her relief, he agreed.

Assistant producer was the lowest rung on the ladder, but McGinnis was just glad to be on the ladder.

*   *   *

When McGinnis arrived at CBS, it was the "Tiffany" network, with a lineup of top-rated entertainment programs and an evening newscast anchored by Cronkite. Each night, about thirty million people tuned in to watch *CBS Evening News with Walter Cronkite*. In contrast, fewer than six million people watched the *CBS Evening News* in 2018.

Although the newscast was beautifully executed, it was a different story behind the scenes. The broadcast center at Fifty-Seventh Street between Tenth and Eleventh Avenues in Manhattan was a grungy building that had once been a milk factory. Its most memorable features were filthy carpets; yellow, smoke-stained ceilings; and piles of papers everywhere. The graphics department was decorated with wall-to-wall *Playboy* centerfolds.

McGinnis remembers one woman in a position of power amid the sea of men. Her name was Joan Richman, and she had become the first female executive producer of a network news program in 1976. McGinnis recalls Richman walking into the building each morning wearing a pair of dark glasses and heading straight to her office without saying a word to anyone. "I liked her and admired her, but she was scary," McGinnis said.

Linda Mason was another member of that early generation of women in broadcast newsrooms. Mason, who became the first female producer at *CBS Evening News* in 1971, said she got ahead by keeping her head down, doing her work as well or better than the men did, and avoiding making waves. "If a man wanted to open a door for me, I'd say, 'Thank you.' If he didn't, I'd open it. And if a man wanted to pay for my lunch, I'd say, 'Thank you,' and if he didn't, I'd pay. I was never a feminist. I was just me, and people responded to it . . . i.e., men," she said.

Mason rose to senior vice president for standards and specials before retiring in 2013 after forty-seven years at CBS. She thinks her approach, which she described as reserved and modest, paid off. She remembers asking for her first producer title and being told that women couldn't be producers. "Holy cow! Did I bring a lawsuit? No," she said. "Did I go complain somewhere? No. And two months later I got the job."

Andrew Heyward, who was president of CBS News from 1996 to 2005, said those early female entrants to newsrooms learned to be tough to survive. He remembers two women who were among the first female producers hired by the network. They kept a water pistol that looked like an erect penis pinned to their office wall. Above the pistol, they taped a tabloid newspaper headline about a snowstorm that read, "12 Inches on the Way." "They were scary, tough and intimidating," Heyward said of the women. "There were no attempts to be friends or pals."

Over time, three other kinds of women emerged in the business, according to Heyward. One group was made up of women who came to the network from schools like Vassar and Barnard. They were smart, sophisticated, and classy. Another group consisted of worker bees; they were smart and tireless but also careful not to stand out or threaten the men around them. "They hid some of their talent," he said. And then there were women like McGinnis, who were "one of the gang, fun, the girl next door." Of McGinnis, Heyward said, "She was competent, hard-working, and fantastic at speaking truth to power."

*   *   *

McGinnis was learning fast, and she thought she was ready to be a full producer with more authority and more control over coverage. Producers were responsible for the setup and execution of "remote" shoots—what the audience saw whenever the anchor wasn't on-air.

McGinnis's opportunity came when Richman, who was heading the special events department, hired a man from a local TV station and asked McGinnis to teach him how to do live TV. McGinnis said she would be happy to train the new hire, but she didn't think an associate producer should be training a full producer. "I think a producer should be teaching a producer, so I want to be made a producer," she told Richman. And, she said, she wanted to be paid one dollar more a week than the male producer. Richman agreed.

It was 1983 and McGinnis was thirty-three years old, working in a prestigious job in one of the most respected divisions of CBS News. She was finally making enough money to stop commuting two hours each way from New Jersey and move to Manhattan. She dated regularly, including many men at CBS, although never anchors and reporters. For a while, she dated lawyers, but they had trouble understanding her hectic work schedule. "They'd say, 'Why do you have to go to Rome?' And I'd say, 'Why do you have to go to court?'" Her friends and family began to worry that she would never marry.

For a while, she dated John Reade, a colleague in special events. They met when she was still a "snooty secretary," he said. They saw each other for several years before he bought her an engagement ring, but then they decided they weren't ready to get married. He returned the ring and bought her some earrings and bracelets instead. They remain close friends decades later.

McGinnis was engaged to one other man, but she never did marry. "I don't know if I didn't love them enough, but they weren't the right guy," she said. "I never made a decision that I wasn't going to get married. I get very annoyed when people say to me, 'Oh, so you chose your career over marriage.' No, I chose something interesting to do and kept succeeding at it, which meant promotions. I wasn't going to say no to a promotion because I might meet a guy and get married."

The next promotion for McGinnis was an unlikely one. She heard that Bob Horner was planning to rebuild a backwater department of CBS News that sent content, typically twice a day, to the local CBS stations. With more sophisticated satellite technology, video could be sent across the country faster and cheaper, and Horner believed the department could develop into the backbone of CBS.

McGinnis knew syndication was considered the dumping ground for people who couldn't make it elsewhere at CBS, and, besides, she already had a great job. In the special events department, she had a front-row seat to the biggest news events in the world. But she was intrigued by Horner's vision, and it would give her a chance to manage a unit of about thirty-five people, something she had never done before. She talked to almost everyone she knew and asked for their advice. Every one of them told her it was a dead end: She would be out of sight and out of mind.

Ultimately, the chance to do something new decided the matter. "Boredom was the thing that propelled me to look for more," she said. "Every time I got a new job, all I thought was, 'This is what I want to be the rest of my life'—until I did it for about two and a half years. Then I wanted to do something more."

But there was an obstacle. The head of syndication wanted to hire McGinnis, but his number two wanted a woman from a local television station. Finally, the two men decided to give the job to both McGinnis and the other woman. Years later, they told McGinnis they figured there would be a "catfight" and the best woman would win.

The two women knew the perils of sharing a job, and they were painfully aware that people thought two women would never be able to get along. "We made a pact that we weren't going to ever turn on each other," McGinnis said. "We were going to do this together, and if we had problems we were going to go off and talk about it ourselves. We were going to prove that two strong women can work together."

It wasn't easy. They had different ideas about how things should be done, and both were extremely competitive. They even competed to be the first to show up at the office each morning. They each kept arriving earlier and earlier until McGinnis finally called a stop. "I said to her, 'If we keep this up, we're going to be in here at six in the morning. Let's just decide between the two of us when we're going to come in.'"

A few years later, McGinnis had the chance to move up to executive producer, the second highest job in syndication. The two candidates were McGinnis and a man who happened to be friends with the department head. Caught in the middle and unable to decide, the department head suggested another job share: his friend and McGinnis could be co-executive producers. McGinnis was having none of it. "Here's the deal," she told him. "If you pick this guy, I will work for him. You won't hear a peep out of me; I'll do whatever he wants. But I can tell you this: I'm not sharing a job with someone where I'm going to be doing all the work and he's going to be sitting in your office smoking cigars and having Scotch."

McGinnis was named executive producer of the unit, then known as NewsNet, just as it was becoming increasingly important to CBS. The staff grew to almost fifty people, and so many of the new hires were women that it became known as the "BabeNet" department.

Three years later, in 1992, the network was looking for a new deputy bureau chief in London, and McGinnis decided to apply. It was considered one of the network's most glamorous jobs, and McGinnis knew she would have competition. But at NewsNet, she had helped establish an integrated system of national newsgathering, and CBS was interested in building the same kind of network in Europe. She got the job and, soon after, was promoted chief of the entire London operation.

London suited her. She visited castles and parks and did "all the touristy things." She became a regular at the London symphony and vacationed throughout Europe. "I loved living there," she said. "I felt very free."

She also was far enough away from CBS headquarters in New York that she could avoid most of the network bureaucracy, and there was little to slow her down. She directed coverage of major stories that included the wars in Bosnia and Somalia, and she built a consortium of international broadcasters to share content.

Then Princess Diana died, and everything changed.

*   *   *

When Heyward called McGinnis back to New York in 1997, he told her he planned to demote his head of newsgathering, who had been McGinnis's longtime friend and mentor, and he wanted McGinnis to take the job. She said she didn't want it. Heyward kept talking. He told her he was determined to bring in a new person for the job and if she didn't take it, it would go to someone else. She finally agreed.

McGinnis knew she would be tested in her job, not only because she was new but because she was the first woman to hold such a high-ranking position in the news division. She just didn't know how she would be tried or when or where. It ended up playing out in all sorts of ways.

Several months into the job, Heyward took a European vacation and McGinnis was left in charge. One day, Dan Rather, then anchor of the evening news and someone she had known back when she was a secretary getting him coffee, called to tell her he was taking a plane that night to Bosnia to cover the war. McGinnis thought it was a terrible idea. The network would have to put a substitute in the main anchor role—never good for ratings—and Rather would arrive in Bosnia with no plan and little likelihood of quickly finding great stories. McGinnis relates the conversation this way:

> Rather: "Marcy, I'm going to Bosnia tonight."
>
> McGinnis: "No, you're not going to Bosnia."
>
> Rather: "I've told them to make the reservations; I'm going to Bosnia tonight. It's a big story. The flight's at 11 p.m. It's a decision I've made."
>
> McGinnis: "I'm on my way to your office. You're not going to Bosnia."
>
> Rather: "Don't bother coming to my office. I'm on my way."

McGinnis said she reacted "like a lunatic. I'm literally running to his office thinking, 'What am I going to say? What am I going to say?' So I get there and I don't even know where this came from—right out of my butt." She told him, "OK, you definitely should go to Bosnia. There's not even a question that you should be going to the story. It's a big story. But you're Dan Rather. If you're going to go, we're going to do it right. We're going to get interviews. We're going to get you with the best camera crews, with the best producers. We're not doing this on the fly. You're Dan Rather. We're doing this right, so let's make a plan for when you go and do it right."

Rather replied, "You got it, Marce."

The incident was vintage McGinnis. Instead of engaging in a showdown, she appealed to Rather's ego. She praised. She smiled. And she got her way.

* * *

When people who worked with McGinnis talk about her, they almost invariably bring up her size. Colleagues once made a video of the newsroom shot at the level of about four feet. They called it the "Marcy-cam."

She was so small she was easy to pick up. McGinnis remembers a top executive walking into the newsroom one day, lifting her up, and twirling her around. He announced, "I'd like to thank the National Organization for Women for this trophy." "Everyone laughed," McGinnis said. "Can you imagine a senior vice president doing that today?"

McGinnis said cameramen and other CBS employees would occasionally try to kiss her or push her onto their laps, but she said she never faced the overt sexual harassment that other women at CBS have alleged. Longtime CEO Les Moonves was accused of forcing women to have sex with him and exposing himself to them. Jeff Fager, executive producer of *60 Minutes*, was accused of groping women. Both were ousted from their jobs in 2018.

McGinnis said her biggest challenge was her "never-ending quest to prove herself." But what people remember most about her is how she managed to run a newsroom without ever appearing to order anyone around.

Tiny but commanding is how Terri Stewart, who became national editor for CBS, described McGinnis. And she was nice. "I have never heard Marcy called the *b*-word, never," Stewart said.

"Marcy acted like she was in charge without being nasty," observed Reade, her ex-fiancé. "What the heck, you're the size of Napoleon, you don't want to act like Napoleon. If somebody was getting out of line, she was very reasonable but very firm."

McGinnis remembers dealing with one male editor, someone she had known for years, who was making a woman in the newsroom very uncomfortable. He would come up behind her as she bent over and make a grinding motion. When the woman asked him for help, he asked her if he should "use his dick."

McGinnis called him to her office. "Oh, Marce, I was just joking," he told her when she explained the problem. He accused her of losing her sense of humor now that she was a "bigwig."

"You know you might be right," she responded. "Let's do this. Let's call your wife. Let's tell her what you did. And if she thinks it's funny, I will agree that I've lost my sense of humor and we'll just move on.'

"He says, 'Oh, very funny.'

"I said, 'It's not funny. If she doesn't think it's funny, it's not funny. If it happened to her at work, would you mind? Would it bother you? So, here's the deal: If you don't want it to happen to your wife, your daughter, whoever, don't do it.'"

He apologized and said it would never happen again. As far as McGinnis knows, it never did.

CBS senior national correspondent Jim Axelrod said McGinnis checked all the boxes for executive leadership: She was skilled and analytical and could implement a plan. In addition, "because of the time she came up as a woman in the business, she developed that rhinoceros skin and toughness," he said. "But it all unfolds in a context of compassion. . . . She never forgot about the struggle up a ladder, and so it left her with a remarkable sense of appreciating other people's struggles and challenges."

*   *   *

McGinnis headed the CBS news operation for almost eight years, managing a staff of more than six hundred around the world and a budget of more than $300 million. She was in charge during the attacks on the World Trade Center, the wars in Iraq and Afghanistan, and Hurricane Katrina in New Orleans.

But as McGinnis was focusing on news coverage, trouble was brewing elsewhere at CBS. In 2005, Rather stepped down from the anchor chair he had held for almost twenty-three years after the airing of a controversial report about then president George W. Bush's service in the Texas Air National Guard. A few months later, Heyward, who had been president of CBS News for nearly a decade, also left. He was replaced by Sean McManus, who had been president of the CBS Sports division, and McManus wanted his own number two.

Within a week, McGinnis had reached a financial settlement with the network and secured an agreement that she would be the one to notify the staff she was leaving. On November 15, 2005, she conducted the editorial meeting as usual and then walked to her office and hit the "send" button on her computer. In her message to the staff, she noted how far she had come at CBS:

> In 1970, just two weeks after graduation from Marymount University in Arlington, Virginia, I began my career at CBS News as a secretary in the Special Events Unit. I had no idea where I was headed and no idea where I would end up. . . . There was no way, thirty-five years ago, that I could have ever guessed that I was going to travel the world for CBS News, get a front-row seat to history and end up the number-two person in the News Division. I consider myself blessed by any standard. . . . As for the future, I approach it with the same zeal I have had through my entire life—searching for a new path that is interesting and adventurous, fun and exotic, stimulating and challenging.[9]

After leaving CBS, McGinnis worked in academia as associate dean of Stony Brook University's School of Journalism. She would have one more brief stint in journalism, as senior vice president of newsgathering for Al Jazeera America, before becoming a professional career and life coach and communications trainer.

But there was one more thing McGinnis felt she needed to do. During all of her years at CBS, she had been uncomfortably aware that not only had she started as a secretary but she had only an associate's degree, while it seemed as if everyone else at the network had degrees from places like Harvard.

So McGinnis went back to college. At age fifty-nine, she was awarded a bachelor's degree in history from the State University of New York.

ADVICE FOR WOMEN LEADERS

JULIA WALLACE

I walked into the Illinois *Rock Island Argus* newsroom in 1975 as an intern and made history on my first day.

I sat down at my desk, grabbed an ashtray and started smoking a Salem Light. I didn't think much about it. The city editor always seemed to have a cigarette hanging out of his mouth, and he just let the ashes fall wherever he happened to be. The whole place smelled of tobacco, ink, and glue.

That weekend, I learned that I was the first woman to light up in the newsroom. For years, the men had puffed happily away at their desks while the women smokers hid in the ladies' room. Even after I continued to smoke at my desk, the other women retired to the bathroom. They were afraid that if the female publisher (her father had owned the paper) found out, she would fire them. She didn't approve of ladies smoking.

One day I rushed up to the second-floor newsroom, smoking as I ran. The city editor dusted the ashes off his pants and told me not to smoke on the first floor where the publisher's office was. "She doesn't need to know," he said. I followed his advice but kept smoking in the second-floor newsroom.

Until we began work on this book, I don't think I truly understood the changes that happened in American workplaces in the 1970s. We all owe a great debt to the women who broke out of the secretarial pools and the research ghettos at news organizations like CBS and *Newsweek*. The "scary" women. The persistent women. The women who filed the lawsuits and did the hard work that gave me and Kristin and so many others a chance to be part of this amazing world of journalism.

McGinnis was a member of the first wave of women to rise to the top of news organizations in the United States. Although times have changed, the story of how she climbed the ladder from secretary to a top executive at one of the largest media outlets in the world remains relevant for women who face many of the same challenges navigating today's corporate hierarchies.

Absorb Everything

Wherever you work, learn as much as you can. Ask as many questions as you can. Yes, you need to master your own job, but the more you know about the company and the work other people do, the more successful you're likely to be. When I was a night reporter at *USA Today*, it was pretty boring most nights, so I watched stories move through the editing system. I was able to see how top editors changed stories, the kind of fact-checking they did, and the writing touches they employed. That's how I learned to edit, and that's exactly how McGinnis climbed out of the secretarial pool and got her first producing job.

Consider Your Career a Jungle Gym

"The most successful people I know don't think of their career as a ladder but rather a jungle gym," said Patricia Sellers, longtime editor of *Fortune* magazine. Sheryl Sandberg, COO of Facebook, liked the concept so much she built one chapter of her best-selling book, *Lean In*, around it. McGinnis followed this advice to a T. Instead of staying in special events and working her way up in that department, she took a chance and moved to the syndication unit to learn about satellite transmission, then a new technology. Later, she moved to London, which steeped her in foreign news. It was the range of her experience, in addition to her performance, that propelled her into the number-two spot at CBS News.

Hang on to Your Humanity—and Your Humility

People who worked with McGinnis invariably say that she was both tough and compassionate. She never seemed to forget where she came from. She never lorded it over others or used her position as a bludgeon. She was able to say and do very tough things because she deployed the right mix of humor, humility, and empathy. Once, when she had to implement layoffs at CBS, she called her managers together for a dinner, told them the news, and agreed with them that what was happening was terrible. That night, she said, they could complain and yell all they wanted to, and that was fine. But the next day, they would get to work and figure out how to make the cuts. They did.

Speak Truth to Power, but in a Way That Gets Results

McGinnis has a giant smile and an animated way about her that makes her fun to be around, but she can be absolutely fearless. Her boss, Andrew Heyward, said one of her strongest traits as a leader was that she was "fantastic at speaking truth to power." McGinnis fought for what was fair, for herself and others, and she wasn't afraid to challenge authority, but she did it in a way that was designed to avoid intimidating or destroying other people. I wonder what trailblazer Joan Richman thought when McGinnis asked for one dollar more than a man with the same job. My guess is that she inwardly smiled.

• 3 •

Dealing with the Lechers among Us

> This public official puts his hand on my leg, and I'm thinking, "You can't make a scene at the White House." What was I going to do? So I held his hand for the whole dinner. I ate with one hand. My theory was the hand couldn't move if I held it.
>
> —Nina Totenberg

For decades, Mi-Ai Parrish quietly navigated sexual harassment at the media companies where she worked. When a friend told her about sexual remarks men in the newsroom were making about her, she laughed. When a boss wanted to take her on an out-of-town trip, she politely turned him down. When he began to retaliate, she quietly found another job. When a public official described her to a colleague as "that hot Oriental chick," she rolled her eyes.

She never spoke up, never made a fuss, until one day when she decided enough was enough.

Parrish, who numbers among the top Asian-American women in journalism, is not alone. Almost all women leaders have stories about inappropriate sexual comments or actions—delivered by bosses, colleagues, sources, and, increasingly, internet trolls. And like Parrish, their response was to either overlook the bad behavior or deal with it themselves.

As the #MeToo movement has demonstrated, sexual harassment is a pervasive and invasive cancer in workplaces of all kinds. The CEOs of Intel, Barnes & Noble, Boeing, and other major companies have been fired or forced to resign for actions that range from making sexist remarks to pursuing a romantic relationship with a subordinate.

In the media industry, sexual harassment has reached crisis proportions. A 2018 study by the Center for Talent Innovation, a nonprofit think tank based in New York City, found that 41 percent of women working in media reported being sexually harassed by a colleague—the highest proportion of any white-collar group surveyed. (The legal profession was the lowest, at 22 percent.)[1]

In late 2017, a former assistant editor at the *New Republic* shook the media world when she circulated a "shitty media men" list containing the names of more than seventy men working at media organizations. The anonymous list included the men's job titles, employers, and their alleged actions, which covered the gamut from general creepiness to rape. Creator Moira Donegan quickly took down the list, which she said she intended to be private, but copies of it continued to circulate on the web, leading to investigations, reprimands, and the firing of some of the men named.[2]

The rogue's gallery of men in media who have been forced out of their jobs for sexual harassment or sexual misconduct just keeps growing:

- Charlie Rose, co-anchor of *CBS This Morning* and host and executive producer of a nightly PBS talk show, accused of parading around naked in front of female employees, groping them, and making sexual comments.[3]
- *Today* cohost Matt Lauer, accused of making lewd comments and engaging in sex with women at NBC. "He couldn't sleep around town with celebrities or on the road with random people because he's Matt Lauer and he's married. So he'd have to do it within his stable, where he exerted power and he knew people wouldn't ever complain," one former producer told *Variety*.[4]
- Fox News chief Roger Ailes and network host Bill O'Reilly, both accused by multiple women of harassing them over decades at the network.[5]
- Michael Oreskes, who led NPR's news division and was a high-ranking editor at the *New York Times*, accused of inviting young women to dinner and pursuing them via email under the pretense of giving them career advice.[6]
- Leslie Moonves, the powerful longtime chairman and chief executive of CBS, accused by a dozen women of behavior that included sexual misconduct, harassment, and retaliation.[7]
- *New York Daily News* managing editor Robert Moore, accused of creating a sexualized work environment and bragging about punishing women who didn't go along.[8]

The list could go on . . . and on. But to understand how it got to this point, it's important to step back in time. Judith Levine, the author of four books and numerous articles about sex and justice, makes the point that "harassment is as old as workplaces with men in charge—to say nothing of slavery and household service. Sexual harassment, in other words, is as old and as wide as work itself." In about the mid-1800s, reports of sexual harassment began showing up in public records, such as newspapers and government reports, according to Levine. They documented young women being coerced in meat-packing plants, garment-sewing factories, and mining towns, among other workplaces.[9]

These women did not call what happened to them sexual harassment because the term did not come into use until the mid-1970s. Lin Farley was teaching a class at Cornell University when she decided that what her students were facing demanded a name. They told her story after story about getting fired or quitting jobs because they had rejected the sexual overtures of a supervisor, she said in a 2017 interview on the New York public radio station, WNYC. "So, when I left the class, I thought that we needed to have a name for what this phenomenon was. We all needed to be talking about the same thing. And so I went to my colleagues at work, I went to other women, we brainstormed. We just couldn't come up with the right phrase. I thought, 'Well, the closest I can get is sexual harassment of women at work.'"[10]

Meanwhile, feminist lawyers like Catharine MacKinnon were discussing how to attack the problem in the courts. Although Congress had passed the Civil Rights Act in 1964, making it illegal for employers to discriminate based on gender, the courts had not decided that the law applied to sexual harassment. It wasn't until 1986 that the Supreme Court unanimously ruled that sexual harassment was covered by the Civil Rights Act. In that Supreme Court case, Mechelle Vinson accused her branch manager at Meritor Savings Bank in Washington, DC, of raping her in a bank vault, fondling her in front of others, and threatening to fire her if she refused his demands.[11]

It was a landmark decision, and it looked like the environment for women in the workplace might change. But five years later, the country watched as Anita Hill told the Senate Judiciary Committee that Supreme Court nominee Clarence Thomas had sexually harassed her when she worked for him. Twenty-seven years after that, the country watched again as Christine Blasey Ford described being assaulted by Supreme Court nominee Brett Kavanaugh. Both judicial nominees were confirmed.

In 1991, 67 percent of Americans surveyed told pollsters that if Hill was telling the truth, Thomas should not be confirmed. In 2018, 69 percent said the same of Ford and Kavanaugh.[12] After nearly three decades, little had changed.

Although the testimonies of Hill and Ford did not prevent Thomas and Kavanaugh from reaching the Supreme Court, they did generate a national debate that moved the conversation about sexual harassment from the quiet corners of courtrooms and classrooms into the nation's boardrooms and bedrooms.

Margery Baker Riker, one of the first female vice presidents at CBS News, remembers the Thomas hearings well. "My husband came home from his office one day and said, 'All of the men in my office think this whole Anita Hill thing is ridiculous. If she wasn't happy, why didn't she leave?'

"So I said, 'OK, sit down. I'm going to tell you things that I've had no particular reason to tell you before because it didn't matter,' and I proceeded to tell him two very specific stories of two very, very powerful men at CBS News with whom I had very awkward situations. The first was the executive producer of a program, and we were on a trip. He would call me each night with the most obscene phone calls you could ever imagine. And then I had to go to work with him the next day and work side by side with him and pretend like nothing happened."

The other incident, she told her husband, took place when she first stepped into the vice president's job at CBS. She often would have closed-door meetings with a network executive in his office. "One day he got up as the meeting was over, walked over to me, and gave me a very intense hug. Not just a simple hug," she said. "I sort of pushed him away and smiled and walked out the door. There isn't a woman at CBS who wouldn't have a comparable story or more. Did we do anything about it? No. Who was I going to report it to? These guys were my bosses, and there was no system in place to do anything about it. I just assumed it was part of the territory."

Barbara Cochran said women of the generation that she and Riker represent assumed there would be sexism in the workplace, and they found their own ways of handling it. "If somebody got overly flirtatious or something happened, you kind of defused it and moved right along," said Cochran, who has held several high-powered jobs, including serving as the first female chief of a TV network's Washington bureau. "You were not eager to call attention to yourself and say, 'You're treating me in such and such a way because I'm a woman.' You just didn't want to do that."

While working at the *Washington Star* in the 1970s, Cochran applied for a position that would require her occasional presence in the composing room, where a crew of men set type and prepared the next day's edition of the paper. "It was the era of miniskirts, and I was told they couldn't send me to the composing room because my skirts were so short," she said. "So I got longer skirts, and I got to go to the composing room."

Paula Ellis, who would become vice president of operations for the Knight Ridder newspaper chain, also started out in the business in the 1970s. She said some of her worst experiences were with people she interviewed for stories, including a minister who made a grab for her. "Back then I didn't think of it as sexual harassment," she said. "We just dealt with it. I didn't give it a lot of space in my head. I had other things to do."

* * *

Mi-Ai Parrish (then Gaber) was in the fourth grade when she learned how dangerous being female could be. She was the daughter of a Korean-American mother, who had fled her war-torn homeland, and a white father of Eastern-European descent. People often told her that, with her glistening black hair and features that clearly displayed each of her parent's heritage, she looked "exotic."

One day her band teacher offered to give her free flute lessons at his home. Her parents, she said, thought he was "doing something nice for this little girl who didn't have money for lessons." Instead, he began touching and caressing her. After a few more "lessons," she quit the band and never told anyone why. She didn't think anyone would believe her.

As she got older, she began to compensate. She wore big glasses and boxy sweaters and eschewed makeup. She did everything possible to be invisible and asexual. She avoided alcohol, convinced that drinking could put her in dangerous situations.

When she entered her first newsroom in 1991 at the *Virginian-Pilot* in Norfolk, Virginia, Parrish tried to blend in, but for a young Asian-American woman, it wasn't easy. When she learned that one of the newspaper's editors was talking about her at a bar, saying how "hot" she was, she withdrew even further.

"I was mortified. I was embarrassed. I wasn't mad. I modified myself even more," she said. "It made me even less fun. I wanted a good job, and I wanted to earn the job. I didn't want people to think I slept my way to the top."

Her glasses got bigger, and her clothes got boxier. She married one of the paper's sports editors and worked hard to prove herself in the newsroom. When she was promoted to assistant business editor, her biggest concern was that people would think she got the job because she was pretty.

A year later, she followed her husband to Chicago and landed a job at the *Chicago Sun-Times*, where she encountered a very different kind of newsroom. "Not only was I not the only Asian, I wasn't even the only Korean," she said. "There were immigrants and children of immigrants. I loved it. I had found all my little misfit friends. . . . It was like *Brigadoon*."

Before long, however, new owners took over the paper and the climate changed. One editor told her she needed to get a new photo for a column she wrote for the newspaper. She remembers him telling her, "For God's sake, woman. You look like a dominatrix. All the men are talking about it." Years later, Parrish wrote about how she felt at that moment: "A whoosh filled my ears, and I tried not to show how mortified I felt."[13] She told her mother what had happened. Her mother asked her what a dominatrix is.

The same editor invited her to dinner with him and his wife. At the last minute, his wife canceled, and Parrish spent an uncomfortable evening with the man at a high-end steak restaurant. She knew there were rumors going around the newsroom that they were sleeping together, but, again, she kept her head down, ignored the chatter, and tried to do her job. But the stress, she said, took a toll on her marriage. She and her husband divorced, and she moved to Phoenix for an editing job at the *Arizona Republic*.

At the *Republic*, Parrish met her second husband, Pulitzer Prize–winning reporter Dave Parrish, and the two decided to start fresh in a new place. They took jobs at the *San Francisco Chronicle*, where he worked as an investigative reporter and she was the editor of the Sunday edition.

On the surface, things were going well. She was promoted to deputy managing editor, with an expanded portfolio of responsibilities, but, at the same time, she felt a growing sense of unease. One of the editors made regular comments about her clothes and looks and began inviting her to meet with him at out-of-the-way bars. He said he didn't want to go somewhere where they would be recognized, and Parrish didn't have the nerve to ask him why there was a need for secrecy.

"I was hoping it wasn't that," she said. "If you call it by its name, it is that. I was hoping I was invited because I was so brilliant and wonderful and not because . . . he wanted to stare at me all night."

When he invited her on a work trip to Los Angeles, Parrish decided to talk it over with her husband. The two agreed the safe course was not to go, but neither of them anticipated the reaction. The editor was furious and threatened to damage her career. Her husband was taken off the investigative team.

Parrish began looking for another job and left as quietly and quickly as she could. She went on to be deputy managing editor of the *Star Tribune* in Minneapolis, publisher of the *Idaho Statesman*, and publisher of the *Kansas City Star*. In each of those places, she said, she encountered people and situations that made her feel objectified and sexualized. She did nothing. Her reason? "I would have lost my seat at the table."

* * *

Some women in the news business have found ways to fight back.

Gaby Darbyshire, a co-founder and chief operating officer of Gawker Media, said she was used to a sexualized work environment in England, where she was a lawyer. "I was told in no uncertain terms that I should stop wearing trousers to the office because the clients liked to see my legs. That's how it was," she said. She decided to move to the United States, believing she would have a better chance of being judged on her skills rather than her gender.

She entered the Silicon Valley start-up world only to find that she still was "batting away the flies of prejudice," so she decided to try subtle confrontation. When a male colleague would say or do something she considered out of line, she would give him a pointed look, perhaps accompanied by an unamused laugh, and say something like, "Wait, did you really just say that?" The effect, Darbyshire said, was that "he knows you clocked him, but you're not making a scene of it. But he also knows not to mess with you."

Kate O'Brian's approach was less subtle but just as effective. When she was twenty-one years old, she landed her first job at ABC News, where she did everything from getting coffee to handing out scripts to people in the control room before each show. One day O'Brian was in the control room—a small, dark, crowded space—when she felt a hand cradling her behind. "I was so shocked," she said. "But right from the get-go, I knew I had to say something. My only question was, can I say the word *ass* in front of all these people? because I was brought up as a good girl, and you didn't swear.

"I very quickly realized, yes, I probably can, so I said in a loud enough voice so everyone could hear in the control room—I said this guy's name. I said, 'Take your hand off my ass.' The control room went silent, which doesn't happen very often, and, very slowly, the hand backed away from me and I just went about my business. No one tried to do that again to me."

O'Brian would go on to become senior vice president for news at ABC and president of Al Jazeera America.

When Parrish decided to fight back, she was forty-five years old and the publisher of the *Arizona Republic*, the paper she returned to in 2015. She was thrilled to be back in the state after fourteen years away. Arizona, she thought, could be a surprising place. While it is politically conservative, it has been a breeding ground for powerful and successful women. The state produced the first female member of the Supreme Court, Sandra Day O'Connor, and it has had four female governors, more than any other state. But there also are clear fault lines on issues of race, ethnicity, and gender.

Parrish discovered this firsthand when the *Republic* made the decision to break with more than 125 years of history and endorse Hillary Clinton for president in 2016. It was the first time the paper had ever endorsed a Democrat for president.

Parrish was taken aback by the vehemence of the response. Businesses pulled their ads. Readers canceled. The staff was bombarded with threats. "People called in screaming that you just made the endorsement because Clinton has a vagina and you have a vagina," she said. "They called me the *c*-word and the *b*-word. All this nasty, misogynistic stuff that I had always pushed away in the past was right in front of me. It woke me up."

She began accepting invitations to speak to women's groups about the challenges women still face pursuing professional careers. For the first time, she felt like she was standing up for herself. But even so, she didn't touch the third rail of sexual harassment. In early 2017, it was acceptable to talk about ways women were discriminated against, but almost no one was talking about sexual harassment and even fewer were outspoken about their own experiences. Parrish was no exception. Female empowerment was a safe topic; her own stories were not.

In July 2016, Gretchen Carlson publicly accused Roger Ailes, the longtime CEO of Fox News, of harassing her. In October 2017, the *New York Times* broke its blockbuster story revealing Hollywood heavyweight Harvey Weinstein's history of serial harassment.

Parrish watched with interest as the national stories unfolded. Then, a month after the Weinstein story broke, another #MeToo story hit much closer to home. Michelle Ugenti-Rita, a member of the Arizona legislature, accused Don Shooter, chairman of the powerful House Appropriations Committee, of sexually harassing her for years.[14] One day later, the local *Capitol Times* newspaper published a story naming seven other women who said Shooter had harassed them.[15]

A year earlier, Parrish and the newspaper's male attorney had visited Shooter to discuss pending legislation. Toward the end of the conversation, Shooter began to talk about how satisfied he was with his life and how he had accomplished everything on his bucket list. Except one thing: "Those Asian twins in Mexico."

As they left Shooter's office, the attorney turned to her and said, "I'm so sorry. I can't believe he said that." Parrish told him there was no need for him to apologize, that she wasn't even surprised by Shooter's comment.

Parrish mentioned the incident to several people in the newsroom, but she didn't think much more about it until the stories about Shooter began to emerge. Editor Nicole Carroll and editorial page editor Phil Boas told her she should write about what had happened to her; they said it was time for her to speak up.

She worried. The comment was a small insult compared to the other allegations against Shooter, but she decided to try to write about it anyway. The result was a narrow, almost clinical recital of the incident, as if it had no relationship to anything else that had happened in her life. A friend read it and gently told her to try again. In the second attempt, she wrote about the boss who told her she looked like a dominatrix. She wrote about telling her attorney that Shooter's comment was no big deal.

And she wrote this: "After so many years, I was used to it. It was just another remark in a long, long list of offensive, obnoxious, ignorant, destructive things said to me and others by people with some power or sway. But the truth of the matter is this: It wasn't OK. And it wasn't OK for me to be OK with it. For me to put up with it. To laugh it off, to excuse it, to use it as a cocktail-party tale. It wasn't OK for me. And it isn't OK for my amazing nieces, for my brave colleagues, for the women coming up behind me."[16]

The same day the column appeared, Shooter's colleagues in the legislature suspended him from his committees and hired a private law firm to investigate the allegations against him. Two months later, the Arizona House of Representatives voted fifty-six to three to expel Shooter for "dishonorable" behavior. Not since 1991 had the House of Representatives acted to remove a fellow lawmaker. CNN noted another first: Shooter was the first state legislator in the country to be expelled from office since the start of the #MeToo movement.[17]

Parrish said she hopes the country has reached a tipping point. She knows that she has. "When I was young, I had this very strong sense of justice," she said. "If I just tell the truth, it will be corrected, and that wasn't what happened, so I had to figure out how to navigate it.

"I was so used to walking away from the 'cute little Asian chick' comments, it actually took a friend poking me with a stick to say this was unacceptable."

* * *

In its early days, NPR was leagues ahead of other news organizations in hiring and promoting women. In 1979, Barbara Cochran (then Cohen) was vice president of news and information. Susan Stamberg hosted NPR's flagship news program, *All Things Considered*, the first woman in the United States to hold a full-time position as anchor of a national nightly news broadcast, and Linda Wertheimer directed the show. The reporting staff included Nina Totenberg and Cokie Roberts, who would go on to become two of the most recognized names in news.

NPR, which began broadcasting in 1971, basically was a start-up with a limited budget and seemingly limited prospects as an alternative news source. Consequently, women were welcome. Margaret Low, who worked at NPR for three decades before moving to the *Atlantic*, described it as a place that has always "embraced women and female leadership in a pretty clear way."

In fact, the men on staff generally were a little younger and less experienced than the women, Cochran said. "It was the reverse of what you would have encountered in most newsrooms because it was such a new enterprise." There were so many women that one part of the newsroom was dubbed the "fallopian jungle."

Women have continued to play a key role at NPR over the years. Both Low and Ellen Weiss served as senior vice president of news at various times, and one woman, Vivian Schiller, was president and CEO from 2009 to 2011.

More than 56 percent of NPR's staff was female in 2017[18]—the same year the station's senior vice president of news was accused of sexual harassment. Michael Oreskes had stepped into the role two years earlier to replace Low. There were problems almost from the beginning of his tenure, according to an independent investigation completed in 2018.[19]

Just seven months after he was hired, two women complained to the human resources department about Oreskes's behavior. Both said he had invited them to dinner, during which he asked personal questions that made them feel uncomfortable. In one case, he made comments of a sexual nature and hugged the employee. Oreskes was given "a stern talking to," and he agreed not to repeat the behavior, according to the report.

Several months later, more questions emerged about expense-account dinners Oreskes had arranged with women as well as several email exchanges with young women and college students outside of NPR in which "he attempted to arrange meetups to provide career advice or discuss other topics that seemed personal in nature," according to the report. Oreskes was given another talking-to; this time he was told he would have to go through his expense reports and provide business justifications for his dinners.

Meanwhile, another woman called NPR to report that Oreskes had forcibly kissed her in the 1990s when they were both at the *New York Times*. NPR decided to send a note asking employees to come forward if they had been sexually harassed, which prompted another woman to report that she had been groped by Oreskes, according to the report.

Interviewees also told investigators that Oreskes "leered at women in the newsroom, engaged in uninvited shoulder rubs and brushed a little too closely when passing by. Women in the newsroom were frequently cautioned to avoid being alone with Mr. Oreskes."

In addition, the report described sexual harassment complaints against two other male employees—chief news editor David Sweeney and investigative correspondent Daniel Zwerdling, both of whom subsequently left the company.

When news of the investigation leaked to the *Washington Post* in the fall of 2017,[20] pressure grew for NPR to do something about Oreskes. He was asked to resign in November of that year.

In February 2018, NPR management called a staff meeting to discuss the investigation. Senior management and board members faced a room packed with mostly skeptical staff members who questioned whether enough was being done to address sexual harassment. When NPR board chairman Paul Haaga stated that NPR did not have a culture of harassment, he was met with "boos and scoffs," according to a story posted on the NPR website. He subsequently apologized but declined to commit to a zero-tolerance policy on harassment, calling that "harsh," according to attendees.[21]

The meeting revealed a generational divide in how women at NPR viewed sexual harassment. Younger women, who had been posting sticky notes in the women's bathroom to encourage one another, were outraged at both the men's behavior and how slow management had been to deal with it.

Totenberg was less critical of how the company handled the case, given the fact that neither the *New York Times* nor the Associated Press disclosed Oreskes's behavior when NPR was checking his bona fides prior to hiring him. She said she wished the NPR women had come to her about Oreskes. "I would have kicked his nuts," she said. "He wouldn't have done anything to anybody after that. I wouldn't have gone to management about him. I would have gone to him and said he's going to ruin his career if he ever, ever did this again, and then I would have gone to management."

Totenberg, who is in her seventies, said she has dealt with many episodes of sexual harassment. "I had bosses who I suppose young women today would say attacked me, but it's not like I didn't have a chance to defend myself, and I did," she said. "They didn't just proposition me. I had one boss who was all over me like a rug. It was very embarrassing. But you just had to get through it and get rid of them, if possible, without offending them. That was the trick, not to offend them. That was always the trick."

She recalled an episode in 1993 when she was at the White House for a small dinner. President Bill Clinton was seated on one side of her and a high-ranking public official on the other. "This public official puts his hand on my leg, and I'm thinking, 'You can't make a scene at the White House.' What was I going to do? So I held his hand for the whole dinner. I ate with one hand. My theory was the hand couldn't move if I held it."

Totenberg laughs when she tells this story. "I consider it a funny story. I do not consider it a trying story, though I may have at the time," she said. Women of her generation, she explained, "rolled with the punches. That's why it's hard for some people our age to understand people who have never had to roll with the punches. We shouldn't have had to roll with the punches, but I'm not convinced you'll ever get rid of this entirely."

Jill Abramson, former executive editor of the *New York Times*, was Oreskes's deputy in the *Times*'s Washington bureau in the early 2000s. She confirmed a report for the *Washington Post* that Oreskes showered an inordinate amount of attention on one young woman while they were both in the bureau.

"If I had to do it again, I would have told him to knock it off," Abramson told the *Post*. "I think I should have raised this with the human resources department. Maybe confronting him would have somehow stopped him from doing it to another woman. I don't really feel it was in a gray area in retrospect. I should have stopped him."[22]

* * *

It wasn't the Nina Totenbergs or the Jill Abramsons of journalism who kickstarted the #MeToo movement. It was someone much more unlikely—a former Miss America and co-host of Fox News.

Gretchen Carlson was among a flock of female newscasters featured on Fox. She was a violin prodigy as a child and, in 1989, became the first classical violinist to be crowned Miss America. She studied at Stanford University and Oxford University before entering local TV news. Her first network job was at CBS News, where she co-anchored the Saturday edition of *The Early Show* before moving to Fox News in 2005, eventually becoming cohost of *Fox & Friends*.

On air, she seemed to dumb herself down, which caught the attention of comedian Jon Stewart, who showed clips of her looking up words like *czar* and *ignoramus* on air. Stewart gleefully pointed out that Carlson was high school valedictorian, graduated with honors from Stanford, and attended Oxford—"not the Mississippi Oxford, the Europe one."

"Baby, Gretchen, come back," Stewart said. "You don't have to stash your IQ in an offshore account."[23]

Carlson thinks that, like many women in the public limelight, she was misunderstood and underestimated. "I've been an advocate for women my whole life. That got lost in the story because I have blond hair, because I'm a former Miss America. I worked at Fox News," she said. "With those things that have happened in my life, sometimes my resume fell off the face of the earth."

Roger Ailes, the Fox News chairman and CEO, had long been one of the most powerful men in media when Carlson joined the network in 2005. He had built the conservative news channel into what *New York Magazine* said amounted to "something like a fourth branch of government; a propaganda arm for the GOP; an organization that determined Republican presidential candidates, sold wars, and decided the issues of the day for two million viewers."[24]

Inside Fox, he ruled by fear. Ailes reportedly had a closed-circuit television system installed to spy on employees in their offices, monitored their emails, obtained copies of their phone records, and leaked negative stories about errant employees to the press.[25] Few people dared cross him. Women, in particular, seemed to be his targets. They were subjected to everything from demeaning comments and groping to demands for sex, according to multiple accusations against him.[26]

Carlson, like the other women at Fox, put up with the behavior until she was demoted in 2013 to an afternoon show, after which she began compiling evidence against Ailes. She reportedly began bringing her iPhone to meetings in Ailes's office and secretly recording him.[27] When Fox declined to renew her contract in 2016, she sued for sexual harassment.

In her complaint, Carlson, then fifty, said Ailes had retaliated against her and "sabotaged her career because she refused his sexual advances and complained about severe and pervasive sexual harassment." When Carlson met with Ailes to discuss the discriminatory treatment to which she was being subjected, Ailes stated, "I think you and I should have had a sexual relationship a long time ago and then you'd be good and better and I'd be good and better," adding that "sometimes problems are easier to solve that way."[28]

The suit prompted more than a dozen other women at Fox to come forward with stories of harassment, and Ailes was forced to resign under pressure. Later that year, Carlson settled with Fox News's parent company, the 21st Century Fox Corporation, for $20 million and received a public apology.[29]

"The final trigger was when they took my career away from me that I had worked so hard to achieve. If I didn't do something about it, then who would?" Carlson said. "It really came down to that. How could we still be enduring this? I didn't want my children to go through this, and I didn't want anyone else's children to go through this."

Ailes, who denied the allegations, died in 2017 from complications from a head injury. Carlson went on to write a book about sexual harassment and established the Gift of Courage fund to support organizations working with women and girls, including survivors of sexual assault and harassment. She said she never expected to become a poster child for women who were sexually harassed at work. "I could have never known that my actions would have unleashed the tsunami within my own company, the cultural revolution we are experiencing right now in the world," she said.

It was clear, however, that the tsunami was gathering force. About a year after Ailes stepped down, the *New York Times* and the *New Yorker* published investigations into Hollywood producer Harvey Weinstein's treatment of women, including at least eight settlements with women who had accused him of sexual harassment.[30] The story, by now, was a familiar one: A powerful man had used his power to exploit women. What wasn't clear was whether the powerful man, in this case, would survive the storm.

Weinstein seemed to think he could. In a letter to the *Times*, he announced he would be taking a leave of absence "to deal with this issue head on." He went on to discuss his plans to make movies that would take on

President Donald Trump and the National Rifle Association.[31] Ailes remained in power for fifteen days after Carlson went public with her accusations. Weinstein was gone in three.

The story of sexual harassment in the workplace is still being written, with more women speaking up seemingly every day about not just physical harassment and assault but also the kind of vitriol they face online. Fifty-eight percent of women journalists and media professionals surveyed in 2018 by the International Women's Media Foundation and TrollBusters said they had been threatened or harassed in person; 63 percent said the same had happened to them online. The vast majority said they believed they were attacked because of their gender, and nearly 30 percent said they considered getting out of the business as a result.[32] Another study of tweets sent to politicians and women journalists in Canada and the U.S. found that women received more than 1 million abusive tweets in 2017 alone—the equivalent of one every 30 seconds.[33]

As this kind of behavior gets more scrutiny—and becomes more public—some men who have been accused of being sexual predators have begun to lash back.

In an anguished article for *Harper's Magazine* in 2018, John Hockenberry, the former host of the public radio show *The Takeaway*, spoke for those who think the #MeToo movement has gone too far. His producers, WNYC and Public Radio International, did not renew Hockenberry's contract after he was publicly accused by female colleagues of unwanted kissing, touching, and sexualized comments.[34]

Hockenberry painted a picture of himself as a paraplegic man with five children, facing a second divorce, living alone, without a job and on the brink of financial ruin—all because of a "misguided" sense of romance that led to "lapses of judgment."

"Despite acknowledgment by my accusers that I am no rapist or sex offender, the unarguable discomfort and anguish of my co-workers have thrown me into a category in which society at large chooses, for whatever reason, not to distinguish between the charge and act of rape and some improper, failed, and awkward attempts at courtship," he wrote.

Hockenberry went further, describing the #MeToo movement as a "license to target," an "open season" on men like him, and an "overcorrection." At one point, he compared it to "Jacobins' Reign of Terror in France" after the French revolution.[35]

Jeff Fager didn't use words like "open season" when he was fired as executive producer of CBS's *60 Minutes*, but he seemed equally incredulous. An investigation by the *New Yorker* into sexual misconduct at CBS had called out both Moonves, the CBS CEO, and Fager, who was said to have made unwanted advances toward women and enabled a culture of harassment at the network.[36]

Fager was fired after he sent what appeared to be a threatening text message to a female CBS reporter who was covering the harassment story in the wake of the *New Yorker* articles. He wrote, "Be careful. There are people who lost their jobs trying to harm me and if you pass on these damaging claims without your own reporting to back them up that will become a serious problem."[37]

Some *60 Minutes* staffers expressed shock that someone would get fired over a text message, as did Fager. He issued a statement that said, "One such note should NOT result in termination after thirty-six years, but it did."[38]

*   *   *

Schiller, the first and only female CEO of NPR, thinks that the real awakening is yet to come. "This is just the beginning of the story," she said. "The fact that we're in 2018 celebrating the fact that a man who unzipped his pants in his office in front of a woman is being told to stop . . . Wow, that's progress?

"The breakthrough we need is when we're at a point where it's socially unacceptable for a panel or conference or boardroom to be all men," she said. "The breakthrough will come when no one finds it acceptable when only one or two women are in anything. We're not anywhere close to a place where there is true assumed equality."

Carlson believes that what is required is more women in leadership positions. Up to now, there have been so few women at the top that they have been forced into a kind of complicity, she said. "They're in this purgatory trap of 'Do I go along with the boys or do I stand up for women?'

"We just have to look at the past and say, 'Yeah, we probably all made a lot of mistakes in not speaking up and going along with the boys, but we need to stop that now.' If we really want to change this for the younger generations, we have to take responsibility for our voices being heard."

*   *   *

ADVICE FOR WOMEN LEADERS

Kristin Gilger

The stories about sexual harassment in this chapter are just a portion of the many, many such stories we heard while interviewing women for this book. No one, it seems, has been exempt. Julia and I certainly were not.

In her gender in the media classes at the Cronkite School, Julia poses a scenario to students that goes something like this: "You are a reporter working on a story about corruption in the local sheriff's office. You have a source who has documentation, but he tells you he'll give it to you only if you sleep with him. What do you do?"

a. Sleep with him and write the story.
b. Laugh it off and try to convince him to give you the documents, even though you have no intention of sleeping with him.
c. Grab the documents and run.
d. Report him to his boss and yours.
e. Tell him you don't want the story that badly and walk away.

The reporter in this story is me, and the choice I made was "e." At the time (the late 1980s), I thought it was a pretty good response, but many of the students in Julia's classes say they would report the incident, and I view that as a good thing. Whenever I start worrying that nothing has changed, I remember the Anita Hills and the Christine Blasey Fords of the world. I think about what Mi-Ai Parrish, Gretchen Carlson, and so many others have done. By breaking their silence, they made it possible to break the cycle.

Many of the experienced news leaders we spoke with say they wish they had done more. They offer no-nonsense advice for young women today.

Call Out Bad Behavior When You See It

You can deal with some situations on your own. If a co-worker or source makes a comment, gets too close, or otherwise makes you feel uncomfortable, tell him he's making you uncomfortable and he needs to stop. This puts the guy who habitually and knowingly does these sorts of things on notice that you're not going to put up with him. And it prompts those men who may not really intend harm to think twice about how their words and actions affect others. Laughing it off does neither.

Report Behavior When It Crosses the Line

It's hard to specify exactly where the line is, but like former Supreme Court justice Potter Stewart said about pornography back in 1964, "I know it when I see it." For me, uninvited touching, a pattern of sexualized and demeaning comments, or any request (or demand) for a sexual favor all require more than just telling the guy to shove off. Most human resources departments have become much more sensitized to sexual misconduct in recent years, and that's where you should go if yours is one of them. If not, tell your boss or your boss's boss. If you can't bring yourself to do that, tell another trusted supervisor. Document what happened and what you have done about it, even if it's just writing a note, dating it, and putting it in a file.

Talk to the Men

The #MeToo movement includes numerous male allies, but many of them are at a loss as to what, if anything, they can do to help. Tell them there's a lot they can do.

Parrish says that when the well-meaning, earnest, thoughtful men in her life ask her, "Has that happened to you?" she responds, "#allofus# everysingleone." Telling these men about your experiences helps them see the workplace differently and may just prompt them to speak up the next time they see harassment play out in front of them.

Talk to Your Daughters—and Your Sons

Cynthia Hudson, senior vice president and general manager of CNN en Español, remembers her mother putting up with harassment from a professor who had the power to deny her a PhD. She remembers the powerlessness she felt early in her career when an executive tried to kiss her at a company event. When she rebuffed him, he got angry. He told her, "Who do you think you are? I can hurt you if I want to." The incident terrified her, but she said nothing because "I honestly knew that if I said anything I would be fired."

Hudson said she hadn't thought about that incident in years until the #MeToo movement, when women all over the country began talking about their experiences. She went to her daughters and said, "Let me tell you my story."

My two daughters often will call me up, sometimes in tears, to talk about something that happened at work that they see as sexist or demeaning. I try to give them advice, but often the best I can do is to listen, certain they know that I know exactly what they're talking about.

Support Each Other

If you're dealing with a bully or worse at work, chances are other women are as well. There is power—and solace—in numbers. Just knowing that you're not alone can help settle you down so that you can think more clearly about how to handle a person or a situation. And when there's more than one of you in a room, you can change that little piece of the world.

The Dollars and Sense of Diversity

If you're not covering the entire community, you're not accurate.

—Wanda Lloyd

*W*anda, I don't think I've ever seen any colored girls being a reporter. You better take some education classes so you have a fallback."

Wanda Smalls Lloyd nearly always took her grandmother's advice, but this time she would not. Lloyd knew she wanted to be a journalist from the time she took her first journalism class at the all-black high school she attended in Savannah, Georgia. She had signed up for the class because she was looking for something she thought would be easy and could break up a load of college prep courses. Before long, other students were coming to her for help with their stories, and her teacher was encouraging her to think about journalism as a profession.

After graduating in 1967, Lloyd headed upstate to Spelman College in Atlanta, a prestigious school for African-American women where, despite her grandmother's admonition, she signed up for journalism classes and went to work for the campus newspaper, the *Spelman Spotlight*. One day, a reporter from *Quill*, the Society of Professional Journalists' national magazine, interviewed her for a story about up-and-coming minority students. When the reporter asked about her career goals, Lloyd didn't hesitate: a top newspaper editor, she said.

Lloyd would go on to editing roles at seven daily newspapers, ranging from the *Greenville* (South Carolina) *News* to the *Washington Post*, and she would get that top leadership job as well, serving as the executive editor of the historic *Montgomery* (Alabama) *Advertiser*. Along the way, she would become one of the country's leading African-American female journalists and a powerful advocate for diversity and inclusion in the workplace.

Lloyd entered journalism at a time when there were few women in newsrooms and even fewer black women. The American Society of News Editors (then called the American Society of Newspaper Editors) didn't start asking newspapers about the number of minorities they employed until a few years later, in 1979, but even then it stood at just under 4 percent.[1] And almost no one thought of grooming people who looked like Lloyd for executive-level positions.

The exception was Gannett, a company that started out with a handful of small newspapers in upstate New York and grew to be the nation's largest newspaper chain. It was headed by Allen Neuharth, a flamboyant man who favored white suits and thought of himself as a dreamer and schemer. He had grown up poor and fatherless in rural South Dakota, and he acted as if he had something to prove.

As early as 1969, Neuharth, then the number two at Gannett, was challenging conventional thinking about women and their place in newsrooms. That year, he spoke at an awards dinner for feature writers, most of whom were women. Instead of applauding them, he issued a challenge: "Why do so many of you with so much talent allow the sex gap between yourselves and the top jobs in your profession to continue or even to grow? Why don't more of you prepare yourselves for, and set your sights on, such positions as publisher, editor, managing editor, city editor, broadcast station manager, advertising or public relations executive—or any of the top communications jobs on which the 'For Men Only' sign should come down?"

He went on: "The climate has never been better than it is today for competent and ambitious women in communications to move to top jobs formerly reserved for men. But you have to push and shove and maybe even scratch and claw a bit to get there. You should do it. And if you do, your readers will benefit most of all because you will vastly improve those areas of the newspaper product which are not designed primarily by men, but primarily for women."[2]

Neuharth didn't have the data to prove it back then, but he intuitively knew that diversity would be good for business. Gracia Martore, a former Gannett CEO who worked with Neuharth, put it this way: "It wasn't just the right thing to do; it was the right thing to do for the business. We were in diverse communities across the country and it made an enormous amount of sense to reflect those communities."

*   *   *

Wanda Lloyd grew up in the segregated South. She went to all-black schools, attended an all-black church, and lived in an all-black neighborhood. Her interactions with white people were mainly limited to shopping trips to downtown Savannah, where many stores would not allow African Americans to try on clothes and other merchandise. A woman from Adler's department store would sometimes drive to Lloyd's grandmother's house with a carful of hats so her grandmother could try on and pick out the ones she wanted to buy.

Once, Lloyd's Girl Scout troop was invited to march in a parade with other children from town and enjoy a luncheon at a hotel afterward. Her troop was assigned a position at the rear of the parade and, once at the hotel, the girls were told to walk through the kitchen to reach the dining room. "When I think about it now it makes me angry, but, then, I was excited to get inside that hotel," Lloyd said. "Black people weren't allowed to go to that hotel as guests."

She never ate in a white-tablecloth restaurant, and she never went to Savannah Beach on the Atlantic coast, even though it was just a few miles from her house. African Americans were not allowed there.

Lloyd's strongest childhood memories, though, are not about what she didn't have but what she did have—a community where everyone knew everyone else and people watched out for one another. "We had fun in our own community," she said. "It was close-knit; it was supportive; it was validating."

Outside of Savannah, the world was changing rapidly in ways that would affect the trajectory of Lloyd's life.

In 1967, race riots engulfed the country, and President Lyndon Johnson commissioned a study, led by Illinois governor Otto Kerner, to determine the cause of the unrest and recommend solutions. The Kerner Commission report, issued in 1968, four years after the passage of the federal Civil Rights Act, included a scathing indictment of the media for ignoring African-American communities and reporting from an entirely white perspective. The media, the report stated, urgently needed to integrate.

In 1970, Lloyd was one of the first two African-American women to win a Dow Jones Newspaper Fund internship, a prestigious program for young journalists that had begun twelve years earlier. After several weeks of training, she was sent to Providence, Rhode Island, for a summer internship at the *Providence Evening Bulletin*. She was an anomaly in the almost all-white newsroom, where she kept her head down—no mean feat for a five feet, nine inches tall black woman in New England—and tried to ignore the stares and slights.

While waiting for a bus to take her downtown to the newspaper office, a policeman stopped and told her she was standing on the wrong side of the street. He assumed she was a domestic worker headed to the all-white, up-scale neighborhood for a day of cleaning.

After graduating from college, Lloyd returned to Providence, where she worked for two years. She also did stints at the *Miami Herald* and the *Atlanta Journal* before following her husband, Willie Lloyd, to Washington, DC, where he had found a job and she hoped to do the same. She thought she would try her luck at the *Washington Post*, and her timing was good: The Los Angeles Times-Washington Post News Service needed help. The news service took the best stories from both newspapers, edited them, and sent them to other newspapers around the world that subscribed to the service. During the next eleven years, Lloyd worked her way up from a junior editor to assistant Washington editor for the news service.

The job required her to attend daily news meetings presided over by Ben Bradlee, the legendary, swashbuckling editor who faced down Richard Nixon over the Watergate scandal and helped end Nixon's presidency. It was the mid-1980s, almost twenty years since the Kerner Commission report, but Bradlee's team still consisted almost entirely of white men. Lloyd was usually one of the few minorities and one of the few women in the room.

While Lloyd was happy to be at the *Post*, what she really longed for was a job in the newsroom where the action was. She applied for several editing posts but kept getting turned down. "They gave me all of the excuses, all of the catch words for not being good enough," she said. "I kept saying, 'How do you know? Have you talked to my supervisor? My supervisor seems fine with my work. He keeps giving me additional responsibility.'"

At one point, Lloyd said she and two or three other black women met with Bradlee and laid out their concerns. She said she doesn't remember exactly what he said, "but his attitude was, 'You guys are black and you're working at the *Washington Post*. You ought to be thankful.' He dismissed us. He wasn't convinced what we were saying was necessary or important."

*   *   *

Just across the Potomac River from the *Post*, Neuharth was busy launching an upstart publication that purported to be a true national newspaper. *USA Today* was about as different from the *Post* as two newspapers could be. Launched in 1982, it was the first paper to embrace color photos, graphics, and short, crisp stories. The editors weren't above putting a sports story on the front page, and the editorial page featured an opposing view to every editorial. Even more startling, the paper bucked the practice of using anonymous sources on its news pages—something the *Post* and other establishment newspapers thought indispensable to getting inside information from politicians and bureaucrats.

Journalists across the country responded with predictable disdain, dubbing the new paper the "McPaper." Bradlee, when asked if *USA Today* was a good newspaper, quipped, "If it is, I'm in the wrong business." Neuharth was unfazed. He was widely quoted as saying, "Bradlee and I finally agree on something. He's in the wrong business."[3]

Lloyd's entrée to *USA Today* came through an exchange of children's clothing. A friend who worked there, Alice Bonner, had a daughter a few years older than Lloyd's daughter and she had some clothes to pass along. Bonner was behind schedule editing a story and asked Lloyd to meet her at the paper to pick up the clothes. While she waited, Lloyd decided to visit one of her old mentors, Ron Martin, with whom she had worked at the *Miami Herald* and who had become executive editor of *USA Today*.

As they chatted, Lloyd mentioned that she might be ready for a job change. Martin immediately picked up the phone and connected her with Karen Jurgensen, who had just been named one of the paper's managing editors. Within a few weeks, Lloyd had accepted a job as deputy managing editor with a portfolio that included overseeing major stories.

Again, her family was dubious. Her mother asked her, "Wanda, you're sure you want to do this? You have a mortgage and a baby." Few people understood why she would leave the venerable *Post* for a paper that drew snickers from many credible journalists and was rumored to be bleeding tens of millions of dollars a year.

Bradlee was on her mother's side. When Lloyd told him she was leaving, she recalls him saying, "Really? Really? I wish you all the luck in the world because this is a terrible decision."

* * *

One of Neuharth's first acts when he became CEO of Gannett in 1973 was to name Gloria Biggs publisher of the *Melbourne* (Florida) *Times*. She was the company's first female publisher. He also brought in Bob Maynard, who headed an institute focused on newsroom diversity, as a consultant to help the company figure out how to attract and retain employees of color. And Neuharth talked to anyone who would listen about how important diversity was to the company's bottom line. His logic was simple: A more diverse staff meant better coverage, which translated into more circulation and more revenue.

Neuharth was encouraged by his second wife, Lori Wilson, who was the only woman in the Florida Senate and who worked on a range of diversity initiatives, such as the passage of the federal Equal Rights Amendment. He also was inspired by his mother, who raised him on her own after Neuharth's father was killed in a farming accident. Neuharth was only two years old when his father died, and he never forgot how hard his mother had to work to support the family. In his autobiography, *Confessions of an S.O.B.*, he wrote, "My mother was the first victim of sexual discrimination that I knew. Gannett and I received repeated recognition in the 1970s and '80s as media leaders in hiring, training and promoting women and minorities. Before my mother died at age eighty-six, I told her all of those awards belonged to her."[4]

As a businessman, Neuharth believed female editors might do better than the men who had so long been running newspapers. "Too many male decision-makers in newsrooms were editing newspapers for themselves or their male associates and the reader be damned," he told author Kay Mills. "It seemed to me that it made professional sense to have more females make those decisions and see if their orientation would be different."[5]

He often pushed women into roles they didn't feel entirely prepared for. In 1974, when he told Christy Bulkeley, whose experience largely consisted of writing editorials, he wanted to make her publisher of the *Saratogian* in Saratoga Springs, New York, she replied that she wasn't ready. He said, "You think you're not ready. You're right. But you're as ready as I've ever been for my promotions and you'll grow into it."[6]

Pam McAllister Johnson was teaching journalism at Norfolk State University when recruiters from Gannett visited her class to talk to the students. The next thing Johnson knew, Gannett offered her a job. "They asked me, 'Do you want to be a publisher? I didn't even know what a publisher did, but I said, 'Yes, sure, I want to be a publisher.'"

In 1981, Johnson was sent to New Jersey to train under the publisher at the *Courier-News*, in Bridgewater, for what she thought would be a year or two. But just three months later, a couple of Gannett executives came to call and told her, "You're going to be a publisher now, and it's in this place in New York, and your rental car is waiting downstairs." Johnson said she went downstairs and got in the car but then realized she didn't remember where she was supposed to go. "I had never even heard of Ithaca!" she said. "I get there and park and I look across the street and it says *Ithaca Journal*, and it's a storefront, and I'm like, 'What? What have I gotten myself into?'" She stayed and became the first African-American woman to serve as publisher of a mainstream newspaper in the United States.

While he was making progress in his diversity campaign, Neuharth wasn't satisfied that the company was moving fast enough. He would know when he had done enough, he often remarked, when there were so many women leading newspapers it was no longer news if he fired one of them.

In 1980, Neuharth recruited a white woman, Madelyn Jennings, to head the company's human resources department, and he gave her a mandate to make diversity happen. Jennings, a gracious and glamorous woman with a backbone of steel, understood that an entirely new system of hiring and promotion was required.

The daughter of a professional golfer from Saratoga Springs, New York, Jennings had been vice president of human resources at Standard Brands, held a variety of executive positions at General Electric, and was on the board of directors of a small newspaper company.

Once at Gannett, she quickly began rewriting the company's policies and procedures. Newspaper properties were required to submit reports tracking the diversity of their staffs and justifying their hires. A bonus system was put in place that rewarded top managers for progress on diversity, and women and minorities were sent to a variety of training programs designed to bolster their management skills.

Jennings thought it important that *USA Today*, the flagship newspaper, set an example for the rest of the company, so she began scouting around for a top female executive and found Cathie Black, who had spent her career in the New York magazine industry. In 1983, Black became president of *USA Today*, making her the highest-ranking woman in the newspaper business who wasn't a member of a family that owned a newspaper.

"Neuharth always struck me as someone who lived outside the lines," said Black, who later became publisher of Hearst Magazines. "He didn't care what was expected. He didn't care about being in the in-crowd. He was a maverick. He enjoyed that role. He was ballsy. And Madelyn was a great catalyst. She was fearless. Together, they changed the course of history."

Dolores Wharton, who joined the Gannett board in 1979 and was the first woman and first African American on the board, called Jennings "the mechanism for which [Neuharth] drove the changes that brought in women and minorities. She did it exquisitely. She was a pro. She was one of the strongest people in human resources in the country, and Allen liked getting the best."

In 1982, Jennings and some other Gannett executives visited a newspaper the company had just purchased in Jackson, Mississippi. The team split up to visit various parts of the building, and Jennings was headed to the pressroom when she saw a bathroom door with the word *Colored* on it. "I went to the department head and said, 'You have thirty minutes to get that painted,'" she said, "and he looked at me as if I was from outer space. I said this was unacceptable. I then went to the personnel director's office and told him what I had done. I noticed a Bible on his desk, and I said, 'By the way, we don't have a Bible on our desk. Get it back in your drawer.'"

By 1988, Jennings could see a real difference in the company's numbers. Nearly 40 percent of all managers, professionals, technicians, and sales agents and about one-quarter of newspaper publishers within Gannett were women. The proportion of minorities was 47 percent higher than the national average.[7] No other newspaper company came close to those numbers. That year, *Los Angeles Times* publisher Tom Johnson credited Neuharth "for doing the best job in the business so far, and it's also been very good for the others because those who say that progress can't be made . . . just look at that organization."[8]

Women and minorities also began to notice what was happening at Gannett, which made it easier to attract talent. Martore, a white woman, was in banking when she agreed to join the company in 1985 as assistant treasurer. As she reviewed Gannett's annual report, she was struck by the number of women on the board, the number making their way up the ranks, and the number who already held key leadership positions. She thought Gannett might be the kind of place where she could succeed, and she turned out to be right. By 2011, Martore was CEO of the company, one of only a handful of women who have been leaders of Fortune 500 companies.

Despite leading the way on diversity, Gannett did not erase all the inequities between men and women. In 2016, the labor union representing many of the newsroom staffers at the *Detroit Free Press* found that men made 6.5 percent more an hour than women.[9] Four women filed a lawsuit at the newspaper in 2017; it was still pending in 2018.

*   *   *

When Wanda Lloyd arrived at *USA Today* in 1986, she immediately knew things were going to be far different from what she was used to at the *Washington Post*. For the first time, she had a woman boss, Karen Jurgensen, who would go on to become the first female editor of the newspaper. The daily news meetings Lloyd attended were filled with women who talked about stories they thought would appeal to a wide range of readers.

Lloyd quickly established herself as a calm and thoughtful voice in a newsroom that sometimes verged on chaos. Other editors were impressed and, more surprising to Lloyd, so was her mother back in Savannah. "It looks like your career is taking off," she told her daughter with no small amount of pride.

Lloyd was selected for an eight-week management training program in Illinois, and her husband, together with friends and neighbors, managed childcare for Shelby, their four-year-old daughter, while Lloyd was gone. At the workshop, Lloyd learned about budgeting, personnel management, marketing, and sales, and when she returned, she was promoted to managing editor for newsroom administration, making her one of the highest-ranking black women in the newspaper industry at the time.

Lloyd's new job put her in charge of hiring and recruiting, and she worked hard to bring in diverse talent from around the country. Often she was competing against the *Post* for talent. She once won over a black female sports editor by telling her to go visit the sports department at each paper and think about where she would best fit in. The woman took the job at *USA Today*.

But even at a place where diversity was baked into the culture, Lloyd didn't always feel at home. Although she grew close to Jurgensen, she was uncomfortable around many of the other white women, she said, and she encountered remnants of the good ol' boy system. One day, Lloyd discovered that a new secretary had been assigned to the newsroom without her knowledge or approval. It turned out that the woman had worked for an executive in another department and a guard had discovered the pair having sex in an office. The woman was reassigned to news, and the executive was sent to a small Gannett paper as publisher. Lloyd was shocked that he wasn't fired.

Because she was in charge of budget and newsroom personnel, Lloyd was viewed as the editor's right-hand person, an arrangement that worked well for ten years under two editors. But in 1994, Dave Mazzarella became editor and promptly promoted four white men to key positions. Lloyd was furious, not just because it was all white men who were promoted but because she hadn't been consulted in her role as senior editor for administration.

Mazzarella said he received "some flak" for the decision, but "I picked the best people for the job at the time. I didn't know any females who would fit into those roles."

This was not a version of *USA Today* Lloyd had seen before. She decided it was time to leave.

*　*　*

Building a diverse workforce has been a long, slow climb in most industries, but it has been especially slow in media companies.

Women made up 20 percent of newsroom employees in 1971, according to a survey by Indiana University. The number jumped to 34 percent by 1982,[10] but then progress slowed. In 1999, the American Society of News Editors began tracking the percentage of women employed in newsrooms. That year, it was 37 percent.[11] In 2017, it had inched up to 39 percent.[12]

For women of color working at American newspapers, the numbers were even worse. According to ASNE, about 8 percent of newspaper company employees were women of color in 2017. Only 6 percent of newsroom leaders were women of color.[13]

While *USA Today* has had three female editors at various times in its history, many major newspapers have never had a female top editor. Those papers include the *Wall Street Journal*, the *Washington Post*, and the *Los Angeles Times*.

Top female executives are even more rare in network television news. Deborah Turness became the first female network news president in 2013, when she took over the news division at NBC. In 2018, Susan Zirinsky was named president of CBS News, becoming only the second woman to ever lead a network news operation.

After Turness became president of NBC News in 2013, it didn't take long for rumblings of dissatisfaction to surface. A *New York Times* article quoted one anonymous staffer as saying Turness brought "a bit of rock-chick swagger to a newsroom full of middle-aged men."[14] Turness, who had a successful career in British broadcasting before joining NBC, replied in a typically understated British way: "The heat that happens here is quite unique." Before the end of 2017, she had been moved to another job.

Craig Robinson, chief diversity officer for NBCUniversal, declined to talk about Turness, but he is well versed in the difficulties of creating a diverse workplace. He said most companies are careful to create promotional materials with photos of diverse workers, and they talk about how diversity is good for business, but they don't do much to explain why it's important. When he's at a cocktail party and tells someone what he does for a living, he typically gets one of three responses. Some people (almost always women or people of color) say, "That's great," and then tell him a personal story about their own struggles. Other people, upon learning he's a diversity officer, ask, "What's that?" The third response is something like, "Oh, that's that quota, HR thing."

Until companies really begin to make the business case for diversity, he said, it's going to be difficult to move forward.

*   *   *

Once Lloyd decided to leave *USA Today*, her first step was to talk to recruiters for Gannett. At the time, *USA Today* was a separate division from the rest of the Gannett enterprise, and its other papers were looking for talent. In particular, they needed editors for a chain of newspapers the company had recently purchased in the Southeast. Lloyd interviewed and was sent to Greenville, South Carolina, as one of two managing editors. There, she would learn how to run a small newspaper, and her appointment would help Greenville acclimate to Gannett.

The African-American community in Greenville welcomed Lloyd, but she had more trouble with the news staff, which was made up of many longtime reporters and editors, mostly white and male, who were a little suspicious of an outsider. It didn't help when she began making changes that went to the core of how things had always been done at the *Greenville News*.

Lloyd was struck by how many mug shots of African-American men who had been arrested for a crime showed up on the front page of the paper. In fact, it seemed to her that getting arrested for a crime was about the only time African Americans made the front page. She announced that the paper had a new policy: Unless the suspect was at large or a threat to society, the photo would not appear on page 1.

Lloyd also began working to "mainstream" the paper to make it more reflective of the community. *USA Today* had been practicing mainstreaming since its launch in 1982, requiring that photos of women and minorities appear throughout the newspaper and that reporters develop source lists that included women and people of color. Inside the Greenville newsroom, Lloyd said there was passive resistance. Photos of black men arrested for small crimes would slip into the paper. "I never felt any personal animosity, but [there were] curmudgeonly attitudes," she said.

Four years into the job, Lloyd got a call from the Freedom Forum, a nonprofit focused on journalism that Neuharth had helped create after he retired from Gannett. As head of the foundation, Neuharth was intent on directing its resources to promote the issues he cared about most, including diversity.

Lloyd joined the staff and was put in charge of developing a diversity institute in Nashville, Tennessee. The concept was for newspapers in various cities to recruit diverse residents who were not journalists but who knew and cared about their communities. The recruits would come to Nashville for training in journalism and then return to their communities prepared to join their local newspaper staffs. It was an innovative program designed to address the difficulties of recruiting minorities by helping papers "grow their own" talent, but it never really got off the ground. Newspapers had begun to lose advertising revenue, and editors had other priorities for spending their money. After three years, Lloyd made a call to Gannett to see if the company was interested in taking her back.

Gannett told her the editorship of the *Montgomery Advertiser* was open, and Lloyd was immediately interested. Montgomery was where Rosa Parks, a secretary with the local NAACP, made her stand against segregation when she refused to move to the back of a city bus and give up her seat to a white man. The 1955 incident sparked a bus boycott that lasted more than a year and set the stage for Martin Luther King Jr. to mount a national crusade against segregation.

It was a thrilling prospect to edit a newspaper in a city with such a rich history. When Lloyd told Charles Overby, a longtime newspaper editor and executive, that she was becoming editor in Montgomery, Overby responded, "Well, Wanda . . . that's like being governor of Alabama."

Like many Southern papers, the *Advertiser* had a complicated history with civil rights. Although a former editor, Grover Hall, won a Pulitzer Prize in 1928 for his editorial attacks on the Ku Klux Klan, the *Advertiser* was more often "on the wrong side of civil rights," said Kenneth Mullinax, a former reporter. In 2018, the *Advertiser* published an editorial acknowledging the city's "sordid history of slavery and lynching" and recognizing "its own shameful place in the history of these dastardly, murderous deeds."[15]

When Lloyd was named editor of the *Advertiser* in 2004, news organizations around the country took note. The number of women who have made it to the top editor post at newspapers is small, but for women of color it is minuscule. Only a handful of women of color have ever been the editor of a newspaper as large and influential as the *Advertiser*.

"Dr. King's ideal of a beloved community was coming true because of her," Mullinax said. "Here we were, this old racist rag, and here she was as the leader of that paper. It was a breath of fresh air."

But amid the buoyancy, Lloyd was worried: Readership of the newspaper in Montgomery's African-American community was low. She got to work, starting with the exasperating police photos of black men on the front pages, and kept pushing for more minority coverage. "If you're not covering the entire community, you're not accurate," she told the staff. As the fiftieth anniversary of the historic bus boycott approached, she oversaw an award-winning project that documented the effect of the boycott on Montgomery and the nation. The package was so powerful that the Target corporation paid for a million copies to be distributed in schools across the country. The presses ran nearly nonstop for more than a week.

Lloyd was comfortable with authority, but she had learned to be careful about how others saw her. She didn't want to push change at the *Advertiser* through intimidation or force. When asked if she shared any characteristics with Rosa Parks, she said, "We were both quiet change-makers."

Still, there were times when she simply put her foot down. Each year, the newspaper would send a photographer to take a photo of a birthday cake baked by a local couple to honor Confederate general Robert E. Lee. Lloyd put an end to that. And when reporters started investigating allegations that public school teachers were rigging student test scores, African-American leaders descended on the newspaper and spent a day and a half trying to convince Lloyd to drop the investigation. She refused.

Sometimes, the issues she dealt with were subtle. During meetings with state officials to discuss the paper's editorial positions, she would ask questions only to have the official de jour address his answers to the white men in the room.

Through it all, Lloyd kept her calm until one day when she received an email complaining that the paper was giving African Americans too much coverage. It was a nasty note, filled with racial invectives and a pointed reference about knowing where Lloyd went to church. Lloyd also discovered that the email had been sent to the publisher and everyone in the newsroom. She ran to HR, closed the door, and started screaming, "I can't take this anymore!"

"I had never in my life lost it like that before," she said. "I sobbed uncontrollably for at least five minutes. My whole body was shaking. I just had never encountered anything like that. I had encountered racism all my life, but this racism was directed directly at me as an employee, as a journalist, as a person. Later, I was surprised they didn't call an ambulance for me; that's how bad it was."

Lloyd remained editor of the *Advertiser* for almost nine years before deciding in 2013 that she was finished with the newspaper business. She still loved being an editor, but she was worn out from dealing with budget cuts that had forced several rounds of newsroom layoffs. She returned home to Savannah and spent three years as the chair of the journalism program at Savannah State University, the oldest historically black college in Georgia, before turning her attention to a personal memoir, tentatively titled *From Jim Crow to Journalism Giant*.

She's satisfied with what she was able to accomplish during more than forty years in journalism, and she's proud of the stories her papers did and the people she mentored along the way. Every once in a while, though, she returns in her mind to that conversation with *Post* editor Ben Bradlee back in the 1980s.

"Here's what I said after I got back from that meeting with Ben Bradlee: 'It's going to take at least a generational change of leadership to make diversity work,'" she said. "We've had a couple of generations since then, and it's still not there. But I'm hopeful that the generation behind us, who have grown up in more diverse environments and have seen women as leaders, will be different."

*   *   *

ADVICE FOR WOMEN LEADERS

Julia Wallace

When I was a reporter in Dallas early in my career, I was convinced that my destiny was to be an editor. I volunteered to work weekends filling in on the city desk, and I loved it. When an assistant city editor position came open, I applied for the job but was told that I wasn't right for it because I didn't dress like an editor.

That was true. There were no other female editors in news. So, no, I didn't dress like an editor!

A year later, in 1982, a friend told me about a new newspaper called *USA Today*. I applied for a job, hoping that my gender wouldn't be the liability it appeared to be at the *Dallas Times Herald*. Beginning with the interview, it was clear to me that this was a different kind of place. A woman, Nancy

Woodhull, held one of the top jobs, managing editor for news, and there were more female than male editors in news.

I got the job and reported for *USA Today* for about a year before deciding to give the editing idea another try. I went to my boss and asked if there were any positions available. We talked about a few possibilities, and then he literally created an editing position for me.

Later, one of the men who worked for me joked that he felt like he was living in a "matriarchal society." I asked if he meant the South. He said no, he meant Gannett. Every one of his bosses had been a woman.

Kristin was a young mother working in Charleston, South Carolina, in the early 1980s when she was recruited by the *Times-Picayune* newspaper in New Orleans. She was hesitant at first; she and her husband had been in Charleston for only about a year, and the move would mean her husband would have to give up a job he liked. Before she could make a decision, she learned she was pregnant with her second child, and she figured that was the end of the conversation with the *Picayune*. When Jim Amoss, who went on to become editor of the paper, called her a second time, she told him, "Well, I don't think you're going to be interested in me any longer; I just found out I'm pregnant."

Amoss said that wasn't a problem. "What about health benefits and maternity leave?" Kristin asked. "I won't be covered because this would be a preexisting condition." Amoss said not to worry; everything would be taken care of. Kristin accepted the job and spent the next ten years at the paper. (The baby was a girl.)

For Kristin and me and Wanda Lloyd, finding the right place to work made all the difference in our careers. We were lucky to find companies that gave us the chance to show what we could do.

Of course, no one place fits everyone, and finding the right match is a little like choosing the right spouse: Caution is required. There was a time when I looked for positions based on what kind of job it was and the city I would be working in. It took time for me to realize that even more important is the company itself. It's just not worth the emotional energy to work at a place where you're not respected, no matter how good the job seems.

Following are some things to think about when you're considering a company, and some things to do once you get there.

Who's at the Top?

Do the people in charge talk about diversity? If they're leaving diversity to someone in human resources, it's not going to happen. What made diversity work in Gannett was Neuharth's personal passion and constant focus. Ron Martin, who was the executive editor of *USA Today* when I was there, was constantly encouraging and guiding women and minorities. He hired me as managing editor of the *Atlanta Journal-Constitution*, and I became editor when he retired. When people ask me about mentors, Martin is always number one on my list.

The Little Things Count, Too

You want to have a good sense of how many women and minorities a company employs and what kinds of positions they hold, but a true commitment to diversity is about more than numbers. What do the company's policies and practices tell you? How are raises and promotions decided? Is there pay equity? What are the family leave policies? Do employees feel like they can leave to pick up a sick child or go to a parent-teacher conference in the middle of the day? Is there a place for nursing mothers? Sometimes it's the little things that count. A reporter once told me she decided to accept my offer of a job because she was so impressed by how clean and modern the women's bathrooms were. (I hate to think what the bathrooms looked like where she worked before.)

Do Your Part

Once you've joined a company, do your part to encourage a diverse and inclusive environment. Try to understand what it's like to walk in someone else's shoes. As a woman of Indian descent who grew up in Puerto Rico and New York, Mitra Kalita, senior vice president for news, opinion, and programming at CNN Digital, said she often acts as a translator and explainer. "I feel like I spend so much time talking to white women about the need to be more inclusive. They're rightfully angry about the ol' boys' club that dictates our lives right now," she said, "but there are a lot of other people who say, 'Look at what I've been up against today.'" Being a good colleague helps build a good workplace.

Remember: It's Not Kindergarten

Understand that in the real world, business is a contact sport and a certain amount of toughness is required. Jan Neuharth remembers her father, Al, as being someone who was always pushing women to stand up for themselves. Once, when she was young, her older brother hit her and she ran to her father, demanding that he do something about it. Her dad turned to her and said, "Hit him back."

A Short History of the First
Female Editor of the *New York Times*

I felt a burden the whole time: "Don't let the girls' team down."
I felt every day had to be great.

—Jill Abramson

In a photo that went viral the day after she was sacked as the top editor of
the *New York Times*, Jill Abramson is poised to hit a punching bag.

She's wearing black boxing gloves, a baseball cap, and a long white tank
top that exposes a tattoo of a subway token on her right shoulder. She's looking directly at the camera with an expression that falls somewhere between a
smile and a grimace. The *New York Post* featured the photo on its front page
with the headline "Sacked Times Editor Ready to Rumble. An-Grey Lady!"

If Abramson is angry, it's a controlled burn.

The first female executive editor in the *Times*'s 160-year history,
Abramson's appointment in June 2011 produced an avalanche of "it's about
time" reactions as well as praise. "Nobody doubts that Abramson, a terrific
reporter and a calm, intelligent managing editor, is totally qualified for the
job," wrote the *Guardian*'s Peter Preston. "Happy, historic days!"[1]

The appointment was particularly momentous for an institution where
being a man, especially a white man, had long guaranteed more pay and better opportunities. In 1974, after years of being told, "No," the women of the
Times sued. The federal class action suit was settled in 1978, and the *Times*
agreed to an affirmative action program, but progress was slow. Twenty years
after the suit, only two women had made it as far as editing roles on the metro
desk, and one of them observed that she wouldn't have made it even that far
if she had been a mother.

Abramson's tenure as executive editor lasted just thirty-two months,
one of the shortest in the *Times*'s history, for a myriad of reasons. There were

pressing financial issues and internal challenges to the long-standing and sacrosanct separation between news and advertising. The role of the editor was changing, with far more pressure to work across departments—and make money. The *Times*, like other American newspapers, was struggling to catch up and compete online.

Such pressures might have done in any number of editors, but Abramson faced an additional hurdle: She was a woman leading one of the world's most important news organizations. No woman had ever come close to doing that before. Abramson's success hinged not just on her performance as an editor, but on her performance as a female editor in a place and in an industry still unused to a woman being in charge.

*   *   *

On the day that Abramson was ousted, Natalie Nougayrède, the first female editor of *Le Monde*, also lost her job, contributing to growing angst about the status of women in journalism. What had seemed to be slow but inevitable progress since the start of the women's movement of the 1970s did not appear inevitable anymore. It was suddenly clear that not only was it the rare woman who could get and hold onto a top news position but women were, in fact, regressing.

In 2014, *Nieman Reports* devoted a special edition to the problem, concluding that fewer women headed major U.S. newspapers that year than they did a decade earlier. The report noted that the very public departures of Abramson and Nougayrède were "merely the latest sign that, with a few notable exceptions and in spite of years of work toward more diversity, men still run the industry."[2]

There are as many reasons for the dearth of women newsroom leaders as there are numbers that prove the point. Often women opt out of the pipeline for top jobs for personal reasons or because they have grown discouraged by their news organization's culture and their chances of success. Some, like Abramson, persist, working their way to the top only to find that when they get there, they are woefully unprepared for the challenges they face.

*   *   *

Abramson grew up in a well-to-do New York family that revered the *New York Times*. Delivered to the family's Central Park West apartment each day were two copies of the paper—one that Abramson's father, Norman, carried to work and one that remained at home.

Norman Abramson was a flamboyant man who, when young and single, liked to date showgirls and play pool. The pool playing got him kicked out of New York University, according to his daughter, and he never did finish college. The owner of a prosperous textile company, Norman had big ambitions for his two daughters, and he didn't countenance mediocrity. When it became clear that Jill, the youngest by six years, was embarrassingly bad at sports, he would hurry home from work, walk her across the street to Central Park, and make her play catch with him until it got dark. Jill never really got the hang of it, but she did learn to fear throwing like a girl.

Her mother, Dovie, was a Barnard graduate who read widely, frequented the theater, and volunteered in schools and on behalf of liberal causes. She was the kind of woman who was always exquisitely dressed and perfectly made up. "Even the week before she died, she would put on full makeup and lipstick every day," her daughter said. "It would never have occurred to her to go out without her face on. She was five feet, six inches tall and never weighed over 120 pounds. She was pretty, and that mattered to her." Jill and her sister, Jane, on the other hand, were completely indifferent to either makeup or clothes—a source of constant disappointment to their mother. "Maybe it was the era I grew up in," Abramson said, "but I don't really know how to put on makeup, although I wore makeup to the Oscars, I'm pretty sure."

Now in her sixties, Abramson seems to strive for unadorned. She favors black shift dresses, black tights, and black boots. Her hair, brown with a hint of gray, is cut bluntly just below her chin. She has never colored it, although her friend Maureen Dowd, the *Times*'s op-ed columnist, has tried to convince her to try highlights. Dowd "works on me," Abramson said. "And she's made me somewhat more fashionable. She sends me ads for things I should buy to this day."

The most memorable thing about Abramson, though, is not the way she looks but the way she talks. In a profile for the *New Yorker*, writer Ken Auletta described her voice as the equivalent of "a nasal car honk."[3] She also has a way of elongating the last word in a sentence (*news* becomes *newwwwws*) before promptly launching into the next sentence. Whether purposeful or not, the effect is to shut people up.

Some say that Abramson's voice is matched by her manner, which has been described as grating, abrasive, brusque, intimidating, high-handed, and condescending. Although she is all of five feet, two inches tall, she is altogether capable of sucking the air out of a room. Others say such characterizations are harsh and unfair. Bill Keller, who was executive editor of the *Times* before Abramson, can't imagine people taking so much note of a man's voice.

Glenn Kramon, who served as an assistant managing editor under Abramson and several other *Times* editors, observed, "Jill had a look on her face that—if you knew her—meant she was thinking. But some who didn't know her took it as scowling and unhappy, and so much of how you are received is how you look. So, without meaning to, she alienated people by implying that she was more upset than she really was."

Abramson seemed oblivious to much of the criticism. She cared far more about the journalism. A longtime investigative reporter before moving into management, she reveled in the chase for a good story, and she hated getting beat. "The cycle of investigative reporting is literally manic-depressive," she explained. "I would convince myself that I would never get another great story again. Any time I got beat on something, I despaired."

It was that drive that helped propel Abramson's rise at the *Times*. She was named head of the Washington bureau in 2000 and managing editor in 2003—the first woman to hold either job.

Keller, executive editor of the *Times* from 2003 to 2011, said he was looking for someone with investigative chops when he picked Abramson to be his managing editor. "I don't have the obsessive quality that makes a good investigative reporter," he said. "I wanted an ME who would supply that."

Keller also thought it was time for the newspaper to promote a woman. "We had been promising since before [former managing editor] Arthur Gelb's day [in the 1980s] that we were going to improve the lot of women, so making Jill managing editor helped that in two ways. One, it sent a message that the glass ceiling has gotten a little higher," he said. Second, the hope was that Abramson would move other promising women into positions where they could advance. "There was a lot of talent that was being underutilized," Keller said. "It was just stupid not to have these talented women in places where you needed talented women."

Abramson delivered, championing women throughout the newsroom and promoting them to department heads and other leadership positions, and she delivered in other ways as well. The *Times*'s investigative work improved, and she was respected in the newsroom, Keller said. She reacted quickly to news, was comfortable with authority, and could be counted on to handle things when Keller was away. And she was loyal. "It's not that hard to find people who will tell you you're full of shit," he said. "But they also tend to be the same people who leak to everyone else that you're full of shit."

Abramson had managed newsrooms before. Early in her career, she served as editor in chief of the *Legal Times* in Washington, DC, for two years before joining the *Wall Street Journal* as a senior reporter, eventually becoming deputy Washington bureau chief. But she mostly learned to manage by instinct. The mother of two grown children, Abramson remembers thinking that being a good manager couldn't be much different from "being a great parent, which I think I really am. I kind of thought: I made that up as I went along, so I thought I could do the same" at the *Times*.

For a long time, it worked. During her eight years as managing editor, "I was pushy," Abramson said, "but I don't think people focused on that. I was within the normal range of being aggressive. . . . It didn't become an issue until I became top editor." That's when Abramson came up against a hard reality: To succeed as the editor of one of the world's largest and most powerful news organizations requires skills she had spent almost no time developing: skills like managing across departments, building a loyal team, and protecting the bottom line.

Abramson readily admits to being unprepared for the top job. She said one of her fatal mistakes was that "I didn't devote one hour of thought to, 'If I ever got Bill's job, what kind of team would I want?'" Instead, she said she appointed her chief rival for the job, Dean Baquet, to managing editor and let him pick the rest of the top leadership team.

While she approved of Baquet's choices, some of them were inevitably more loyal to him than to her. Two editors who Abramson thought "had my back" took buyouts, leaving her isolated at the top. "No one ever said to me, 'Jill, the most important thing when you get to the top of a big operation is building your team.' I didn't invest my time in building relationships and cultivating a team . . . and seeking their input on important issues. . . . I thought Dean and I could decide everything."

She said several people warned her about Baquet trying to usurp her, but she brushed it off. "I didn't do anything because I really enjoyed working with Dean. I didn't feel threatened. We had very similar tastes—we both love investigative work. Journalistically, we were a good team."

As executive editor, Abramson became a minor celebrity. She was in demand for speeches and public appearances, and there were invitations to the Oscars, White House dinners, the Kentucky Derby, and the Sundance Film Festival. She jetted to Cairo, China, Cuba, India, Pakistan, London, and Israel. It "was my shot to see the world," she said, "and I was going to take my shot." In the newsroom, there was grumbling about how often she was gone, leaving Baquet to run the news meetings and to make the big decisions about coverage.

She liked to entertain, frequently hosting *Times* staff members at her loft apartment in Tribeca, even though, she said, the "bathrooms were disgraceful." She once asked *Times* publisher Arthur Sulzberger Jr. for a $50,000 loan to renovate the bathrooms, a request she said the paper's human resources eventually turned down, despite the fact that other loans had been made to senior executives and at least one editor had been given a clothing allowance.

Travel and parties aside, there were parts of the job Abramson detested. She had little control over her schedule, which was divided into fifteen-minute increments, and there were endless meetings, very few of which "involved talking about journalism," she said. "It made me crabby and upset."

A number of the meetings involved the need for the paper to build its digital presence and find a way to draw in advertisers who were no longer interested in the print product. Kramon, who had worked with Abramson dating back to her days in the Washington bureau, said, "When we began taking digital seriously, there were many wrong turns. We didn't know what would work and what wouldn't work. So much time was invested in dry wells that produced little return but consumed a lot of time, and I think she became more and more frustrated by that."

There also was pressure to tap the newsroom for revenue-generating ideas and to dissolve some of the separation between the business side of the operation and the news side. Abramson said she fought the moves. She remembers at least one heated conversation with Publisher Sulzberger and CEO Mark Thompson, during which she told them, "If that's what you expect, you have the wrong executive editor."

"I didn't understand fully how desperate the revenue situation was," she said. "I knew it was bad, but I didn't think it was so bad that these traditions had to go away. And I was wrong; I was too hard line. I saw native advertising as immoral. Eventually I stood down, but probably I was too doctrinaire."

Those meetings helped contribute to a reputation that she was "not a great collaborator," Abramson concedes, and a handful of incidents in the newsroom reinforced that perception.

A widely circulated 2013 story in *Politico* described several occasions when Abramson snapped at colleagues.[4] During one meeting, she pointed out that the headline on a story posted on the *Times*'s website was incorrect. When the editor responsible for the page didn't get up immediately to fix it, Abramson asked him what he was still doing in the room.

Abramson confirms the story but insists she never shouted at people or deliberately humiliated them. "I think some reporters would say I banged my fists, but I didn't. I think it's like my kids—if I talked to them in a stern voice and expressed disappointment, they would say, 'Mommy, you have to stop yelling at me.' It's because it came from me—an authority figure—that it was perceived as yelling."

She also thinks she was judged more severely because she's a woman. She was incredulous when people began comparing her behavior to that of Howell Raines, the *Times*'s executive editor from 2001 to 2003, who was widely viewed as a tyrant. Her actions, she said, didn't approach Raines's level of rancor and "wouldn't have been viewed in the same way if I were a man."

The question of a double standard came up again when Abramson had a run-in with Baquet that lit up the *Times*'s newsroom. Abramson had called Baquet into her office to complain about coverage that she didn't think was sharp enough. Baquet barreled out of her office, slammed his hand against a wall, and disappeared from the newsroom for the rest of the day. He later apologized for throwing "a tantrum."

"If I put my fist through the wall, I would have been fired or committed to an insane asylum," Abramson observed. Instead, the newsroom seemed to sympathize with Baquet, who was a popular leader with strong people skills, and the story fed the narrative that Abramson was the one who was difficult to work with.

Abramson largely ignored the criticisms of her management style (although she said the *Politico* story made her cry). She had no time or patience for office politics. She wasn't chummy with her boss, and she didn't particularly care whether people liked her. "I'm Popeye," she said with a laugh, referring to the cartoon character who drew strength from eating spinach. "I am what I am. I'm like, 'deal with it.' That's how I've always been."

When Abramson is most animated, she's either talking about her children or a big news story. She rattles off the stories she's proudest of: coverage of the 2008 financial crises and national security breaches; offshore money coming into the Clinton-Gore campaign; the scandals that brought down former New York governor Eliot Spitzer; a series on homeless children in New York.

Journalistically, the *Times* was doing well. In 2013, the newspaper was awarded two Pulitzer Prizes; the next year it was four, one of the best Pulitzer showings in the paper's history. The paper also was making progress on the digital front, debuting "Snow Fall," a multimedia story about an avalanche that was so beautiful it set a new standard for digital storytelling. Abramson felt she was on a roll.

Then in early 2014, two and a half years into her editorship, she got a wake-up call in the form of a letter from Sulzberger.

"He handed me this letter and said, 'This is a tough letter. I'll leave you to read this,'" Abramson recalled. "I said, 'No, I want you to stay here while I read it,' and I read it. The first question I asked was, 'Do you want someone else in this job?'"

*   *   *

Abramson is not the first woman who has struggled after making it to the executive suite, and she won't be the last. Gail Evans thinks she knows the reason why: Women don't know how to play the game. Evans, who wrote the book *Play like a Man, Win like a Woman*, was the first female executive vice president at CNN. She believes women need to stop thinking of politics as a dirty word and learn how to build powerful coalitions that help secure their positions.

"Guys move in packs," she said. "So one guy gets the big job, and he brings his team with him. She gets the big job and she believes you give everybody a fair chance, so she leaves everybody in place where they were. . . . When you get into a position like the editor of a newspaper, you need to have somebody who can watch out for your back [and] who can really tell you the truth. And clean up your mess."

Pat Fili-Krushel, who rose to one of the top TV jobs in the country as chair of NBCUniversal News Group, learned that lesson the hard way. She thought she was a star at the Lifetime Channel, well positioned to become the next CEO. Instead, the job went to someone who had spent time cultivating relationships with the board of directors. She vowed never to let that happen again.

"When you're driving a car, you don't look at your feet; you look through the windshield so you look out to where you're going," she said. "You've got to look through that windshield to make sure you are positioning yourself for what comes next, which includes looking sideways to your colleagues. I'm not saying be political, but you need to be politically astute."

A 2017 McKinsey & Company study, "Women in the Workplace," identified other common factors that hold women back. The study noted that women occupy only 21 percent of C-suite jobs in American corporations and even fewer are CEOs or serve on corporate boards. Among the reasons: Women don't get as many assignments as men that prepare them for the next job, and they don't get meaningful mentoring support or much honest feedback.[5]

For the top jobs, publishers, boards of directors, and CEOs don't just want someone with excellent skills who knows how to get things done. They want someone who thinks strategically, inspires large numbers of employees, networks well, and projects a strong executive presence. While the word "gender" is not mentioned, that string of characteristics is almost universally associated with men. Women simply have a harder time convincing others they fit the bill.

In a 2007 *Harvard Business Review* article, psychology professors Alice Eagly and Linda Carli offered a different way of looking at the problem: Women, especially those in top management jobs, face conscious and unconscious bias from all directions—their bosses, their peers, and their employees. They face the challenges of balancing work with family life, and they are allowed a much narrower range of acceptable leadership behaviors than men. Women don't face a glass ceiling so much as they face a labyrinth, with mind-bending twists and turns every step of the way.[6]

For Abramson, the labyrinth at a place like the *New York Times* was especially murky. And it was about to get even more so.

* * *

The letter Arthur Sulzberger handed Abramson that morning in January 2014 struck her as incredibly personal. It outlined her faults—that she could be abrupt and pushy and that her management style was not as congenial as it should be. "It was all about the style and not the substance of the job," she said. When she asked why she had heard none of these complaints before, Sulzberger told her he had only recently learned of them. He said he was not asking for her resignation, but he wanted this to be "a wake-up call," she said.

Abramson was convinced she was being evaluated by a double standard. "I'm sure he had legitimate criticisms," she said of Sulzberger, "but I think a lot of it was the she's-too-sure-of-herself version of too aggressive."

She took Sulzberger's letter to an attorney specializing in sex discrimination and asked if it meant she was about to get fired. She said the attorney told her it didn't look good and she might have a case. Then she went to Michael Golden, vice chair of the New York Times Company, and asked to be assigned a management coach. She knew the *Times* was paying for another editor—also a woman—to get management coaching, and the woman was enthusiastic. She told Abramson it was "like getting someone to organize your closet."

Abramson said she met with the coach, who agreed with her that the letter was sexist. "She thought I was being railroaded. She never thought I'd ever be able to make improvements that would satisfy what she saw as a double standard. She told me to be prepared to be fired." Still, the coach offered some suggestions on how Abramson might temper her style and, over the next months, Abramson said she tried to be less argumentative, especially in her dealings with other departments. It seemed to work. That spring, a couple of months after delivering his warning letter, Sulzberger took her to lunch and told her she had "cured" the problem, and he had gone to the board to get a raise for her, Abramson said.

At about the same time, a newsroom salary study revealed gender inequities, and Abramson became convinced that hers represented one of the biggest inequities of all. She discovered that in her former position as managing editor, she had been making less than her male counterpart had, and she was making significantly less than Keller did when he held the executive editor job before her. Instead of talking to Sulzberger about her concerns, Abramson said she wrote a letter that "basically said, 'You guys have screwed me out of a lot of money.'"

The answer she got was that the salary differential was justified because Keller had been with the company far longer than she had been, she said. She was offered a raise, but the amount was far below what she had in mind, so she hired an attorney to represent her in salary negotiations. "That flipped them out. They thought it was very un-Times-ian," she said. "But it didn't seem unbelievably bananas to me. After a glowing review, I thought I could ask for justice on my money."

Abramson doesn't believe she would have been fired just because she was pushing for more money. What really did her in, she said, was her effort to hire Janine Gibson, editor of the *Guardian*'s American digital operations, as the *Times*'s second managing editor. Abramson had gotten to know Gibson while their two companies were preparing to publish stories about National Security Agency surveillance based on leaked material from Edward Snowden. Abramson wanted Gibson to lead the *Times*'s digital operations. It was a sensitive negotiation because Baquet could be expected to be unhappy about sharing the managing editor title with someone else.

Abramson talked to Baquet in general terms about how the *Times* had often had two managing editors and that she needed someone who could focus exclusively on digital, which was becoming increasingly important, but she concedes that she wasn't as forthcoming with him as she should have been. Thompson and Sulzberger, though, were fully up to speed, she insisted. She even arranged for Gibson to meet with Sulzberger.

When Baquet got wind of the meeting, he went to Abramson to complain that he hadn't been consulted. "He was mad and had reason to be mad," she said.

She was concerned, so she asked Sulzberger to take Baquet to dinner to calm him down and reassure him that he was next in line to be executive editor. She said Sulzberger agreed and told her he would call her afterward to let her know how it had gone.

The night of the dinner, Sulzberger made the call as promised. Abramson said he reached her at home and told her things had not gone well. "He said it was a very tough dinner." It has been widely rumored that Baquet gave Sulzberger an ultimatum to choose between him and Abramson, but Abramson said she doesn't know if that's true; she only knows she feels betrayed by someone who she thought "had my back." Baquet turned down requests to be interviewed on the record.

1. Diane McFarlin is the only woman attending a news meeting at Florida's *Sarasota Herald-Tribune* sometime in the 1980s. McFarlin rose to executive editor and then president and publisher of the paper. *Courtesy of Diane McFarlin*

2. Christiane Amanpour, CNN anchor and chief international correspondent, makes no apologies for her style and encourages others to follow her lead. "Look, I think that women have been playing nice for an awfully long time," she says. "I think that we have to start kicking the door down." *Courtesy of Christiane Amanpour*

3. Audrey Cooper, the first female editor-in-chief of the *San Francisco Chronicle*, was often the one cutting cakes at newsroom celebrations. "Then I thought, 'Why am I the one cutting the cake every single time?'" she says. *Mike Kepka; 2015 photo*

4. Cynthia Hudson, head of CNN en Español, describes herself as having "Cuban passion in my bloodstream." She realized that when she got excited about something, she could come across as loud and angry. "I'm not abrasive," she says, "but sometimes my style comes across as dominant, so I pull back." *Courtesy of CNN en Español*

5. Marcy McGinnis began as a secretary at CBS News and rose to the number two job in the news department. Here, she is part of a twenty-fifth-anniversary celebration for then-anchor Walter Cronkite. *Courtesy of Marcy McGinnis; 1975 photo*

6. Marcy McGinnis quiets the crowd during a good-bye party for CBS anchor Dan Rather in 2005. McGinnis served Rather coffee when she started at the network and went on to become his boss. *John Filo*

7. Linda Mason became the first female producer of the *CBS Evening News* in 1971. She eventually was named senior vice president for standards at the network. In 1995, she traveled to Cuba with anchor Dan Rather (left) to interview Cuban leader Fidel Castro (middle). *1995 photo*

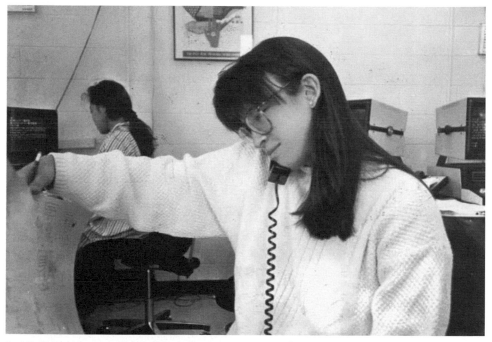

8. Mi-Ai Parrish was editor of her college newspaper at the University of Maryland. She avoided alcohol, dressed in boxy sweaters, and wore giant glasses, all in an attempt to be as invisible as possible. *Courtesy of Mi-Ai Parrish; 1991 photo*

9. While publisher of the *Arizona Republic* in Phoenix, Mi-Ai Parrish wrote a powerful column about a state legislator who had made a crude sexual comment to her. She says the #MeToo movement was a wake-up call for her and many other women. *Courtesy of Mi-Ai Parrish; 2017 photo*

10. In 2017, Gretchen Carlson sued her former employer, Roger Ailes, CEO of Fox News, for sexual harassment, helping launch the #MeToo movement. She says she wants things to change for her children, Kaia (right) and Christian (left). *Courtesy of Gretchen Carlson; 2018 photo*

11. When Kate O'Brian was twenty-one years old, a co-worker grabbed her in a dark, crowded TV control room. She yelled, "Take your hand off my ass!" "No one tried to do that again to me," she says. O'Brian went on to top jobs at ABC News and Al Jazeera America. *David Douglas; 2016 photo*

12. Wanda Lloyd's grandmother told her "colored girls" didn't become reporters, but Lloyd refused to listen. She would have a long career in newspapers, including serving as editor of the *Montgomery Advertiser* in Alabama. *Courtesy of Wanda Lloyd; 2012 photo*

13. Allen Neuharth, CEO of Gannett (right), hired Madelyn Jennings (left) in 1980 as vice president of human resources. Together they made Gannett one of the most diverse newspaper companies in the country. *Courtesy of Madelyn Jennings; 1994 photo*

14. Pam McAllister Johnson was a journalism professor when the Gannett company asked her if she wanted to be a publisher. "I didn't even know what a publisher did, but I said, 'Yes, sure, I want to be a publisher,'" she says. In 1981, she was named publisher of New York's *Ithaca Journal*, becoming the first African-American woman to serve as publisher of a mainstream newspaper in the United States. *Courtesy of* Black Enterprise *magazine; 1985 photo*

15. Jill Abramson, the first and only female editor of the *New York Times*, found the top position a difficult one for a woman. Her daughter, Cornelia Griggs, snapped this photo of her mother at a gym and posted it after Abramson was fired from the *Times*. *Courtesy of Cornelia Griggs; 2014 photo*

16. In 2006, Monika Bauerlein teamed up with another woman to propose a co-editorship of *Mother Jones* magazine. The two women shared the top spot for nearly ten years, despite skepticism that two women could get along. *Kristin Gilger; 2018 photo*

17. Clara Jeffery was the other half of the female editing duo at *Mother Jones* magazine. During her tenure, the magazine aggressively covered gun violence, parental leave, and other issues facing working families. *Kristin Gilger; 2018 photo*

18. Sandy Rowe sometimes wondered whether it was possible to succeed as both a mother and an editor. Here, she reacts to an announcement that her newspaper, the *Oregonian*, has won a Pulitzer Prize. She is pictured with the newspaper's managing editor, Peter Bhatia (left) and reporter Richard Read (center). *Courtesy of Sandy Rowe; 1999 photo*

19. Sandy Rowe and her husband, Gerard, are retired and live within a mile of their children and their children's families. Pictured are (back row, left to right) Gerard Rowe, Sandy Rowe, Mims Rowe Copeland, Joe Copeland, Sarah Rowe, and Mike O'Connell and (front row, left to right) Sadie Copeland, Timothy Copeland, Nick O'Connell, and Andy O'Connell. *Pete Perry; 2017 photo*

20. Judy Woodruff, managing editor and host of *PBS NewsHour*, returned to work after her son, Jeffrey, was born in 1981, even though people expected her to stay home. It was a more difficult decision to return to work sixteen years later when Jeffrey was partially paralyzed. Pictured are (left to right) Judy Woodruff, sons Jeffrey and Benjamin, daughter Lauren, and husband Al Hunt. *Courtesy of Judy Woodruff*

21. As a local TV news director, Carrie Hofmann spent days away from home during big news events. "I tell people who work for me now that there will be another tornado, another big story, but missing a big event in your kid's life—that's not going to happen again," she says. Hofmann is shown vacationing with her daughter, Brooke, and husband, Robert. *Courtesy of Carrie Hofmann*

22. Aminda Marqués Gonzalez, executive editor of the *Miami Herald*, says she wouldn't have been able to manage a newsroom and children without the help of a very hands-on husband and "a good Cuban mother." She is pictured with Dave Wilson, senior editor for news (left), and Rick Hirsch, managing editor (right), in the *Herald* newsroom. *Courtesy of Aminda Marqués Gonzalez; 2013 photo*

23. Melissa Bell, publisher of Vox Media, was more interested in changing journalism than changing the makeup of newsrooms. She is now convinced that women need a larger voice in media. Pictured are Bell (center), Lauren Williams, Vox editor-in-chief (left), and Allison Rockey, executive editor (right). *Christina Animashaun; 2018 photo*

24. Q McElroy, a digital director at Cox Media Group, was drawn to digital journalism because she felt there was more opportunity for advancement. Women do better when audience traffic, not office politics, determines success, she says. *Courtesy of Q McElroy; 2018 photo*

25. Cory Haik started out in newspapers but didn't think they were adapting to digital fast enough. She made the move to the digital startup *Mic* in 2015 and was promoted to publisher in 2017. *Courtesy of Cory Haik*

Mitra Kalita, a senior vice president at CNN, says her generation put up with a lot in newsrooms. Her daughter's generation is much more likely to say, "Burn it down." She is pictured in her New York office with Richard Galant, CNN's senior editor for opinion. *Bernadette Tuazon; 2018 photo*

Roller derby was one way Tracy Greer escaped the stresses of her job at a Phoenix public radio station. She loved her work but ended up quitting because of what she called a toxic environment for women. The *-30-* on her arm is a journalism term for the end of a story. *Courtesy of Tracy Greer; 2017 photo*

28. Maycie Timpone became director of social media at Buzzfeed in Los Angeles before she was thirty. She enjoys a work environment that she describes as having a feminine vibe. "I think things must have been different for my mom and grandmas," she says. "I imagine they had to be more aggressive or act like one of the guys. I would hope that women my age can be more themselves and not worry so much." *Courtesy of Maycie Timpone; 2017 photo*

Two days after the dinner, at 8:45 a.m. on a Friday, Sulzberger summoned Abramson to his office and she "figured the jig was up." She said he told her, "I'm making a change" and handed her a press release that announced her decision to step down. "I said, 'I will never agree to this; I've devoted my life to truth-telling.'" If she was going to be fired, she wanted the world to know, and she wanted Sulzberger to take responsibility.

She left Sulzberger's office, walked out the front door of the *Times* building, and stopped. "I just stood there on the sidewalk. I didn't feel like crying, and I didn't feel that upset. . . . I was feeling a strange sense of relief. I loved being executive editor—being introduced as executive editor. And it was incredibly cool and very meaningful to me to be the first woman executive editor. But I felt a burden the whole time: 'Don't let the girls' team down.' I felt every day had to be great."

Baquet was on jury duty, so the plan was that Abramson would be in the newsroom when the announcement was made the following Wednesday. Then late Tuesday, the night before the planned changing of the guard, Sulzberger called her at home and told her she need not come in. Abramson already had been mowed down; now she felt like she was being plowed under. "I never had a chance to thank the newsroom or say good-bye or anything," she said. She pointed out that Raines, who left in disgrace in the wake of the Jayson Blair plagiarism and fabrication scandal, was allowed to say good-bye while she wasn't. "And I wasn't in disgrace."

Abramson's firing was dissected in the *New Yorker*, *Vanity Fair*, the *Daily Beast*, and dozens of other media outlets, many of which were critical of the way the *Times* handled the affair. Neither did it sit well with many in the newsroom. Shortly after Abramson's departure, HBO *Girls* actor Lena Dunham, who writes *Lenny's Letter*, a weekly online feminist newsletter, published a widely circulated piece with the title "Jill Abramson Is a Pushy Broad." In it, she included an email exchange with the late *Times* media columnist David Carr, in which he asked what a lot of *Times* staffers were asking: "Even if you accept that Jill was a handful . . . did she deserve to be dragged into the public square and be stoned to death for being a bitch?"[7]

Aron Pilhofer, who ran the interactive unit at the *Times*, a team focused on the digital transformation of the newsroom, counted himself among Abramson's supporters. He said he was impressed with her journalistic ability and her understanding of the need to move into digital publishing more aggressively.

"It was the classic 'the man is decisive and the woman is difficult' story," he said. "You just watched it happening in slow motion. It was jaw-breaking to see what ultimately happened. Flat-out sexism was a huge part of it."

Abramson is matter-of-fact about her decision to make her firing public. Lots of people get fired, she said, and she doesn't feel like she has anything to be ashamed of.

While she won't provide details about the exact financial terms of her severance, she said she was happy with the offer. It wasn't nearly what Raines reportedly got, but "I thought it would be just fine," she said. And she didn't consider suing because she doesn't believe she was fired because of sex discrimination. "I was fired because after two and a half years of me, [Sulzberger] valued Dean more than me."

*   *   *

When Abramson was appointed executive editor in 2011, it was a historic moment for the *Times*—and an emotional one for many in the newsroom, especially the women. Susan Chira, an assistant managing editor, told the *New Yorker* at the time, "I can't believe how far we've come. To see Jill take the mantle, I felt tingling. You have to praise and savor [it] when a woman can earn it through merit."[8]

Kramon said he felt the same way. "There was an exuberance, as when [Barack] Obama was elected," he said. "One hundred and fifty years, and she was the first woman to run the *New York Times*."

After her unceremonious dumping, women in the newsroom were alarmed. "The whole thing was not handled graciously at all," said one female staff member who did not want to be named. "To see a woman make it and then be fired like that was very difficult. No one is going to forget it. It was amazing and wonderful to have a woman at the helm. To have it end this way was crushing. It still seems weird and a puzzle."

Part of the puzzle is figuring out how big of a role gender played in Abramson's fall from power. As one female staff member put it, "You have to wonder, if a man did exactly what she did, would he have been fired? It's the old expression about how she had to dance backward in high heels instead of just walking."

In an emotional piece titled "Editing While Female" for *Politico*, the news outlet's then editor Susan Glasser wrote about the "awful sameness" of the criticisms leveled against Abramson and other female news leaders. "The women are always labeled smart, but difficult, unapproachable and intimidating. It is always, of course, not a question of their journalistic merits but of their suitability, their personality," she wrote. "Maybe there were serious policy disagreements, fights about how to handle change or even plain old-fashioned power struggles. But that is never what's cited as the official rationale when the axe falls on these women. And why should it be? There is already a narrative out there, a convenient excuse. It's about 'management style' or 'communication.'"⁹

Sharon Rosenhause, managing editor of both the *South Florida Sun-Sentinel* and the *San Francisco Examiner* before her retirement, put it even more bluntly: "A man who had been as aggressive as Abramson was would have been rewarded, not fired. That's almost always like it is." Abramson said her daughter had much the same reaction. She told her mother, "It wouldn't have happened if you were a man."

In the days after the firing, Abramson's friends closed ranks around her as best they could. Two served as Abramson's "medieval tasters," reviewing media coverage and passing on only those items they thought she should see. Dowd, the *Times* columnist, took her to lunch and presented her with a pair of Steve McQueen sneakers and a brass plate that said "Pushy." Jane Berentson, former editor of *Inc.* magazine, and Ellen Pollock, former editor of *Bloomberg Businessweek* magazine, both of whom worked with Abramson at Steven Brill's monthly law magazine, the *American Lawyer*, early in their careers, decided to start getting together regularly as a sort of support group. They called it the "Fired Ladies Brunch."

* * *

In early 2017, three years after Abramson's departure, Liz Spayd, then the public editor of the *Times*, wrote a scathing column about the status of women at the paper. Women "have skidded down the power structure," Spayd wrote, with fewer women leading big news departments and fewer still coming up the pipeline.

"Men run the paper's national news, foreign news and metropolitan news as well as both business and sports," she continued. "The next editing tier is also heavily male, a climate that led one group of women to wryly fantasize one day about how differently a story might read if no man touched it throughout the editing chain. Among reporters, men often outnumber women, in some cases by significant amounts: three to one in the Washington bureau and in sports, almost two to one in metro. Men claim a comfortable majority on the foreign staff, among the arts critics and on the opinion pages, where male columnists take up ten of twelve spots. Around the room, testosterone is not in short supply."¹⁰

Two years after Spayd's indictment, some progress had been made: four of the ten editors listed on the *Times* masthead as running the news operation were women, although none ranked above deputy or assistant managing editor, and the *Times* could take credit for leading the country in coverage of sexual harassment. Beginning in 2017, under Baquet's watch, the *Times* broke one major story after another that led to the downfall of CEOs and politicians and changed the national conversation about how women are treated in the workplace.

The coverage began with a meeting filled with female editors and reporters, some of them hired or promoted by Abramson, to discuss how to cover the fallout from an *Access Hollywood* story about then candidate Donald Trump. The video in which Trump brags about being able to do anything he wants to women prompted dozens of women to write to the *Times* about their experiences with sexual harassment.

The conversation was heavily focused on Trump until reporter Jodi Kantor pointed out that the problem was much larger. She said, "We need to unmask the abusers," recalled Carolyn Ryan, who was then political editor. "I could just feel the drive and the sense of mission. Did it matter that they were in a room filled mainly with women? I think it did—just in the boldness of that declaration. The reporting took on a real sense of momentum and that was partly because there were so many women in the newsroom who cared deeply about it."

A year later, the *Times* broke the story about Harvey Weinstein's history of assaulting women. Since then, more than 250 high-profile people have been accused of sexual harassment and/or assault in the workplace.[11]

*   *   *

A week after leaving the newsroom, Abramson got a call from her alma mater, Harvard University, that turned into a job offer. That fall, she began teaching narrative nonfiction in the English department, introducing students to the writings of Gay Talese, Isabel Wilkerson, and others among her favorite authors. She split her time between Cambridge and New York, where she keeps an apartment in Lower Manhattan, with side trips to Connecticut, where she and her husband of nearly four decades have a house. For a while after leaving the *Times*, she stayed in Cambridge with her daughter, a surgeon who graduated from Harvard in 2005, and her daughter's husband, also a doctor. She eased their crazy schedules by taking charge of her granddaughter in the morning before heading to campus. She also began writing political columns, giving speeches, and working on book projects.

"I love my life now," Abramson said in spring 2017 as she settled into a chair behind the large wooden desk that dominates her office in a corner of the basement of Harvard's Barker Center. The firing "turned out to be perfectly timed," she said. "I wouldn't be able to be doing any of this if I were still there. I had a fantastic ride. It ended probably a little before I wanted it to at the *Times*, but if I had waited until the end of my sixty-fifth year, I wouldn't have come here; I wouldn't know my granddaughter the way I do; I wouldn't have my students."

She also reminds herself that she has been through worse. In 2007, she was hit by a truck while crossing a street at Times Square. Her right foot was crushed and her pelvis and her left femur were broken. She spent four weeks in the hospital and months more in rehabilitation learning to walk again while wearing the only shoe that would fit—a size 13 men's shower shoe. When she returned to the newsroom two months after the accident, it was in a wheelchair.

To deal with the pain, she gave herself morphine injections in her stomach, and then she began taking oxycodone. Soon, she said, she was addicted. Getting off the pain medication was one of the hardest things she has ever done, she said, and it was followed by a serious depression that drove her into nine months of psychotherapy treatments.

Abramson said she emerged with the realization "that I'm much more resilient than I imagined." The experience may very well have colored how she reacted to losing one of the nation's top newspaper jobs in a particularly public way. "I could see that maybe it wasn't the end of the world," she said. "Anything can happen to you at any moment."

* * *

ADVICE FOR WOMEN LEADERS

Julia Wallace

When Kristin and I walked out of Abramson's basement office at Harvard University, we were a little shell-shocked. Abramson was not what we had expected based on the many news reports about her rise and fall as the executive editor of the *New York Times*. When a student bounded in, announcing he had secured a good summer internship, Abramson jumped up and hugged him. "I'm so proud of you," she told him.

She was funny, self-aware, and even a little bit humble. This was not the iron lady we had been prepared to meet.

We were even more surprised when almost two years after we interviewed her, just before this book was to go to print, Abramson was accused of plagiarism and sloppy journalism in her book, "Merchants of Truth" about changes and challenges in the news industry. While she had come in for plenty of criticism for her management style, she had always been respected as a journalist.

But given what we know about the newspaper business, we were not surprised by her rise and fall at the *New York Times*, and we believe her story holds important lessons for all women who aspire to top management jobs.

Act the Part

As a manager, you are always on stage. Abramson admitted to having good days and bad days and letting that show. The higher up you go, the more you need to understand that your every move is being watched. For women, this can be especially precarious: Be too abrupt and you're a bitch. Be too warm and you aren't taken seriously. But it also can be an opportunity to define a style that works for you and the culture you're in.

When I was the managing editor at the *Arizona Republic* in Phoenix, the newspaper was for sale and tensions were high. Staff members worried about who would buy the paper and whether their jobs would be secure. Every day, people would wonder if this was *the* day. I struggled to find a way to calm the nerves. Since it was Phoenix, I went with a solution that fit the place: I started wearing blue toenail polish (before it was popular) and told the staff I was not going to be wearing blue polish when the new owners arrived; so they could just check my toes, and if they spotted blue, they could relax. And, yes, when the new owners were announced, I put on my pumps. For the record, I could not have done this in Chicago or Atlanta!

Tell Them What You're Worth

Good girls might not talk about money, but you need to do it early and often. Keep in mind that women make less than men. It varies by job, but on average women earn eighty-two cents for every dollar men earn.[12] Do your research so you know what the job pays, and ask other people what they make. They may not tell you the exact number (experts say men typically inflate the number by 10 percent), but you'll have something to work with. Ask for raises and negotiate.

During my eight years as editor in chief of the *Atlanta Journal-Constitution*, a parade of men would come to my office each year around raise time to tell me what a good job they had been doing and why they deserved more money. Almost no women did that. And once they received a raise, men would be appreciative, but they also made it a point of telling me how deserving they were. Women were more likely to simply say thanks and walk out. Think about it: If you're a manager who doesn't want to lose talent, who's going to get more money next year: the employee who lets you know that money matters to him or the employee who is grateful for whatever she gets?

When Abramson accepted the job as editor, she didn't even ask what the pay would be, and only later did she learn it was lower than the editor before her. She was so excited by the job offer, she just said "yes." "I figured it would be more than I made and that would be great," she told us.

It's important—from the beginning—to establish that pay matters to you. And when you find inequities, remain calm and leverage your relationship with your boss, which means actually talking to him or her—with facts in hand—before you hire an attorney or shoot off a demand in writing.

It's about the People

Relationships are the key to success in any business, and the higher up you go, the more this rule applies. Men have developed a lot of ways to build relationships—from sports talk and poker nights to golf games. Women need to build their own teams, inside and outside the workplace, that they can depend on.

I was very fortunate during my time at the *Atlanta Journal Constitution* to work with James Mallory as my managing editor. When the door was shut, he would tell me when I was wrong, and we could vent to each other about anything and everything, knowing it would remain confidential. We got so close that we could literally finish each other's sentences. It's important to cultivate those kinds of trusting relationships at work, but strong leaders need even more: They need a whole posse behind them. Your posse should be made up of people you have brought along and rewarded and with whom you regularly interact.

Then there's the all-important relationship with your boss. I always insisted on weekly meetings with my boss. I felt it was important to have regular sit-downs so we weren't seeing each other only when there was an emergency or crisis, when neither of us was apt to be at our best. Some weeks, my boss and I had important issues to discuss; other times, our weekly meetings were a chance for us to get to know each other better and for him to gain a little better understanding of my organization—things that mattered when the crises did come along.

Finally, you need to win the room. When Frank Blake was CEO of Home Depot, he set aside an hour every Sunday to compose handwritten notes to high-performing staffers. With almost four hundred thousand employees, he clearly couldn't reach them all, but he gained a reputation as a leader who cared.[13]

Sometimes women, in an effort to show they are tough, hide their human side and lose their effectiveness. You don't have to be a baby-kissing politician, but you do have to work to be approachable and even likable. A tough-talking, take-no-prisoners management style may work for some men, but it seldom works for women. Figure out a style that suits your personality, your company's culture, and your gender.

Changing the News

How Women Shape Culture and Coverage

This is what I've always wanted—to work in a newsroom led
by women.

—Becca Andrews

Mother Jones was in search of yet another editor, and Monika Bauerlein
and Clara Jeffery had a decision to make: Should they compete against each
other for the magazine's top job or bow out and let an outsider take over?

They had both applied for the position just a year earlier, in 2005, and
it had gone to a man—Russ Rymer, whose credentials included two well-
regarded books, dozens of articles for major magazines, and a reputation as
an "evolved male," thanks at least in part to his marriage to feminist writer
Susan Faludi.

But Rymer had little interest in developing the magazine's web presence,
and the magazine was veering off track, according to Jay Harris, the publisher
and CEO at the time. Subscriptions and newsstand sales were falling, the
staff was in turmoil, and the liberal-leaning political magazine was struggling
to find relevance as a six-time-a-year print publication. In August 2006, the
Mother Jones board decided Rymer had to go. He was the second editor—
both of them men—to be forced out in just two years.[1]

Mother Jones had a history of colorful, if somewhat erratic, leaders. Ten
years earlier, Michael Moore had served as editor for all of four months before getting fired in a dispute over editorial decisions. He sued for wrongful
termination, reportedly settling for $58,000 and using the money to fund his
first film, *Roger and Me*, about his hometown of Flint, Michigan.[2]

The magazine had "been through some tumult over the years and sort of
had a rap," Jeffery said. She and Bauerlein, the highest-ranking women in the
newsroom, were tired of it, and they were worried about the magazine's future.

The two were confident that either of them could run the publication, but the board had already turned them down once before. So they came up with a novel idea: What if they both got the job? They could be co-editors, pooling their talents and managing the magazine as equal partners.

They pitched the plan to Harris, who was intrigued. That night he went home and asked his wife, Marcia Cohen, an associate dean at the Stanford University School of Medicine, what she thought of the idea. "Of course they can do it," Cohen told him. "They're women."

Madeleine Buckingham, the magazine's chief financial officer who would go on to succeed Harris as CEO, said she was at first "a big skeptic." She worried about whether two people could really lead in unison, who would make the final decisions, and if the staff would be confused about who was in charge. But the idea of doing something so different, so "open-minded," appealed to her, and she had been around Bauerlein and Jeffery long enough to know they worked well together. She told Harris, "Let's give it a shot."

The reaction was swift, with bloggers and media critics lampooning *Mother Jones* for its benighted optimism in pairing two women to do anything. The celebrity and media blog *Jossip* sniped, "Of course it takes two women to do the job of a man."[3]

"It was galling," Bauerlein said. "There's a power vacuum, so cue the cat-fights." Beyond the catfight jokes was an even more hurtful assumption—that neither of them was "good enough or strong enough," as Bauerlein put it, to do the job on her own.

They also were annoyed by people who assumed they would be working part-time in order to spend more time with their families. "People would go, 'Oh, you're so cute; you job share,'" Jeffery said. "We both work really long hours; this is not a job share. Nobody says to the founders of Google, 'Oh, this is cute; you're job sharing. What an unusual situation that you could work so well together.' If you're a woman, there's an assumption that it's both easier to do and yet harder to do—like you're going to rip each other's eyes out or something."

The women knew that almost no one believed the arrangement would work. They set out to prove the doubters wrong.

*   *   *

While women were slow to rise to the top ranks of U.S. newspapers and network television, the magazine industry was more welcoming.

Sarah Josepha Hale edited *Godey's Lady Book*, a nineteenth-century literary magazine for women, for forty years while also managing to write poetry, including the ditty that became known as "Mary Had a Little Lamb."[4] Other iconic female magazine editors include Helen Gurley Brown, who ran *Cosmopolitan* for thirty-two years beginning in 1965, helping to bring about the so-called sexual revolution; Anna Wintour, who has edited *Vogue* since 1988; and Tina Brown, who served at the helm of both *Vanity Fair* and the *New Yorker* at different times in her career.

Only a handful of women, however, have risen to the top editing jobs at so-called thought leader magazines that focus on "hard" topics like politics and money. This select group includes *Mother Jones*, the *Atlantic*, the *Nation*, the *National Review*, and the *Economist*.

Mother Jones has had more women in charge than any of them. Deirdre English was the publication's first female editor in chief. She held the position for eight years in the mid-1980s before leaving to join the faculty at the University of California, Berkeley, and write books about women's health and sexual politics, including one with the provocative title, *Witches, Midwives and Nurses: A History of Women Healers*.[5]

However, before Bauerlein and Jeffery, *Mother Jones* had never had a formal co-editorship, much less one made up of two women. Co-editorships, while not unheard of in the magazine industry, are unusual. *Variety* and *U.S. News & World Report* have had co-editors at various times, and H. L. Mencken, the famous literary critic and journalist, co-edited the literary magazine *Smart Set* with theater critic George Jean Nathan in the early 1900s. At around the same time, the husband-and-wife team of Bruce and Beatrice Gould were building the *Ladies' Home Journal* into the best-selling women's magazine in the world. Only death broke up what may be the most famous editing duo of all—Robert Silvers and Barbara Epstein, who co-edited the *New York Review of Books* for more than forty years. Not one of these duos was made up of women.

If any media organization was going to take a chance on something different—two women sharing power at the top—*Mother Jones* seemed a likely candidate. The magazine had long championed feminism and other liberal causes, and women had always been part of the magazine's story, starting with its namesake, Mary Harris Jones.

Jones was an early-twentieth-century labor organizer who helped found the U.S. Social Democratic Party. She dressed up like an old lady, all the better to grab attention and get away with saying and doing things that were out-of-bounds for most women in her time. She traveled the country espousing then-radical causes like worker rights and the end of child labor. She never supported the suffragists, believing they were a distraction from the more important cause of erasing class inequality, but she certainly did speak her mind.[6]

As the story was passed down to Harris, who joined the magazine about fifteen years after its launch in 1976, the name for the new publication was supposed to be *New Dimensions*. But at the last minute, a trademark claim nixed that idea, and the founders had to scramble to come up with something else. They consulted with Bill Jayme, a well-known master of direct marketing,[7] who flipped through a history book and spotted an obscure item about Mary Harris Jones.

Mother Jones's founders Paul Jacobs, an activist and journalist, and Adam Hochschild, a journalist and mining heir, wanted to create a magazine in the best muckraking traditions of journalism. It would be a passionate advocate for social justice, unafraid to take on corporate and political power. It would get attention. Who better, then, to name the magazine after than Mother Jones herself?

*   *   *

To get to the *Mother Jones* offices in downtown San Francisco, you walk through a grand lobby lined with marble, check in at the security desk, and ride the elevator to the sixth floor. A narrow hallway leads to an unmarked door that requires employees to swipe a security card and visitors to linger in the hope that someone will emerge to let them in.

Once inside, there's a reception desk but no receptionist, a stretch of carpet stained beyond hope, and a maze of cubicles that make up the newsroom. Reporters work quite tamely beneath a massive circus poster that reads "Political Circus: Freaks! Wild Beasts! It's Fun Inside!"

Behind the glass walls of a conference room lined with awards and a single church pew, editors gather around a conference table to discuss the news of the day. The stories they pitch are vintage *Mother Jones*: questionable donations to a political campaign; sexual harassment charges against members of the National Academy of Scientists; uncapped oil wells in neighborhoods; queer visibility; a documentary about transgender body builders; and plenty of stories about pot—legalization of pot, health benefits of pot, and pot convictions, among them. There are jokes about Chick-fil-A and a Dave Matthews concert, and a spirited debate about whether honey really cures seasonal allergies.

Bauerlein and Jeffery sit with an empty chair between them at one end of the table, asking questions now and then but mostly letting the conversation flow around them. When the meeting breaks up, Jeffery picks up her small shaggy dog, a mutt she calls Cabbage that she brought to work because he wasn't feeling well, and carries him back to her office.

The two women have known each other since the late 1980s, when they were both in their twenties. Bauerlein had just finished a graduate degree in journalism at the University of Minnesota and was working at *City Pages*, an alternative newspaper in Minneapolis. Jeffery was a student at Carleton College who was reporting a story for *City Pages* about sexual assaults on campus. Bauerlein was impressed.

They met again at *Mother Jones* in 2002, when Jeffery, who had gone on to work for the *Washington City Paper* in DC and then for *Harper's Magazine*, was hired as deputy editor. Bauerlein had come to *Mother Jones* more than a year earlier to head investigations.

While they don't quite finish each other's sentences, it's clear the two have an easy camaraderie. As the mothers of ten-year-olds, they bond over things like erratic school schedules and what to do with the kids on election nights. They were both pregnant in the first year of their co-editorship, and their children were born six months apart. "It was her third child," Jeffery points out. "She was a little bit more prepared than I was."

They also share a keen sense of what makes a good *Mother Jones* story and the best way to run a newsroom.

When describing their bosses, staff members invariably say their styles are complementary. Bauerlein displays a casual friendliness that makes her easy to talk to; Jeffery's manner is at once more abrupt and more guarded. But both women, the staff agrees, are strong, direct, and decisive. Both will tell you exactly what they think.

Whatever the similarities or differences in their styles, what makes the relationship work more than anything else "is a profound reservoir of trust," Bauerlein said. "We each have a lot of respect for the other. Any decisions we do disagree on rest on a bedrock of, 'Well, if it goes your way, that's OK, too, because your judgment is just as good or better than mine.'"

* * *

The cover of one of the first magazines produced by co-editors Bauerlein and Jeffery featured a story about Hillary Clinton and the often contradictory opinions people held about her.[8] In an interview with the *Nation* shortly after the Clinton article came out in 2007, Bauerlein said the magazine was interested in taking a different tack in covering the former first lady—one that took into account Americans' complex reactions to a woman in power.[9]

It was the kind of story Bauerlein and Jeffery have cultivated at *Mother Jones*. While the magazine still tackles plenty of hard-core topics—corporate corruption, environmental scandals, and political outrages (taking particular delight in pillorying Donald Trump)—it also seems to be steeped in the editors' own experiences as women. The stories may not be strictly about women, but women are never entirely left out either.

In 2011, the two editors collaborated on a cover story about the "dirty secrets of the jobless recovery," describing an economic recovery that benefited corporations at the expense of workers. They called it "The Great Speedup" and, in it, they spoke directly to readers: "Mind racing at 4 a.m.? Guiltily realizing you've been only half-listening to your child for the past hour? Checking work email at a stoplight, at the dinner table, in bed? Dreading once pleasant diversions, like dinner with friends, as just one more thing on your to-do list?"[10]

Jeffery and Bauerlein insist the magazine would report on many of the same topics regardless of who was in charge, but stories about parental leave, reproductive rights, and challenges facing working families also resonate personally. And, as women, they gravitate toward stories that focus on people and their experiences.

"We made the decision to cover the hell out of gun violence five years ago," Jeffery said. "I don't know if that's because we're women or moms, but I suspect in large part it's because we're parents and we're concerned."

Buckingham, the former CEO who encouraged the gamble on a co-editorship, said having women in charge does more than influence news coverage—it changes the culture and environment of the workplace. "Monika and Clara and I embrace our nonworking lives, and we don't shy away from acknowledging that we're mothers and we have kids and they're important," she said.

Staff members, including the two editors, bring their children (and sometimes their pets) to the office, and they feel free to leave in the middle of the day to pick up a child or attend a soccer game. "The magazine takes family-friendly policies seriously here," said Becca Andrews, the assistant news editor. "And it's a workplace that feels safe for women. I don't feel on edge here . . . and I never felt that way in my other jobs."

Andrews, who is in her late twenties, remembers her first staff meeting in 2015, when she arrived at *Mother Jones* as an editorial fellow. "Monika and Clara and Madeleine were at the head of the table, and I got unexpectedly choked up seeing them there. I thought, 'This is what I've always wanted—to work in a newsroom led by women,' and it never felt like a possibility until I got here."

*   *   *

The question of whether women leaders change the news and newsrooms is one that mass media scholars have tried to answer. They observe that since women began entering newsrooms in significant numbers in the 1970s, news coverage has shifted toward the kinds of stories that women generally say they want—human interest and personality-based stories as well as stories about education, safety, health, family, and personal relationships. But it's not clear the shift can be attributed to the presence of more women in newsrooms.

Some research points to a difference in the way women report on some topics. A 2017 Women's Media Center study showed that the gender of the journalist affected coverage of campus rape and reproductive rights,[11] and another concluded that women gave the HPV vaccine more frequent and more prominent coverage.[12] Other studies have said that gender makes little difference in coverage of political topics or campaigns.[13]

There is little academic research on the effect women managers have on coverage, although one 2010 study concluded that newspapers with female managing editors published somewhat more feature stories.[14] Many women, researchers say, seem to absorb the news values of the dominant male culture and end up making the same kinds of editorial decisions a man would make.

This dichotomy was intriguing to Tracy Everbach, an associate professor at the Mayborn School of Journalism at the University of North Texas, so she decided to test for herself whether a female-led newspaper was any different from a male-led newspaper. In 2002, she headed to western Florida and the *Sarasota Herald-Tribune*, a midsize newspaper then owned by the New York Times Company that was distinctive for being the country's only top-hundred-by-circulation paper led by all women. The paper had a female publisher, executive editor, managing editor, and two assistant managing editors, earning it the nickname "Amazonia."

What Everbach discovered was another inconsistency. Her analysis of the *Herald-Tribune*'s front pages, local news pages, and business, sports, and lifestyle sections indicated that the content was pretty much the same as in any other newspaper. The stories covered mostly what researchers refer to as "masculine topics"—politics, crime, and finance—and relied overwhelmingly on male sources.[15]

But while Everbach concluded that female management did not change what appeared in print in the *Herald-Tribune*, she did find that the women had a significant effect on the culture of the workplace. A previous study in 2000 by the Readership Institute at Northwestern University had examined the cultures of a hundred American daily newspapers and characterized the vast majority of them as aggressive and defensive places. The dominant culture was one of confrontation and perfectionism, where "people are expected to avoid all mistakes, keep track of everything and work long hours to meet narrow objectives."[16] They were, in other words, very masculine.

The *Herald-Tribune*, Everbach found, was a far different kind of place. Instead of unilateral decision-making, problems often were resolved through teamwork and consensus. Editors encouraged employees to speak up, and they accommodated those who needed time or flexible schedules to deal with family obligations. Staff described the newsroom environment as comfortable, personalized, and nurturing.

The women in charge in Sarasota at the time of Everbach's study were Publisher Diane McFarlin, Executive Editor Janet Coats (then Janet Weaver), and Managing Editor Rosemary Armao. In separate interviews, all three agreed that Everbach got it right: The *Herald-Tribune* newsroom was different because women made it different.

McFarlin said she started implementing family-friendly policies, offering job sharing and flexible hours, when she was executive editor of the paper before becoming publisher. She did it because she was convinced that a more flexible, supportive workplace produced happier and more productive employees. Then in 1997, she hired a new, young managing editor, Janet Coats, and things really began to change.

Coats had two small children and made no apologies for leaving the newsroom in the middle of the day for a pediatrician's appointment or a baseball game, and she encouraged other employees to do the same. It wasn't just women who responded. She remembers one male staff member who came to her office to thank her for not making him and other men in the newsroom feel guilty about going to a parent-teacher conference or taking their kids to a game on occasion.

"We modeled more openness for people with more balanced lives," Coats said. "We treated people as people and not just as journalists and recognized that people had other things going on in their lives, and we tried to live that out loud."

The newsroom was different in at least one other way that reflected a female ethos. "We talked in circles," Coats said. "We were open to indirectness. We were more comfortable with open-ended conversation. . . . We used to joke that we would start at point A and then we would meander around to point N, and then we would go back to point C. We were not so hung up in linear conversations, and I think people felt more welcome to contribute that way because you knew you weren't going to be automatically shot down if you voiced your ideas and opinions. It was not a foregone conclusion what the decision would be."

The new openness extended to readers as well. The editors got out into the community and encouraged readers to comment and criticize. "Taking time to consult and discuss is not a sign of weakness, but a sign of respect," McFarlin said. "When you do it internally, it shows respect for your colleagues. When you do it externally, it shows a level of respect for the audience and customers."

McFarlin, Coats, and Armao said they were a little taken aback by Everbach's conclusion that the newspaper product didn't change under their leadership. McFarlin said they made a concerted effort to put fewer stories about bureaucracy on the front page and more stories that "related to people's lives—stories about schools and classrooms, the challenges of day-to-day living, more personality profiles, and more of a focus on people who were making a difference in the community."

Other differences were more subtle, as when Armao put a stop to the sports department running story after story (and picture after picture) of a particularly attractive—but mediocre—Russian tennis player. Armao sent an email to the sports department, telling editors, "I'm declaring a rule that we can't run another picture or story of Anna Kournikova until she wins something."

Coats remembers being on the job in Sarasota for only about six weeks when Princess Diana died. A desk editor called her at home to give her the news that the English princess had been injured in a car crash and the plan was to put the story on an inside page. Coats told him it was a much bigger deal than that and to clear space on the front page. "The guys were not happy," she said.

She also recalls a dispute about coverage of a sexual abuse case. The paper had reported on a father who had been convicted of sexually abusing his children when they were small. It was treated like a typical courts story, and, in most cases, that would have been the end of it. But Coats, who said she had been sexually assaulted by a male relative when she was a child, thought the paper needed to do more. She assigned a reporter to interview the victims, which resulted in a powerful portrayal of what it's like to be abused by a loved one. "I got a fair amount of pushback from the [male-dominated] copy desk saying this is too explicit, [that] we can't do this," Coats said. She told them, "This is an important story to tell, and we're going to let these people tell their story."

She tried to steer reporters away from "true crime" angles and go after the story behind the story. Later, when she was working as executive editor of the *Tampa Tribune*, the paper published an in-depth piece from the parents' point of view about what it's like to lose a child. It ran under the headline "Losing Rachel." "No one else did the story the way we did because we had a different point of view," Coats said. "It wasn't a crime story; it was a story about loss."

*   *   *

Women leaders say their personal experiences as mothers, wives, daughters, and friends frequently inform their news judgment—and sometimes spawn their best ideas.

Ann Moore was considered one of the most powerful women in media when she was publisher of *People* magazine and then CEO of Time Inc., the first woman to hold that position. As she was moving up the ranks at *Time*, she remembers worrying about her young son's lack of interest in reading. But she knew he loved sports, and she figured he might read a sports magazine aimed at kids. That, she said, was the genesis of *Sports Illustrated Kids*. The monthly spin-off of the popular adult magazine launched in 1989 and has since grown to more than four million readers around the world. Her son loved it.

Linda Mason, who was the first female producer on *The CBS Evening News with Walter Cronkite* and eventually rose to become senior vice president at the network, said she once produced a two-part series about the dangers of birth control pills after a friend of hers, who was only twenty-three at the time, suffered a stroke that was linked to the pill.

Women and minorities experience things and see things that their white male counterparts do not, said Arlene Morgan, assistant dean at Temple University's Klein College of Media and Communication and former associate dean of the Columbia Graduate School of Journalism. Without women, news organizations can't truly reflect their communities or serve the interests of readers and viewers.

Morgan speaks from experience. In 1969, when she began her thirty-one-year career at the *Philadelphia Inquirer*, she was one of seven women in the newsroom, five of whom were assigned to features. The women news reporters wanted to be treated as equals, and that did not leave room for questioning the news judgment of the white male editing staff. But over the next three decades, as more and more women and minorities were hired, coverage began to change. Stories about Philly's neighborhoods, health care, and consumer issues that had never gotten much attention before began to make their way into the newspaper and sometimes onto the front page.

Morgan only wishes the women had spoken up sooner. "That's where I think my generation made a mistake—by 'putting on the pants' and not actually forcing more of those kinds of stories onto the pages," she said.

Vivian Schiller, the former president and CEO of National Public Radio, has similar regrets. While producing documentaries and specials at the Discovery Channel and CNN earlier in her career, she was intent on doing stories about terrorism, war, and politics, and she avoided doing anything that smacked of a "woman's show." "You think, 'I'm in the boys' club now, and I'm going to be one of the boys,'" she said. "Shame on me."

Schiller, who began her career in the 1980s, thinks journalists coming up in the business today are much more likely to push for coverage that reflects the experiences of both women and minorities. "I admire them a lot," she said.

* * *

A little over a year after Bauerlein and Jeffery became co-editors, the American Society of Magazine Editors named *Mother Jones* one of the best magazines in the country, alongside *National Geographic*, *GQ*, and the *New Yorker*.

Bauerlein and Jeffery were elated. It was the first time the magazine had won the award in seven years, and it told them they were on the right track. But they also knew the real measures of their success would not be in the number of awards they won but whether they could build readership and revenue.

When they took over in 2006, the magazine was losing readers and money, and there was talk of discontinuing the print publication altogether. And while *Mother Jones* had been one of the first national magazines to launch a website, it, too, had lagged under editors who either didn't understand digital publishing or preferred its old-fashioned counterpart.

One of the first things Bauerlein and Jeffery did was craft a digital strategy aimed at making *Mother Jones* relevant in a 24-7 media world. Instead of a small staff working with a large pool of freelancers, the magazine needed a critical mass of its own reporters to aggressively pursue stories and break news online. In 2007, when other news organizations were downsizing, *Mother Jones* opened a six-person bureau in Washington, DC, and staffed it with seasoned reporters. "We entirely flipped the model," former publisher Harris said.

To pay the bills, Harris said he helped persuade investors that the time was right for an expansion and that there were "important stories that weren't getting the attention they needed." The new strategy paid off. Web traffic rose sharply, as did subscriptions and donations.

Working in *Mother Jones*'s favor has been a national political climate that favors nonprofit journalism. Other nonprofit investigative news outlets, like the Center for Public Integrity, also have reported a surge of support in the wake of President Donald Trump's election and his attacks on journalism.[17]

There have been setbacks at *Mother Jones* along the way. Bauerlein and Jeffery were accused of abandoning the magazine's populist principles by seeming to favor presidential candidate Hillary Clinton over Bernie Sanders[18] and for paying interns so little they qualified for food stamps.[19] Jeffery was taken to task for tweets that disparaged millennials. And they were both embarrassed when David Corn, their Washington bureau chief, turned up on the "Sh*tty Men in Media List," circulated just as the #MeToo movement took hold in 2017. The anonymous list included the names of purported sexual abusers, harassers, creeps, and bullies of various kinds within media organizations, mostly on the East Coast. *Politico* later uncovered two emails written by *Mother Jones* staff members several years earlier complaining that Corn commented on women's bodies and gave women in the office shoulder rubs or otherwise touched them.[20]

Bauerlein said some women in the DC office had complained several years earlier that Corn was making them uncomfortable and the complaints had been thoroughly investigated. Corn was told to change his behavior, and Bauerlein said she's satisfied that he did. Still, she and Jeffery had some damage control to do with a staff that wondered how such behavior could have occurred on their watch, so they cued up sexual harassment and inclusion training, met repeatedly with staff members, and encouraged people to come forward with complaints.

"I hope it has made a difference," Bauerlein said. "One of the things that surprised me is recognizing how far we have yet to go as a culture to make sure people feel comfortable bringing these concerns to someone. Even at a woman-led news organization, it took a while."

* * *

In 2015, Madeleine Buckingham decided to step down as *Mother Jones*'s CEO to spend time caring for her ailing mother. She recommended that Bauerlein take her place, and the board agreed, ending a nine-year experiment with a co-editorship that few had thought would work.

Jeffery remains editor in chief, with responsibility for the newsroom, while Bauerlein concentrates on growing the business, although she still drops in on news meetings and shepherds the occasional big project. She said she and Jeffery frequently consult on stories and sound each other out about the direction of the magazine. "It remains very collaborative," Bauerlein said. "We very much still share the leadership position. There are no major decisions for the organization that get made without both of us."

Marcia Cohen, the Stanford associate dean who encouraged Harris, her husband, to consider the co-editorship more than a decade ago, said she's satisfied that the decision to put Bauerlein and Jeffery in charge was the right one.

"*Mother Jones* had some interesting years when the men who were leading the organization maybe didn't get along so well and it was more about egos and what made them look good," she said. "Women have egos, too, but that manifests itself in different ways, and they are able to see how they can achieve together something better. They can put aside personal recognition for a larger ideal, a bigger goal. And it worked."

* * *

ADVICE FOR WOMEN LEADERS

Kristin Gilger

The *Statesman Journal* in Salem, Oregon, in the late 1990s was not quite "Amazonia," as people were fond of calling the *Sarasota Herald-Tribune*, but it was close. Julia was editor, I was managing editor, and the newsroom reported to a female publisher, Sara Bentley. We knew of no other newspaper at the time where three women were in charge.

I'm not sure if the newspaper's content changed under our leadership, but I like to think it did. We responded as any journalist would to big breaking news (and, yes, there was the occasional murder, flood, and political scandal, even in relatively sleepy Oregon). But we also pushed deeper, once devoting a sizable portion of our staff for a year to write about the devastation alcoholism causes in families, in part because of my own experience growing up in an alcoholic family. And we appreciated the kind of stories readers could cheer about. When Keiko the killer whale—the one of *Free Willy* movie fame—was to be moved from Oregon to his home waters off the coast of Iceland after twenty years of captivity, we didn't think twice. We sent a reporter and photographer to record for our readers the moment Keiko finally swam to freedom.

But even if we didn't entirely transform news coverage, I am certain that the newsroom was a very different place under our leadership than it had been under the mostly male editors before us.

After a female assistant city editor joined the staff, there were so many jokes about all the women running the place that Julia declared we would begin observing "Barbie Day." On the appointed day, we all showed up in Barbie costumes inspired by the news. The state was engulfed in a debate about whether to legalize assisted suicide; ergo, I was assisted suicide Barbie in scrubs dabbed with red nail polish. Prison reform also was in the news, so our assistant city editor dressed like a prison guard and wrapped her desk in wire fencing. Reporters had to make their way through the fence to get their stories edited.

We didn't spend much time in news meetings; we preferred walking the room, and people wandered into our offices all day, every day. I remember closing my door just once, and that was for a police reporter who needed a good cry.

It wasn't exactly an orderly place, but we did get things done. The features editor (a man) once offered this advice to a new city editor (also a man) about how to navigate this strange, new workplace. "When they ask you a question," he said, referring to Julia and me, "it's really not a question. They want it done."

The women in this chapter—Monika, Clara, Diane, Janet, Rosemary, and many others—all had their own ways of getting things done as women leading news organizations. In the process, they changed what journalism looked like and felt like for the people who worked for them and, in some cases at least, for their readers. Following are some of the takeaways from their stories.

Power Really Can Be Shared

Men often see power in terms of rank and status, while women tend to perceive power as influence and connections to others, according to communications research. This may explain, in part, why Monika Bauerlein and Clara Jeffery were so quick to hit on the idea of a co-editorship. They might have to share a title, but they knew their influence would be far greater than if they did nothing.

The two women proved that power can be shared successfully, but they are quick to caution that it works only if the people involved are fully committed. Neither of them thinks the arrangement would have succeeded if it had been forced on them. Since it was their idea, they had a full stake in making it work.

Give Others Credit

One of the striking things about Bauerlein and Jeffery is how little personal ego they seem to bring to the job. They almost never use the word *I*. Instead, they talk about "we" and "us." They are, however, hugely ambitious, even egotistical, when it comes to the magazine they edit. *Mother Jones* is both their personal conceit and a collective accomplishment.

Similarly, Diane McFarlin, the former publisher of the *Sarasota Herald-Tribune* who is now dean of the University of Florida College of Journalism and Communications, gives her former managing editor, Janet Coats, the lion's share of the credit for creating a family-friendly work culture at the newspaper they headed. And Coats, who now works on grant projects for the journalism school at Arizona State University, says it was McFarlin who set the tone for the paper and made it the kind of place where people loved to work.

These are all strong women who are not prone to false modesty. They know that journalism is a team sport, and they recognize that part of being a great leader is sharing credit—lavishly and often.

Collaboration Can Be Messy

There is one good thing about an autocratic work environment: You don't spend a lot of time talking things out. Orders are issued and people get to work.

There are plenty of bad things about an autocratic workplace, however. Among them: Creativity is squelched; people don't learn to think for themselves; emerging leaders aren't cultivated; and the organization is only as good as the person in charge.

A collaborative workplace, like a democracy, can be a time-consuming and messy business. Coats described conversations at the *Herald-Tribune* as circular, wandering from point to point before reaching any resolution. At *Mother Jones*, an art director told me her job was much simpler when she had to get cover art approved by only one editor rather than two.

Yet it's clear from the women we interviewed and from management research that collaboration more often than not produces better decisions and more buy-in from employees. You just need to learn patience to get to the payoff.

Disagreements Should Be Private

No workplace and no work relationship are entirely free of conflict. In fact, they would be pretty boring places and pretty boring relationships if they were.

Newsrooms tend to "get" conflict; there is almost never a shortage of people willing to express their views, and their arguments rarely lack passion. But serious arguments in any workplace should never take place in a meeting, in the middle of the room, or in front of anyone but you and the person with whom you're having the argument.

When Bauerlein and Jeffery became co-editors of *Mother Jones*, they knew they had to speak with one voice or risk confusing the staff about who was in charge. After more than a decade on the job, they're still careful not to disagree in front of others. Those conversations take place behind closed doors, and they always start with the premise that they both want the same thing. There just may be different ways of getting there.

News Judgment Isn't Science

Each person's judgment is born out of both professional and personal experiences, so the greater the diversity of people making news decisions, the better the news judgment is likely to be.

Even if you don't have years of experience in the profession, you have something valuable to offer. Most news organizations, for example, are trying desperately to figure out a way to reach a younger generation of viewers and readers, so if you're a millennial or even younger, you have something important to contribute. The same is true if you're a person of color, live with a disability, raise children, or take care of an elderly parent. You know something that others don't, so speak up.

Watch and Learn

All of the women we interviewed mentioned at least one person—usually another woman—who taught them important aspects of being a good manager.

Most of the people doing the teaching weren't formal mentors who would sit down and spew words of wisdom; they were simply doing their jobs in a way that modeled how those jobs should be done.

Coats said she was impressed with how her boss, McFarlin, delivered bad news to people in a way that was both honest and kind. She asked McFarlin if she could sit in on the next difficult conversation with someone on staff. She wanted to learn how it was done.

Becca Andrews, assistant news editor at *Mother Jones*, wishes she was more like Jeffery, who is "sure of herself and says exactly what's on her mind. It inspires me to watch what she does and model myself after that."

These women are smart enough to know that it's not enough to be the beneficiary of good management; you need to be a student of it.

• 7 •

What Could Possibly Go Wrong?

Balancing Work and Family

We had a shared view of responsibility in the family. I never dictated to her and she never dictated to me.

—Gerard Rowe

*M*other-daughter relationships are often difficult, and Sandy and Mims Rowe were experiencing the worst of it. There had been an argument, and a teenaged Mims had stormed out of the house, car keys in hand. Her mother ran after her and tried to block the car from leaving the driveway, but Mims just gunned into reverse and drove away.

It was one of the many times Sandy Rowe wondered what had gone wrong. Her oldest daughter, whose first name was Rowe's own maiden name, actually seemed to hate her.

Maybe it was a lie that you could have it all, Rowe thought. She had a demanding career, yes, but she had the financial resources to make it work, including a housekeeper and a supportive husband. She made sure she was there for all the important moments and, still, it didn't seem to be enough.

Rowe, who was regarded as the most successful female newspaper editor in the country, was facing what almost all women who pursue careers must deal with at one time or another: how to split your life between work and family in a way that doesn't destroy either.

Balance is an issue for women in any job. More than one hundred thousand people "liked" tennis star Serena Williams's 2018 tweet lamenting that she had missed her daughter's first step. "I was training, and I missed it. I cried," Williams wrote.[1] Many of her followers responded with their own stories about lost moments in their children's lives.

The competitive, twenty-four-hour-a-day nature of journalism makes it an especially challenging profession for women who face almost daily choices

105

between the personal and the professional. And when something really big happens—a flood, a hurricane, a mass shooting, a Super Bowl, an election—there usually is only one choice.

Jan Leach remembers being in the *Akron Beacon-Journal* newsroom for four days straight after the September 11, 2001, terrorist attacks. When the news broke that Tuesday morning, her husband called and asked, "Where are the kids?"

"I don't know," snapped Leach, who was the newspaper's editor at the time. "I'm busy." He left work and picked up their three girls—a fourth-grader and twins who were in kindergarten—from their Catholic school and took them home. "I feel sad about that because they were little kids," Leach said. "I needed to be there to say, 'Here's what's going on; you're safe; nothing's going to happen to you.'"

Another time Leach was supposed to attend her oldest daughter's grade-school soccer game, but she got busy in the newsroom and forgot. "The game comes and goes, and there's nobody there to take my daughter home," she said. "The entire team is gone; everybody leaves except for the wife of the managing editor, whose daughter was on [the] team. She calls me up and says, 'Cara is here by herself. Are you coming?' I can't believe this. I forgot my own child. I forgot her!"

Work-life balance? Leach scoffs: "I was a miserable failure at it."

Carrie Hofmann's Twitter profile reads, "I am a working mom who juggles running a TV newsroom and her family but loves every minute of it." What Hofmann doesn't tell everyone on social media is that the juggling act comes with a large measure of guilt. "With moms there's definitely more guilt," she said. "My husband, he has no issue if he misses something, and I feel like I've scarred my daughter for life if I miss something."

TV news is especially unpredictable, said Hofmann, who is news director of KSHB-TV in Kansas City, Missouri, and before that was executive producer at KMGH-TV in Denver, Colorado. "I remember in Denver once there was a tornado on my daughter's birthday," she said. "She was young, so it's not something she would remember, but I remember being at work and getting teary-eyed. [Co-workers were running around yelling, and I was thinking,] 'You're yelling at me and you're frustrated, and I'm missing my daughter's birthday!'"

Like Leach, Hofmann once didn't go home for four days—in her case because of a blizzard. The roads were bad, but it was really the station's wall-to-wall coverage of the storm that kept her away. She missed her husband's fortieth birthday that time.

Hofmann said she learned her lesson one night when she and her husband planned to take their daughter and a friend to see Selena Gomez. It was the girls' first concert, and it was a big deal. But NBC was airing a Kansas

City Chiefs football game that night, and Hofmann's station, the NBC affiliate, was offering extended coverage. It was all hands on deck, and Hofmann felt she needed to be there. So she decided to do both. She showed up at the station for the pregame coverage and then met up with the rest of the family in a parking lot and drove to the concert. Afterward, she dashed back to the station for the postgame coverage.

"I'm thinking, 'I'm a rock star.' I'm feeling great. I took care of everything," she said. But then someone at the station commented that a real leader would have been there for the entire game. "That was my aha moment," Hofmann said. "Here I busted my butt to do multiple things, and I realized I might as well pick one. That's the moment when I realized I could have just spent the entire night with my daughter. We could have gone out to dinner beforehand and spent the whole evening, but instead I tried to split myself three different ways to Sunday. Somewhere, someone loses, and you have to decide what's most important. And, you know, the station would have been just fine without me."

Hofmann said she now runs her newsroom differently. Weekend events are divided among top managers so no one is overburdened, and when one of her anchors wants to take time off in the middle of the day for a child's event, she tries hard to make it work.

"I tell people who work for me now that there will be another tornado, another big story, but missing a big event in your kid's life—that's not going to happen again. There are moments that have to take precedence," she said. "If I get fired, the people who will be with me are my family. If I mess that up, it will be a cold day where I don't have anybody. I think you need to keep that in perspective."

* * *

Sandy Rowe grew up in Harrisonburg, Virginia, the daughter of the editor of a small newspaper and a stay-at-home mom.

She didn't aspire to be a journalist, but she was comfortable in the world of newspapers. On trips with her father to the office late at night, she would head straight to the pressroom, lured by the giant machines that churned out piles of neatly bundled papers. Sometimes the men operating the equipment would let her push the button to start the presses rolling. "It was all so visceral," she said. "The noise, the smell."

For the most part, though, Rowe was not easily satisfied. She describes herself as a difficult child, unhappy to the point that her parents grew worried. Her father decided there was only one thing to be done: He would become his teenage daughter's best friend.

Even if Rowe had wanted to, it would have been hard to ignore her father. Lathan Mims was a larger-than-life character, charming, persuasive, and well connected. One of his best friends was Harry Byrd Jr., the legendary U.S. senator from Virginia. Lathan Mims's way of paying attention to his daughter was to engage her in conversation. He would be waiting when she came home and keep her up late into the night talking about politics and school and events around town. He made her laugh even though she didn't think he was quite as funny as he thought he was.

To her surprise, Rowe was named editor of her high school newspaper. She knew it wasn't stellar grades in school that got her the position, so she suspected it had something to do with her dad running the local newspaper. The job made her nervous. She fretted about every story, got anxious on deadline, and worried about making mistakes. She once showed her father an editorial she had written that she thought was particularly well done. Her father read it and zeroed in on the phrase *very unique*. A modifier, he told her, should never precede the word *unique*. While none of this made Rowe fall in love with journalism, she did discover one thing that greatly appealed to her: "I liked being in charge," she said.

Rowe headed to college with little idea of what she wanted to do. She thought she would graduate, get married, and maybe find some kind of job. If she was lucky, she would "marry a lawyer and have a house with a white picket fence," she said. "It's how I thought my life would unfold."

Her college options were limited. In 1966, the University of Virginia had not yet begun admitting women—a fact that still astounds and angers Rowe fifty years later. The family didn't have the money for a private school, so she ended up enrolling at East Carolina University in Greenville, North Carolina.

In college, as in high school, Rowe was an average student. "I was just sort of middling along and trying not to embarrass myself," she said. "There was nothing in my high school or college life or academic life that said, 'This girl is going to be successful.'"

After getting a degree in English, Rowe moved to Richmond to help her father, who had taken a leave from the newspaper in 1970 to run one of Byrd's Senate campaigns. One night, Rowe went on a blind date with a freckled young man who sported a head of curly black hair. "I just thought he was the cutest thing in the world," she said. Gerard Rowe had recently graduated first in his class from the University of Richmond's law school and had just passed the bar. She liked him. Her father liked him. There was just one problem: Gerard was leaving to take a job in Norfolk.

Rowe decided she was moving, too. "You're not going there to chase that boy, are you?" her father asked.

"Of course not," she told him.

"You don't have this expectation that we're getting married, do you?" Gerard asked.

"Of course not," she said.

Within a few months, Gerard was asking Lathan Mims for permission to marry his daughter.

Rowe said one of the things that attracted her to her husband was his unflappable sense of himself. "I was charmed by the whole thing of how comfortable Gerard was with being Gerard," she said. "At that point, I was not comfortable being Sandy." And she still didn't know what she wanted to do with her life.

She got a job as a newsreader at a radio station but didn't like it. "I have a terrible voice and would have such anxiety every time I went on the air. My knees actually knocked," she said. Then she saw a classified ad for a news clerk, answering phones and performing other clerical duties, at Norfolk's afternoon newspaper, the *Ledger-Star*. She was comfortable being back in a newsroom, and she liked the smart, quirky people she worked with and the fast pace of the news. Soon she got her chance to be a reporter.

But while her career was finally launched, Rowe was worried about starting a family. She was twenty-seven, and her gynecologist told her she had better get busy if she wanted to be a mother. Without doing extensive testing, he told her she might be facing premature menopause and put her on a fertility drug. "I went home weeping," Rowe said. "I was absolutely petrified."

When she did get pregnant a few months later, Rowe switched doctors and started trying to figure out what she would do after the baby was born. The newspaper offered no maternity leave and barred employees from using sick leave for that purpose. Rowe and her husband considered the options: She could stay home, she could freelance, or she could go back to her job and find some other way to care for a baby. The newspaper wanted her to come back, and that made all the difference to Rowe.

"There are so many points in a young person's career where someone, not meaning to, can get people, particularly women and minorities, to drop out," she said. "That birth moment was one such moment for me. The fact that they wanted me back, that they asked me to come back, meant so much. I just as easily could have gone the other way. None of my friends in the neighborhood who had children, none of them worked outside the home."

She would have done the same if her husband had asked her to. Instead, Gerard told her, "I think you'd be better off working." Rowe asked the newspaper for three months off without pay and then placed an ad in the newspaper for a "housekeeper," because there was no readily available day care in 1974. Arrie Mae Owens, an African-American woman who already had raised children of her own, was looking for work. It was the first and most important hire that Rowe would ever make.

During Owens's first week on the job, she told her new employer, "The good Lord sent me here." Rowe responded, "I just hope he doesn't send you away." Owens stayed with the family for the next eighteen years until Mims left for college.

At the *Ledger-Star*, Rowe was moving up. The editors had decided to transform a traditional women's section into something called "The Daily Break," and they wanted it to be colorful and contemporary. Rowe was named editor of the new section.

Like many working women at the time, Rowe did her best to keep her home life separate from her work life. She rarely mentioned the baby in conversations at work, and she certainly never cited the baby as an excuse to come in late or leave early. "You didn't talk about it," she said. "You'd pretend you were a man in a woman's body."

Five years later, during her second pregnancy, Rowe was assistant managing editor of the paper, and she was determined to work up until the time the baby was born. As the due date neared, she attended a farewell luncheon for a longtime columnist at the paper. The contractions started almost as soon as she sat down. Rowe began timing them, surreptitiously glancing at her watch, until they were four to five minutes apart and she didn't feel she could wait any longer. She got up, said she needed to leave, and fled the restaurant, stopping to pick up her briefcase and the afternoon paper before racing to the hospital to give birth to her second daughter, Sarah.

* * *

The birth of children is one of the main reasons that women opt out of the workforce; they simply decide that family is more important to them than their careers, while men place more value on their careers. Or so the theory goes.

In reality, researchers have been steadily debunking that explanation since the 1990s. Men and women value pretty much the same things when it comes to their personal and professional lives, according to one recent study of more than twenty-five thousand Harvard Business School graduates. The study concluded that when high-achieving, highly educated professional women leave their jobs after becoming mothers, "only a small number do so because they prefer to devote themselves exclusively to motherhood; the vast majority leave reluctantly and as a last resort, because they find themselves in unfulfilling roles with dim prospects for advancement."[2]

Judy Woodruff, anchor and managing editor of the *PBS NewsHour* and one of the most widely recognized women in television news, decided to return to work after her son Jeffrey was born in 1981, at a time when people didn't hesitate to ask why she wasn't staying home like a good mother should. In her typically understated way, Woodruff would tell them that she and her husband, journalist Al Hunt, thought they could make it work.

At the time, Woodruff was White House correspondent for NBC News. She remembers going into labor after a hectic day at work, and she recalls an NBC photographer coming to the hospital to take photos soon after the birth. The birth announcement, along with the photos, made the *Today* show and the nightly newscast. In her 1982 book, *This Is Judy Woodruff at the White House*, Woodruff wrote that then-anchor John Chancellor "told me later that it was the first time he could remember in his twenty years with NBC that the newscast carried the announcement of the normal birth of a baby who was not related to either a president or royalty."[3]

The decision to continue working was much harder sixteen years later when Jeffrey, who was born with a mild case of spina bifida, underwent what was supposed to be routine surgery and emerged partially paralyzed. His vision was affected, and he was unable to eat, speak, or use his arms and legs on his own.

"He almost didn't survive," Woodruff said. "I took off work for six weeks and then I came back part-time for three months. . . . I did think seriously about stopping work and just taking care of our son. The doctor said to me, 'You really want to think hard before you do that (because) there's only so much you can do for him. He has his own struggles ahead, and you'll need to be there for him emotionally, but you can't change the course of his recovery.'

"That was pretty powerful, and I spent a lot of time thinking about that. I was consumed with grief; his injuries and the disabilities that resulted from them are lifelong. It's something we live with every day. It's a heartbreak that never goes away. I just plowed through it. I was suffering. Jeffrey was suffering the most. To see your child change forever—it tears you up inside. I thought, 'I can't be strong for him if I don't keep going with my own life, if I don't have a purpose.' Thankfully, journalism gave me that purpose."

Karen Pensiero was fully intending to return to her full-time job doing development work for the international division of the *Wall Street Journal* when a phone call changed her mind. She was raising a stepdaughter and a biological daughter, and she also was pregnant with her son when her teen-aged stepdaughter called her at work one night. "Are you going to be able to make it to back-to-school night?" her stepdaughter asked.

"I got off of the phone and burst into tears immediately," Pensiero said. "I forgot her back-to-school night. Of all of the adults involved in her life, I was always the one to do those things. She was my kid. I had tucked her into bed every night and read to her. I had totally let her down."

Pensiero decided to ask the *Journal*'s editors if she could return part-time after taking maternity leave when her son was born. They came up with an arrangement that allowed her to work 60 percent of the time for 60 percent of her previous salary but with full benefits. At some point, her boss wanted to boost her pay because she was putting in more than the required time, but Pensiero turned her down. "Maybe this is a crazy woman thing, but I didn't want anyone to think I was taking advantage of it," she said, and she wanted to be a role model. "I'd watch other people, and usually women when they had kids, they scaled back. They kept their full-time jobs and started leaving earlier, and I didn't like that. I didn't think that sent the right message."

There were times when she was tempted to quit and stay home full-time, but her husband, Jim, who also worked at the *Journal*, encouraged her to stay. He told her, "One day you're going to want to be master of the universe." Pensiero was named the *Journal*'s managing editor in 2017.

Kate O'Brian left a full-time job as a producer for ABC News when her husband was promoted to producer for the network's Rome bureau. ABC told her there was no position for her in Rome. "They basically said to me, 'You can't work because it's a small bureau and you can't work together,'" she said. "It was ridiculous." O'Brian wound up working for the network anyway, but as a freelance producer rather than in a staff job.

A few years later, O'Brian became a trailing spouse again when her husband was posted to London. With two small children and a husband who was on the road 75 percent of the time, "I made the decision that I did not want a job that would put me on the road a lot," she said. Instead, she continued freelancing.

When the couple returned to New York in 1994, O'Brian still wasn't ready to go back to work full-time. This time, ABC found a way to make it work, offering her a job-share producing the evening news. Sharing the job with another producer allowed her to spend more time with her children and still keep her career on track. Eventually, she became senior vice president for news at ABC, in charge of global newsgathering, and then president of Al Jazeera America.

O'Brian said that in a strange way, being on the "mommy track" early in her career helped her get ahead. She had planned, like many of her peers, to get firmly established in her career before having children sometime in her thirties. But as it turned out, she was twenty-six and twenty-eight when she had her children. By the time the girls were in school, she said she was "poised to get back really hard into the workforce at an age when my peers were actually starting to take time off or work fewer hours to have their children."

She also thinks that being a mother first made her a better manager. "I always wanted to write a book called *All Management Is Motherhood*," she said. "I have a theory that mothers make good managers—not just that they have to be more organized but because they understand discipline. You have to be compassionate, but you have to be straight. And they understand how to build teams. It's not just a female thing, but when you're already doing those things with your children, it's easier to see the world in that way and exhibit those behaviors elsewhere. . . . You want to be a good person for your kids? Well, you have to take that into the office, too."

*　*　*

The women who built successful media careers while also juggling mother-hood have one thing in common: support and lots of it. For the most part, they defy the trap that ensnares so many other working women—putting in a full day at the office or factory and then working another full-time job at home. Mothers in 2016 spent almost twice as much time on childcare and housework as fathers, according to the Pew Research Center.[4]

Early in her career, Hofmann from KSHB-TV split childcare pretty much fifty-fifty with her husband, a teacher. He worked days, getting home early enough to handle after-school duties and dinner while she headed off to a night shift at her television station. "If I didn't have a strong partner in my husband, I would never be where I am today," she said.

Aminda Marqués Gonzalez, executive editor of the *Miami Herald*, said she and her husband, a physician's assistant, had a similar arrangement. He worked an early shift so he could be home when their three children got out of school. "My husband was a hands-on dad before it was fashionable," she said. Marqués said she also had the support of "a good Cuban mother."

Janet Coats met her first husband, Mark, when they were in journalism school together in the early 1980s. They both worked in newspapers until their son, Sam, was born, when her husband quit to be a stay-at-home dad. He was the primary caregiver for the next decade for Sam and his younger brother and sister while Coats (then Weaver) was executive editor of two Florida newspapers, first the *Sarasota Herald-Tribune* and then the *Tampa Tribune*.

"Other women in the business would tell me, 'You are one lucky woman. I wish I had a wife,'" Coats said. "There were awkward moments, but it was his idea to do it, and he enjoyed it." He spent so much time with mothers on play dates and at pools that he got comfortable saying, "I raise kids," when people asked him what he did.

*　*　*

Sandy Rowe had Gerard and Arrie Mae.

Once when her children were young, Rowe was sent to a management training program for midlevel supervisors. The instructor asked the trainees to write down the person most critical to their success. "I was just absolutely struggling," Rowe said, "because I had no idea, if I had to list one person, would it be Gerard or Arrie Mae," who had become a critical part of the family. She kept the house in order and made sure the two girls got where they needed to go. The girls adored her. She was so much a part of their lives that one friend thought Owens was their mother. "There was no question in my mind it was one of the two of them," Rowe said. "It never occurred to me it was anyone else."

As they went around the room, every other person, all of them men, listed their bosses or assistants as the people most critical to their careers. Rowe worried that she had gotten the answer wrong, but the more she thought about it, the more convinced she became that she had not. "There is no way I could have done what I did or been successful without Gerard doing what he did and being supportive of any move I made, and if I didn't have Arrie Mae," she said.

She also understood that privilege and circumstance gave her options unavailable to many women. Throughout those years, when people would ask her how she managed both a family and a successful career, Rowe would say, "Why don't you ask the checker at Safeway who is a single mom with two or three kids who has to get them dressed and out the door by herself and doesn't have the financial resources?"

Gerard said he and his wife had a "shared view of responsibility in the family. I never dictated to her and she never dictated to me. I early on knew she was going to be a force in some way. I think that was obvious to people who knew her."

Rowe and her husband were both doing well in their careers. He had become a partner in his law firm and had built one of the firm's most profitable client lists. She focused on honing her leadership skills and continued to be promoted, eventually becoming editor of the *Ledger-Star* and its sister paper, the *Virginian-Pilot*. In 1985, the combined papers won the highest award in journalism, the Pulitzer Prize, for coverage of a corrupt local economic development official. It was the first Pulitzer for either paper in a news category.

In 1993, Rowe was approached about becoming the editor of the *Oregonian* newspaper in Portland, Oregon. She was dubious. Everything and everyone they knew were in Virginia. They had never even been to Oregon. But she and Gerard decided to check it out. Without telling the girls where they were going, they flew to Portland for a weekend and discovered they liked both the city and the newspaper. Mims was in college, so her life wouldn't be disrupted, and they thought Sarah, who was entering high school, would benefit from a change.

Telling his senior partners, who had taken him in and mentored him, that he was quitting was "really tough," Gerard said. "But the opportunity at the *Oregonian* for Sandy was tremendous."

Sarah, however, did not understand why her parents were uprooting her for some "dark and hilly and spooky and cold and rainy" place on the other side of the country. "I thought it was bananas," she said. "I had never heard of this place. I thought it was a terrible, horrible idea." Portland, she declared, was "lame."

Whom did she blame? Her mom, of course. She refused to speak to her mother—at least civilly—for almost a year. "It's hard to blame my dad for much," Sarah said by way of explanation. "He's just super nice. My mom is the driving force—her ideas, her energy. She was the boss of the family. Dad's role was the supporter, the doer, the rock."

Gerard never worked full-time again. He took over management of the house and drove Sarah to school and soccer games. He never missed a game, although Rowe was seldom able to make one. She was focused on some formidable challenges at work.

At her first staff meeting, she was explaining her plans to make the *Oregonian* a great newspaper when one editor raised his hand and said, "Why should we think that a woman with a features background from a smaller paper in the South can help us be better?" Rowe took a deep breath and said something equivalent to "Buckle up, baby."

She told everyone they had to reapply for their jobs, restructured the way the newsroom worked, and expanded the staff, hiring talented journalists from all over the country. "She walked into their slow, bloated, complacent newsroom and rolled up her sleeves," said Therese Bottomly, an assistant city editor at the time, who was named editor in 2018.

The *Oregonian* was known as the "velvet coffin" because it was the kind of place where people settled in, got comfortable, and rarely left. Rowe changed that, Bottomly said. "She had a clarity of vision about where she wanted to go, and she valued an inclusive process. She was a leader who knew what she wanted, and she was able to articulate that."

Six years after Rowe arrived, the paper won its first Pulitzer Prize in more than forty years. It went on to win four more Pulitzers before she retired in 2009.

While she was editor of the *Oregonian*, Rowe was elected president of the American Society of News Editors, only the second woman to hold the position. She promptly launched an effort to improve media credibility, twenty years before it was widely accepted that trust and credibility were pressing concerns for American journalism.

And she was a tireless mentor to many other journalists, particularly women. In 2011, she received the Richard Clurman Award, honoring her work as a mentor. Two tables full of women from all over the country flew to New York for the award presentation.

* * *

Joyce Purnick managed to create a fair amount of controversy during her graduation speech to Barnard College's class of 1998.

At the time, Purnick was the metropolitan editor of the *New York Times*, an unusually high position for a woman, and she had something urgent she wanted to say. She would never have gotten her job, would never have risen as far as she had, she told students and their families, if she had had children. "If I had left the *Times* to have children and then come back to work a four-day week the way some women reporters on my staff do, or taken long vacations and leaves to be with my family, or left at six o'clock instead of eight or nine—forget it. I wouldn't be where I am."[5]

The outrage was fast and furious. NPR's star reporter Cokie Roberts and her husband, Steven, wrote a scathing column for the *New York Daily News* that read, in part, "This is a damaging and demoralizing message to many young women who are already tormented by the conflicting demands of work and family."[6]

But what Purnick said that day at her alma mater was nothing new. A decade earlier, Felice Schwartz, president of a nonprofit for working women, had written an article for the *Harvard Business Review* that sparked the "mommy track" theory. She argued that there are women who want careers and there are women who want families and the business world needs to accommodate both groups. Otherwise, businesses were just wasting money training and developing women who would eventually drop out.[7]

Patricia Schroeder, a Democrat who then represented Colorado in the U.S. Congress, derided the concept as "tragic" because "it reinforces the idea, which is so strong in our country, that you can either have a family or a career but not both if you're a woman."[8]

The division, of course, is not quite as stark as Schroeder suggested. Most women have little choice but to work, and most will have children at some point in their lives. But there are exceptions.

Paula Ellis decided when she was in her late twenties that she was not going to have children. "I made a conscious decision that I couldn't be good at both," she said. "Other women much more talented than me could do it [but] I really felt like I had to make a choice." Ellis focused on her career, rising from a reporter and midlevel editor in Gary, Indiana, to editor of the Knight

Ridder newspapers' Washington bureau and eventually vice president of the chain, then one of the largest media companies in the country.

Ellis said she told her boss of her decision early in her career. She explained that, as far as she could tell, the only successful career women who also had families employed someone else to raise their children, and she didn't want that. "I don't feel a huge void or hole in my life, but I didn't feel like I could do the kind of work I did and be the kind of mother I would like to be," she said. "I would not have sacrificed the well-being of a child for a career."

Ellis's first marriage ended in divorce, and when she remarried, she gained stepchildren as well as a new husband. In some ways, she feels like she got the best of both worlds, but her mother wasn't so sure. When her mother was ill and close to dying, she told her daughter, "I'm worried you didn't have children because you and your brother are such a comfort to me, and I worry about you being alone, that you won't have that." Ellis said she told her mother, in her "usual smart-alecky" way, "They would have been shits, so don't worry."

Diane McFarlin, the former editor and publisher of the *Sarasota Herald-Tribune* who went on to be dean of the University of Florida's journalism school, never had children either. At first, it was because she was so focused on her career, and then her marriage grew shaky. "It would be nine at night and my husband would call and ask, 'When are you coming home?' I would say, 'I'm heading out the door now,' and then someone would come into my office and want to talk," McFarlin said. "That just got harder and harder, and I started diving deeper and deeper into my career." After seventeen years, the couple divorced.

McFarlin said she doesn't regret anything in her life, but she does sometimes wish she had children and grandchildren. When people ask her if she has a family, she tells them she has three thousand children, all of them students at the college she leads.

Meredith Bodgas, editor of *Working Mother* magazine, doesn't think woman would have to make the kind of choices Ellis and McFarlin made if companies were more supportive of working moms.

She has two small children herself and knows how difficult it can be to juggle work and family. She vividly described a night when her four-year-old woke up at 3:00 a.m., followed by her four-month-old two hours later. She decided that, as long as she was awake, she might as well get some work done, so, from about 3:00 a.m. to 6:00 a.m., she fired off emails to her staff while nursing the baby and comforting her older child "who just wanted to sit on my lap and snuggle," she said. She messaged her staff explaining why she was sending emails in the middle of the night and told them not to expect her at the office until late the next morning.

Bodgas thinks all businesses could learn something from the medical profession. Doctors are not typically on call twenty-four hours a day, seven days a week, she points out. Instead, they take shifts to respond to emergencies. "There needs to be a backup and a backup and a backup to the backup," she said.

U.S. companies also could learn from their counterparts in Sweden, where parents are entitled to 480 days of maternity or paternity leave, which they can take until a child is eight years old, Bodgas said. Pay varies but can reach 80 percent of a standard salary.[9] And she thinks companies should provide on-site day care. Even technology companies that offer employees perks like free meals and dry cleaning rarely offer day care.

All of this may seem strange coming from a women's magazine editor, a type immortalized in the 2006 movie *The Devil Wears Prada* in which Meryl Streep plays the dragon lady editor who demands perfection, obedience, and twenty-four-hour dedication from her staff. Bodgas said she once worked for an editor who joked that she was the "Devil Wears L.L. Bean."

"I found that troubling," Bodgas said. "It doesn't matter what the devil is wearing. It's still the devil. The real change is when there is no more devil."

*   *   *

It's chaos and confusion at the Rowe family home in Portland. Rowe's daughters and their husbands, with four children between them, drop in for something to eat, to collect laundry, or just to say hello. All three families live within a mile of each other, and they get together often for family dinners. Gerard makes Costco runs for all of them.

On a single day, Rowe makes three different trips to summer camps for various children and brings one sick child home with her for some special care. Retired from the newspaper business, she serves on local nonprofit boards, but her family gets the lion's share of her attention.

Sarah said she never imagined she would end up being so close to her mom. "We went a little more extreme in how far away we went from each other and a little more extreme in our closeness today," she said. And after declaring Oregon "lame," she now considers it a wonderful home.

"Our families wouldn't work without our mom and dad living in the same neighborhood and helping us out," Mims added. She can no longer remember why she got so angry with her mother that day she tore out of the driveway in a huff.

Neither woman believes she will reach the level of high-profile success their mother did, but both say they're comfortable with that. And then there's ten-year-old Sadie, Mims's oldest, who already displays some of her grandmother's independence. What does she want to be when she grows up?

Sadie smiles. "President of the United States," she says firmly before twirling off to play with a friend.

* * *

ADVICE FOR WOMEN LEADERS

Julia Wallace

My first daughter was about six months old when I got the call asking if I was interested in becoming managing editor of the *Chicago Sun-Times*. It was a job I never imagined for myself. I had gone to college in Chicago and thought the *Sun-Times* was the best paper in the country (sorry, *New York Times*!). But my husband and I were deeply connected to Washington, DC, and we had a newborn. It would be a much more demanding job, and I was discovering just how demanding motherhood could be. We kept weighing the pros and cons until finally my husband turned to me and said, "My dream was to be a White House correspondent and I've done that. This is your dream. Let's do it." I do love this man!

I know there were lost times with my daughters that I will never get back, and there were times when they weren't the first things on my mind. Like Jan Leach, I also had a September 11, 2001, moment. I was at work directing news coverage, immersed in the story. While other parents rushed to pick up their children from school, our daughters were the only ones still there when the buzzer rang at the end of the day.

All working moms have moments like that, and we all feel a certain amount of guilt. Sandy Rowe felt it and, for a time, she thought she had lost her children. Seeing her with them and their families made me think back to 1978 when I arrived in Norfolk for my first job. Rowe had just been named assistant managing editor for news, and I knew right away that she was going to be my role model. She was, and she still is. She made me believe a woman can succeed in both worlds, as dozens of the women in this book have done. Here are some of the lessons that can be gleaned from their experiences.

Don't Be Afraid to Ask

Several of the women we interviewed were able to manage both work and family because their companies valued their contributions enough to make accommodations for them.

People didn't quite know what to make of Arlene Morgan, who may have been the first working mom in the newsroom of the *Philadelphia*

Inquirer in the 1970s. She told the editor she needed a predictable schedule so she could arrange childcare. He agreed to put her on the night desk doing page design, but her direct supervisor began shifting her work times to start an hour earlier or stay an hour later. When she complained, he asked her, "Well, can't your mother come to help?" Morgan didn't give up. She marched into the editor's office and got what she wanted. Morgan eventually became assistant managing editor of the *Inquirer*.

Even women who can multitask at record speed need flexibility when their children are young. In her book *The Fifth Trimester*, Lauren Smith Brody, former executive editor of *Glamour* magazine, offers guidance for new mothers returning to work and who are facing everything from sleep deprivation to finding a place at work to pump breast milk. She said one grateful reader wrote to her, "Your book empowered me to ask for a thirty-two-hour work schedule this summer and one work-from-home day a week. They agreed."

Your Partner Is a Career Decision, Too

Rowe was doing well in Virginia, but her career really took off when she moved to Oregon, and that never would have happened if her husband had been unwilling to put his own career on hold and follow her.

Nearly every woman we spoke to made the point that without a partner who is truly a partner, their jobs would have been infinitely harder and their chances of success much less. Kristin's husband, Gary, stayed home for more than a decade to raise their three children while she worked. She knew it had been a triumph when her mother, who rarely complimented anyone, told her, "Gary did such a good job with those kids." (Kristin tried to overlook the fact that her mother apparently thought she had nothing to do with the way they turned out.)

A partner doesn't have to stay home full-time, of course, but you need someone who is willing to share the load. Otherwise, you're doing multiple jobs, and a hard job becomes even more difficult.

Find a Village

In addition to the support of a partner, most women need good day care and the help of friends and other family members. Finding high-quality, affordable childcare is a pernicious problem for most women. A 2016 study by the Center for American Progress in twenty-two states found that half of the neighborhoods didn't have affordable day care.[10]

Not everyone has "a good Cuban mother" who lives close by and is willing to help out, like Aminda Marqués Gonzalez has, but there are sometimes surprising alternatives. Karen Pensiero was talking to a neighbor about the trouble she was having finding day care, and the woman agreed to take her children. As Meredith Bodgas said, banding together and having "backups to the backups" are essential to avoid living from one crisis to another.

Embrace Your Motherhood—Even at Work

Smith Brody said that when she worked at *Glamour* in the early 2000s, the staff was predominantly female, but the evidence of motherhood was uneven. Some moms had desks adorned with baby pictures and children's artwork and were open about taking off for a school event or a child's illness. Then there were the mothers who sneaked out, "and the only person who would know would be their assistant," Smith Brody said. "They had coded things on their calendar" so no one would know what they were doing.

Aside from the fact that having children—and being open about it—makes you human and very possibly, as Kate O'Brian suggests, a better manager, it's good for your kids to be part of your working world. During one year in Chicago, my husband commuted to and from Washington, DC, so if I needed to go back to the office in the evenings, my daughter came with me. Even now, friends laugh when they see her, remembering the times they caught her coloring under their desks.

My daughters have probably been to more journalism dinners than most journalists have, and it has helped them develop an awareness of the world. Once, my oldest, then fourteen, was seated next to Zbigniew Brzezinski, former national security advisor to Jimmy Carter, at a luncheon. They spent more than an hour discussing world affairs. When my youngest was thirteen, I took her with me to the National Association of Black Journalists convention to hear then-U.S. senator Barack Obama speak. All of this meant they were well prepared to jump into the working world, and I'm incredibly proud of them.

Don't Sweat It

You will not do everything right at work, and you almost certainly will get at least some of motherhood wrong. Every working mom we talked to had a story about forgetting to pick up a child or missing a big event in her child's life.

Marqués, the mother of three and editor of the *Miami Herald*, said the key to balancing work and family is to understand that it's not a fifty-fifty proposition day in and day out. "The reality of it is that it comes in waves," she said. "Sometimes you put your family first and your job takes a back seat, and sometimes you put your job first and your family takes a back seat to your job. It's a constant shifting of priorities."

Most of the women we talked to are happy with the tradeoffs they have made. I asked Rowe what, of all of her accomplishments, she is most proud of. Her family, of course, she replied. "But work is a close second."

The Unfulfilled Promise of Digital Media

I lead one of the largest nonprofit local news organizations in the country, and I'm the co-founder of it. I should be like an ingénue: I'm young. I can dance. I can do whatever you want. But nobody calls me.

—Elizabeth Green

*M*elissa Bell and Ezra Klein were delighted. They had landed a glowing feature in the *New York Times* about their digital news start-up, Vox. The launch of the new site was, the *Times* declared, a "watershed in the news business: a moment when young talent began demanding superior technology as the key to producing superior journalism."[1]

There was one catch: Klein is prominently quoted and appears center stage in two photographs. Bell isn't mentioned until paragraph 13. In one photo, viewers catch a glimpse of her back and one ear.

It wasn't just the *Times* that largely ignored Bell. In 2014, there was intense media interest in Vox, which promised to cut through the noise of too much news and offer explanation and context. The headlines rolled in:

- "Ezra Klein's Vox.com Aims to Make Readers Like the 'Vegetables' of Journalism," *New York Magazine*[2]
- "Vox Media CEO Jim Bankoff on Ezra Klein's Plan to Re-imagine the News," *AdAge*[3]
- "Vox.com Is Going to Be a Great Test of Ezra Klein's Critique of Journalism," *Columbia Journalism Review*[4]
- "Ezra Klein Launches News Site Vox.com," *USA Today*[5]

The oversights didn't particularly bother Bell. As a rule, the tall brunette with the big black glasses avoids attention. She is far more comfortable behind a computer or in front of a whiteboard than she is talking publicly, particularly if the talk is about her.

But there was one article her friends said she simply could not overlook. Emily Bell (no relation) wrote a column for the *Guardian* lambasting Vox and other digital start-ups for their lack of diversity. "Indeed, it's impossible not to notice that in the Bitcoin rush to revolutionize journalism, the protagonists are almost exclusively—and increasingly—male and white," she wrote. "Remaking journalism in its own image, only with better hair and tighter clothes, is not a revolution, or even an evolution. It is a repackaging of the status quo with a very nice clubhouse attached."[6]

Melissa Bell is mentioned just once, as "a back-end publishing expert" whose work is "unglamorous but considered vital." It was all the more infuriating for being written by a woman.

Libby Nelson, who had just joined Vox to cover education, said she was standing on a subway platform waiting for a train when she read the column. "I remember it vividly. I was insulted and hurt by it," she said. "Melissa was incredibly pivotal to the founding, but in the external commentary she was treated as a footnote."

Several women who worked at Vox confronted Bell. She needed to respond, they told her. She needed to tell the real story. Bell was reluctant. "I was held back by my own insecurities, my own shyness, so it was very convenient to have partners who were much more comfortable in a public role than I am," she said. "Then I realized I was damaging our team and our future team if I stayed silent."

She sent Emily Bell an email and tweeted: "I am not @ezraklein's hire. I am his partner and co-founder @Voxdotcom. I am an editor, and a leader on the technology side at @VoxMediaInc." It may have the most *I*'s she had ever strung together at one time.

Since then, Bell has barely paused, accepting speaking engagements, panels, and interviews, even though she would rather stay in the office. "It feels weird to have a piece about me," she said when she sat down to be interviewed for this book. "I know it shouldn't, but it does. I guess that's the whole root of the problem."

*   *   *

When digital media began upending traditional news institutions in the 1990s, there was a glimmer of hope that it was the beginning of a new, more inclusive way of doing business. Here was a new medium being created; it was a chance for a redo.

For more than twenty years, mainstream news organizations had been giving lip service to diversity, but the numbers of women and minorities were still abysmal, especially when it came to leadership positions. Digital media offered a new, more level playing field: Everyone walked in with roughly the same level of experience, which is to say practically none at all.

It's difficult to know the exact gender split among those working in digital newsrooms. Many organizations do not share their data, and it has not yet been collected in one place. A 2017 Women's Media Center report put the proportion of women working in "internet media" at 46 percent—the highest among all forms of media, but many digital news organizations were not included. Newspaper workforces, by comparison, were 38 percent female.[7]

In a two-year study of women in digital media completed in 2013, Meg Heckman found about the same proportion of female leaders in digital media and legacy news organizations, but the number dropped off sharply at the biggest start-ups, dipping to as low as 19 percent in the larger, high-profile operations.[8]

Digital media also have struggled with a "bro culture" endemic to the technology world. It begins with money. Mostly male venture capitalists fund mostly male-led start-ups, which then hire large numbers of mostly young, tech-savvy men and put them in workplaces with precious few rules, much less a human resources department. The result, as Google and other technology companies have discovered, can be hostile territory for women.

Mandy Jenkins, who spent fourteen years in various digital organizations and served as board president of the Online News Association, said new media companies have been the most toxic places she has ever worked in "by a long shot."

"So many new media start-ups are built around a personality and their ideas and their core DNA—and they're men," she said. "They're pretty young, and there are no adults in the room and often no women in the room. It creates a frat house culture."

It's easy to conclude that new, technology-based media look a lot like old media, with all the same gender problems plus a few new ones. The reality, however, is that digital media offer both advantages and disadvantages for women.

Q McElroy was focused on the advantages when she made the move to digital in 2007 to take charge of the entertainment website for the *Atlanta Journal-Constitution*. In 2017, she was promoted to director of engagement and optimization for the newspaper's parent company, Cox Media Group.

McElroy said she was attracted to digital because it represented "a more democratic workplace. It was less about hierarchy and less about job titles and more about a team environment. In digital, it was about the metrics."

Many women in digital news operations talk about the power of metrics. In more traditional newsrooms, they say, the person who yells the loudest is the one who usually wins the argument and whose ideas get adopted. But digital metrics show how many people in the audience are actually reading, sharing, and viewing content. With data behind them, women are less likely to be talked over and ignored.

That doesn't mean, however, that they get recognized, as Melissa Bell discovered. With a few exceptions like Arianna Huffington, one of the founders of the Huffington Post (HuffPost, as it came to be known after her departure), attention tends to go to the Ezra Kleins of the world. This is despite the fact that many of the pioneers in digital media were women. Meg Heckman names women like Lorraine Cichowski, who led *USA Today*'s early forays into digital; Jennifer Musser Metz, a key innovator at Philly.com; and a series of other pioneers—among them, Retha Hill at *Washingtonpost*.com, Michelle Johnson at Boston.com, and Emily Bell at the *Guardian*. She writes that it was "fairly common in the 1990s for women to hold leadership roles in the digital arms of legacy news organizations, either because they viewed those departments as free of glass ceilings or because newspaper executives saw the web as less important than print. Fast-forward twenty years and that perception has flipped." Women today, she said, just "aren't getting the same attention as men."[9]

Elizabeth Green is co-founder, CEO, and editor in chief of Chalkbeat, a nonprofit focused on providing high-quality journalism on local education issues. In 2018, the company raised $6.8 million and provided in-depth coverage in eight cities.

"There have been a hundred stories in the past year about local news, and I've been quoted in zero of them," Green said. "I lead one of the largest nonprofit local news organization in the country, and I'm the co-founder of it. I should be like an ingénue: I'm young. I can dance. I can do whatever you want. But nobody calls me."

* * *

Melissa Bell grew up in San Diego, California, the daughter of "hippie parents," as she describes them. After graduating from Georgetown University, she headed to New York City, where she got a job with a law firm in Lower Manhattan. She thought she would work there a few years as a legal assistant and then head to law school. But something didn't feel right. She was unsettled and unsure about what to do next.

Then the Twin Towers fell. On that day in 2001, Bell was late for work. She was trying to decide if she could turn one of her scarves into a belt when her boyfriend called to tell her that a plane had plowed into the World Trade Center. He told her to stay home.

Bell called her parents back home in San Diego, waking them up to tell them about the plane. She said she was heading to work, but she wanted them to know she was OK. They echoed her boyfriend's advice to stay home. Instead, Bell headed for the subway.

The train she was riding stopped before it reached the World Trade Center station, and passengers began hearing reports of a terrorist attack and another plane hitting the second tower. They got off the train and climbed to street level, emerging onto a scene of chaos and terror, the memory of which still brings tears to Bell's eyes. She tried to help some young men find their mother. She comforted an injured woman. She watched in horror as people jumped to their deaths from the burning towers.

"It showed me trauma like I'd never seen before," she said. "It caused a lot of uncertainty and fear to well up."

At the same time, Bell was frustrated with news coverage of the attacks and the aftermath; she didn't think reporters were asking the right questions. "I spent the next few years feeling like the public story had really gone astray, been depersonalized," she said. "I felt a lot of anger and sadness. I didn't know quite what to do. Being young, I ran away from it all."

She headed home to California and spent a summer waiting tables at a racetrack. That winter she devoted to snowboarding in Vail, Colorado, and waited more tables at night. Her mother, a successful real estate agent and developer, began to worry about her rudderless daughter, so she arranged for Bell to meet with a career consultant.

Bell talked about her yearning for purpose and her love of travel, which prompted the consultant to suggest she think about becoming a missionary. Bell said she wasn't enough of a believer, but she did like to read and she thought it would be amazing to become a book editor, finding and nurturing great authors. Maybe she could be like her heroine, Sophia Tolstaya, the wife of Leo Tolstoy, who helped mold and develop her husband's genius.

Journalism school might be a good option for a budding editor, the consultant suggested. That seemed like a reasonable idea to Bell, so she enrolled at the Medill School of Journalism at Northwestern University, where she quickly found her calling.

"On the first day our assignment was to go out on the street and report. I thought, 'This is the best thing ever. I get to go out and be nosey,'" she said. "I couldn't believe this was a job that people wanted me to do. I fell madly in love with journalism. It saved me from my wandering rambling-ness."

For her internship, Bell jumped at the chance to go to the *Hindustan Times* in New Delhi, India. While she was there, she heard about a new business newspaper that was being created by Raju Narisetti, who had been one of the top editors at the *Wall Street Journal*. She emailed him and, shortly afterward, "This tall, bright-eyed woman shows up, and that was Melissa," Narisetti said. "She was this wide-eyed Californian in Delhi."

He was impressed with her curiosity, which he thought went well beyond that of most journalists. She wanted to understand the process, the strategy, the technology—every aspect of the business—so Narisetti hired her as a "super trainer" to get the staff up to speed on new technology, including a content management system. "She was a key part of making sure the newsroom embraced this new technology and other new ways of doing things," Narisetti said. "Melissa was one of the true believers and one of the true salespeople."

Bell loved it. She enjoyed the energy of a start-up and was fascinated with Delhi. She began writing a personal blog sharing her experiences and reported feature stories for the weekend section of the paper. Of the original newsroom staff of ninety, she was one of about a half-dozen non-Indians and one of the least experienced, but Narisetti lists Bell as one of the top ten people who contributed to the start-up's success.

*   *   *

The opportunity to launch a new publication—sans printing press and bureaucracy—has lured a number of women into becoming digital entrepreneurs. One of the most successful, and certainly the best known, is Arianna Huffington.

Huffington was an unlikely digital media pioneer. She had never been a journalist and had no technology experience, but she did have money, connections, and vision. She and former America Online executive Ken Lerer began talking about the need for a left-leaning version of the popular website Drudge Report. They specifically wanted to go after the National Rifle Association.[10] Huffington was responsible for raising half the money they needed to get started, and she did it in a week.[11] Then, in 2005, she and Lerer recruited digital expert Jonah Peretti and launched the Huffington Post.

Unlike the Drudge Report, which mainly published curated content under provocative headlines, the Huffington Post recruited an army of bloggers to cover politics, entertainment, business, and breaking news as well as write opinion pieces and personal essays. It was a novel idea. Few people at the time understood the power of original content on the web, and even fewer recognized there was a market for journalism with a distinct point of view.

The site met with "decidedly mixed reviews," according to Huffington. "As I remember it, critics were lining up to predict it wouldn't last. One hour after we launched, a reviewer compared the Huffington Post to a combination of *Ishtar*, *Heaven's Gate*, and *Gigli*. A year later she emailed me and asked if she could blog for the site, and of course I said yes."[12]

In 2011, Huffington and her partners sold the business to AOL for $315 million. Huffington remained president and editor until she left in 2016 to launch another digital start-up. In 2018, the HuffPost was one of the ten most popular websites and one of the most recognizable media brands in the country.

In many ways, the most important part of the brand was Huffington herself. A savvy marketer and promoter who wasn't afraid to use her connections, she got plenty of press—some of it unfavorable. In 2016, *Vanity Fair* published a two-part series about her titled "The Arianna Chronicles" that focused on her "capricious management style."[13] No one had to ask who Arianna was.

Huffington believes there is still resistance to women in leadership roles, and digital media is no exception. Women are called "difficult or driven for voicing opinions and taking actions that would be called bold if a man did it," she said in an email interview. "But I learned to carry on despite those voices and despite the so-called 'likeability paradox.' As my mother used to say, fearlessness isn't the absence of fear but rather the mastery of fear."

Q McElroy, who is African American, said gender bias is just one of the obstacles she encountered in digital media. "For me, the most prominent factors were race and age," she said. She often felt that her colleagues thought her "too brown," too young, and too inexperienced to be taken seriously. And as someone whose job it was to push a legacy print newsroom into the digital world, she was viewed as an interloper at best and a threat at worst. But McElroy had been raised with her cousin, the musician T. I., in a black neighborhood in Atlanta, and she had learned not to back down.

In 2009, she was assigned to head a team of more than a dozen columnists at the *Atlanta Journal-Constitution*. They held some of the most coveted jobs at the newspaper, each writing a couple of weekly columns that got prominent play in the print edition. McElroy's task was to convert them to the web. A few already were blogging effectively, but most were not, and a few didn't even know what a blog was. McElroy, then in her early thirties, realized that most of them had been journalists longer than she had been alive. She could just see them thinking, "Who is this young brown girl coming in and telling me what to do? I've been doing this for decades. Who are you and why should I pay any attention to you?"

In one meeting, she explained how the columnists should go about attracting and engaging with audiences online. She set out new rules for their blogs—how many times they should post content, when they should post, and the kind of content they should post. One staff member turned red in the face and started screaming that he wasn't going to do it.

"I pulled him into a room by himself and told him, in a very respectful way, that he would never speak to me that way again as long as he lived," McElroy said. "I told him he was going to do the job as laid out or else." He did.

Cory Haik had similar experiences as the new kid on the digital block of the *Times-Picayune* newspaper in New Orleans.

Haik was a college student, newly married, and with a new baby when she began working for NOLA.com, the *Picayune*'s nascent website in the early 2000s. She was frequently dismissed as the "digital kid," but she was convinced that the days of "a bunch of crusty editors sitting around a table deciding what people needed to know" were coming to an end. "The web was talking back," she said. "I thought, 'Hot damn, I want to be a part of this.'"

Within a few years, Haik was managing NOLA.com, where she worked on two Pulitzer Prize–winning projects before moving to the *Seattle Times* as assistant managing editor of that newspaper's website. In 2010, she was recruited by the *Washington Post* to help merge the print and digital sides of its news operation. Nearly 175 digital staff members who had worked in separate buildings in separate cities were moved to one gigantic desk in the main newsroom in Washington. "My job was to run that desk and figure out what the next stage of digital would look like," Haik said.

At age thirty-nine, Haik was one of the youngest women on the *Post*'s senior team. Her title was executive editor of emerging products, but it might as well have been disruptor in chief. She was one of the people who pushed, pulled, and cajoled traditional print journalists into the digital world. It was not an easy task. When Amazon founder Jeff Bezos bought the *Post* in 2013, Haik was elated. "It was like Christmas came early," she said. Here, she thought, was an innovator who understood digital completely.

But even with Bezos at the helm, Haik felt that digital remained an afterthought at the *Post*, and when she was offered the publisher's job at Mic, a digital-only news and media company that produces content aimed at college-educated millennials, she took it. She was intrigued by the chance to do "professional, high-integrity journalism built natively for digital platforms," exactly what she had been trying to do at the *Post*. But at Mic, she could do it without being tethered to a legacy print product.

Haik was convinced that Mic had found a secret sauce for digital content, one that combined respect for audience with deep engagement. A prime example, she said, was a Mic video about the plight of Alice Johnson, "a lovely grandmother" who was serving a life sentence for a nonviolent drug offense. The video went viral in 2018, and among the viewers was reality television star Kim Kardashian West, who lobbied President Donald Trump to commute the woman's sentence. Trump promptly did.[14] The story, Haik said, is "a testament to the power of social media and the power of digital journalism. It's the kind of thing that lights me up."

But even with $60 million in venture funding and an audience of around forty-five million in 2018, Mic, like many digital start-ups, wasn't able to pull in enough revenue to maintain a sustainable business. In early 2019, the company was sold to Bustle Digital Group for a reported $5 million.[15]

Haik knew that when she left the relatively safe world of a major national news organization, she was taking a risk. But she notes that a number of other women have done the same, including Bell. She suspects that like her, they saw more opportunities for women in the digital space. "We all had really great opportunities come up for us, but I didn't see a path ultimately. I didn't see a path for executive leadership at the *Post*, even though I was in a very high-powered position. . . . I still didn't see a path to be in a position that I really wanted."

* * *

Bell arrived at the *Washington Post* at about the same time as Haik. At first, she filled in for a reporter who was on maternity leave; then, her old boss and mentor—Narisetti, who had joined the *Post* as a managing editor—encouraged her to apply for a job writing a new blog, chronicling topics that were gaining traction on the web. "I didn't necessarily want the job, and the woman who was hiring didn't want me for the job, but somehow she hired me, and I took the job. Raju was very convincing," Bell said.

Narisetti said the *Post* needed to create a real-time blogging environment. "We needed someone—and I say this in a good way—who could be an inch deep and a mile wide. I knew that Melissa had eclectic interests."

He also understood that he was putting her in the middle of a pitched war between two factions. "The print newsroom thought the digital folks had no respect for the brand and they would destroy it," he said. "The digital newsroom thought the print people were really old-school Luddites who didn't want to do anything different or new."

"Those were tough years," he added. "People like Melissa didn't get the benefit of doubt. They were always seen with suspicion."

But Bell loved writing *BlogPost*, which was filled with whatever was newest and most interesting on the web. "I was addicted to the stream of information coming at me," she said. She also began trying to solve problems for the other bloggers, not the least of which was an unfriendly content management system.

At first, Klein, who wrote the *Post*'s popular public policy blog, *Wonk-blog*, was confused. He was a blogger. Bell was a blogger. Why was she in meetings about *his* blog? In an organization filled with hierarchy and rules, her role made no sense to him. But Klein soon realized Bell got results: somehow she was able to bring together journalists, designers, technologists, and data in a way no one else had been able to do.

When Bell was named director of blogging, Klein said he didn't care who did the job as long as technical problems were fixed so that bloggers could more easily post their stories. Bell did that and more. She shepherded new blogs that attracted larger and larger audiences, and she began spending more and more time with Klein. The longer they talked, the more they realized they shared the same concerns about the way news is reported. They believed that, too often, journalism doesn't provide enough context, explanation, or insight for busy readers. Over espressos and more espressos, they decided that what was needed was a new kind of approach to news to fill that void.

They came up with the idea of creating card stacks, a digital form of index cards, to provide background on stories. It was a way of helping readers get caught up on a subject without weighing down the narrative of a story. The cards became one of the early innovations that distinguished Vox from other news sites.[16]

Klein and Bell pitched their idea to the *Post* as a stand-alone brand, but the publisher said the time wasn't right. The two then began talking to potential investors. One of the companies that showed immediate interest was Vox Media, a company founded in 2003 by an Oakland Athletics fan so unhappy with coverage of his beloved team that he started his own blog. It grew into the popular sports website SB Nation.

Former AOL executive Jim Bankoff had taken over as the company CEO in 2009; he renamed it Vox Media and began acquiring non-sports sites. He thought the concept Bell and Klein laid out during lunch at an obscure Chinese restaurant in Washington, DC, was a good match for what he had in mind for Vox Media. As they got closer to a deal, Bell and Klein brought in Matt Yglesias, a blogger at Slate.com, as part of the founding team.

*   *   *

One of the biggest obstacles for female digital entrepreneurs is raising money. In 2017, only 2 percent of venture capital funding went to all-women teams.[17] The main reason? Almost all of the people making decisions about who gets money are men, and their idea of a great investment prospect is someone who looks like Mark Zuckerberg. In 2017, only 7 percent of the investing partners in venture capital companies were female.[18]

Dyllan McGee looks nothing like Zuckerberg, but she had what she thought was a great idea: tell the stories of one hundred amazing women. She wanted to produce five-to-six-minute YouTube–like videos, share them online, and then mold them into a PBS documentary. It took her three years to raise the money.

Here are the kinds of questions she said funders asked her:

- Is this going to be too feminist-y?
- Shouldn't these stories be about men too?
- Is mainstream America ready to sit down and listen to a bunch of women's stories?

McGee eventually got support from AOL (now Verizon Media), after Nancy Armstrong, the wife of then CEO Tim Armstrong, heard her give a talk about the project.

Makers.com launched in 2012 as an unabashedly feminist website with videos featuring women ranging from Ruth Bader Ginsberg to Oprah Winfrey. With a reported 4,500 videos, it may be the world's largest single collection of its kind, with a viewership that numbers in the millions.[19] And in 2013, PBS aired a *Makers* documentary—narrated by Meryl Streep.

McGee has just one thing to say about all the male investors who turned her down: "We proved them wrong."

Jennifer Brandel was working for WBEZ, a public radio station in Chicago, when she decided to make a podcast that would flip the way journalism traditionally works. Instead of reporters coming up with stories they think are interesting or important and then delivering those stories to listeners, she wanted listeners to drive content decisions. Her *Curious City* podcast proved popular with viewers, answering such questions as "What happens to all of the stuff we dutifully recycle?" and "What's at the bottom of the Chicago River?"

Brandel eventually took the concept national, but she has struggled to convince investors to invest or news organizations to pay. "I just know that some men have had an easy time getting money for stupid things, and I've had a helluva time getting money for something we all agree is very important," she said.

It was stories like those of McGee and Brandel that turned Susan Lyne into a venture capitalist.

Lyne began her career at alternative newspapers in the Bay area in the 1970s and went on to work for some of the biggest names in media: the Walt

Disney Company, Martha Stewart Living Omnimedia, AOL, and the Gilt Group. When Martha Stewart was sentenced to prison for offenses related to a stock sale, Lyne was tapped to fill in as head of the company. Part of her job was visiting Stewart in prison.

It was while she was CEO of Gilt.com, the online luxury clothing company, that Lyne realized just how serious were the challenges facing female digital entrepreneurs. She began to meet "a lot of young women who were choosing to start companies as opposed to going to work for companies," she said. In the start-up world, they saw an easier path to success. They would no longer have to spend all of their time figuring out how to break through the old gender barriers; they would have ownership from the start.

Lyne was especially impressed with the companies that were focused on "making life for other women better": companies like Rent the Runway, which rents designer dresses and accessories to women online, and Learn-Vest, the financial planning service that was purchased by Northwestern Mutual for $250 million.[20]

But while these companies got funding for what proved to be very successful businesses, the women who headed them "had to spend a whole lot more time fundraising," Lyne said. "And they all had stories about walking into rooms full of guys who just didn't get what they were doing."

Lyne saw an opportunity. In 2014, with backing from AOL, she launched her own business, BBG [Built by Girls] Ventures, a small, seed-stage venture capital fund that invests in women-led technology companies.

"From day one we were flooded with women who wanted to come in and tell us what they were doing," Lyne said. "We've seen over three thousand companies, all with a female founder, so that tells you that the world is changing."

The venture capital world is beginning to adjust its profile of what a successful entrepreneur looks like, she said. At a time when digital businesses are increasingly built on top of existing technologies and platforms, the new "superpowers" tend to reflect what women are good at: understanding how to talk to consumers and how to market to them.

*   *   *

Bell never set out to be a poster child for female leadership. If anything, she said, she has been an "unwilling crusader." But the company she has helped build has both a large number of female employees and a culture that could be described as leaning female.

According to figures posted on Vox, 52 percent of the staff in 2018 were female and 33 percent were nonwhite.[21] When Klein stepped down as editor in chief in 2017, Lauren Williams, an African-American woman, moved into that leadership job. She named as her number two Allison Rockey, a white woman. Klein became editor at large, focusing on his blog and podcast and various strategic initiatives.

Melissa Bell, meanwhile, took over as publisher of not just Vox but Vox Media, which includes six other networks, employs about 1,000 people, and reaches about 750 million people a month.

Libby Nelson said many of the company's female employees have young children, and work schedules are arranged so they can leave by 5:00 p.m. for day-care pickup. But the biggest difference between Vox Media and other workplaces, she said, is an atmosphere that feels comfortable to women.

She remembers Bell once walking into a meeting visibly upset. She had just come from a funeral, and she was crying. "I remember her forthrightly addressing it and saying, 'Hey, I'm upset about something. I'm having an emotional reaction to it. Please ignore it and focus on what I'm saying,' and then launching into whatever she was saying. And she was so professional. I never thought you could be crying in meetings and be professional about it. It was an eye-opening moment for me."

Bell acknowledges the incident. "I'm a passionate person," she said. "My response is to cry. I don't think it's good to cry at work because I would like to be calmer and not have my direct reports worry about me crying. But starting my own company, being in a place where I'm much more comfortable, my relationship to crying has completely changed. I no longer feel ashamed. It's a very feminine signal, and we don't accept feminine signals like that. We don't think a leader should be able to cry. The more I accepted it, the more it became clear it was an empathy builder."

As she walks through the sleek Vox offices in New York City, Bell is clearly proud of what the company has accomplished. She talks about shows like *No Passport Required*, which airs on PBS, and *Today, Explained*, a daily podcast that attempts to explain each day's news. She talks about her team, which she says deserves all the credit for the work that has been done.

Bankoff, CEO of Vox Media, thinks otherwise. Bell, he said, "is in the middle of every initiative. It's one thing to be a smart and insightful person, which she is. But she can leverage those insights because of her strong ability to build relationships inside the company and with our partners."

Klein wants to be sure people understand something else about Bell: she is the highest-ranking editorial leader in the company. "Melissa could fire me—I think," he said. "And that's appropriate."

When told what Klein had said, Bell laughed, but she didn't say he was wrong.

* * *

ADVICE FOR WOMEN LEADERS

Julia Wallace

When I began reporting for this chapter, I called Kara Swisher, the co-founder of the popular technology news website Recode. I asked her about all the stories I had read and heard about the lack of opportunity for women in digital media.

She snapped, "Show me the numbers," and proceeded to rattle off a list of powerful women at digital companies.

What I subsequently learned is that the digital space is a mixed bag for women, which shouldn't have been a surprise based on my own experience at a start-up, which is what *USA Today* was in 1982. It was crazy, chaotic, and exhilarating all at the same time. You could break the rules and invent jobs for yourself and others. Best of all, no one ever said, "This is how it's always been done."

The start-up climate didn't appeal to everyone, though. I watched a number of people come and go, uncomfortable riding the roller coaster that inevitably comes with inventing something new.

The women in this chapter all share a spirit of adventure. They are all risk-takers. I imagine many of them would be miserable in a slower-paced and more traditional and bureaucratic environment. They are truly writing their own rules.

It's OK If You're Lost for a While

Cory Haik was a pregnant college freshman with no idea where she would end up. For several years, Melissa Bell didn't have a clue what she wanted to do with her life. Part of the reason these women found success is that they were open to change. They gave themselves time to figure things out, and they took chances in order to find the work they love.

Another digital innovator remembered a speaker coming to her junior high school and telling students that most of the jobs they would one day hold didn't yet exist. She was relieved, because she didn't know of a single job that interested her. Even in junior high, she was ready to try something new.

Learn from Failure

Dyllan McGee at Makers.com was curious about what the hundreds of re-markable women the website has profiled had in common, so she sent them a survey to identify their personality traits. It turned out that, on the surface at least, the women had little in common. But as she thought about the video interviews her company had done with the women, she realized they did share two things: They were all ambitious, and they had all experienced a significant failure that they had overcome. "All of these women refused to take no for an answer," McGee said.

We're naturally afraid of failure, but that's what often forces us to dig in and do better. I still credit one of my former bosses, Nancy Monaghan, for my success. The most important thing she did for me was to demote me and force me to work on my weaknesses.

Partnerships Are Powerful

It's difficult to imagine that Vox would have been as successful without either Klein or Bell. Bell thinks strategically about how to fuse content and technology, and she knows how to bring people together to make it happen. But she's not comfortable center stage, and she can seem hesitant and a little unsure when she's speaking. Klein, on the other hand, speaks with ease and conviction whether he is in front of one person or one hundred people. Together, they were a powerhouse. Bell is dubious they would have been able to find funders without Klein. I'm doubtful what came after would have succeeded without Bell.

Titles Matter

One of the reasons some women get overlooked in digital media is that they have titles that are confusing to traditional journalists writing about them. Bell and Haik eventually were named publishers of their companies, which immediately established their credentials. Sometimes it's worth fighting to get the right title. It may seem like a small thing, but it helps establish you in the pecking and prestige order.

Men Matter, Too

It was striking to me how many people mentioned Raju Narisetti as being an important mentor to them, so I called him up and asked him why he had spent so much time developing and mentoring women. He said he has worked for many strong women and hiring and encouraging women was something he was expected to do. But over time, it became a personal commitment. In early 2018, about a hundred newsroom leaders gathered at the Newseum in Washington, DC, to talk about the #MeToo movement and what newsrooms must do to combat sexual harassment. Only a handful of men attended, and Narisetti, who was then running Gizmodo Media, was the only male CEO.

My Narisetti was Ron Martin, whom I worked for at both *USA Today* and the *Atlanta Journal-Constitution*. Kristin's were Jim Amoss at the *Times-Picayune* and Christopher Callahan at Arizona State University. There are many men out there who can and do make a difference for women. "There need to be more of them," Narisetti said.

About the Crying

Kristin and I have been known to warn young women not to cry in newsrooms (hence the title of this book). That made perfect sense for the newsrooms we grew up in, but hearing about Bell, who isn't afraid to show her emotions, made me think twice about this advice. Too often, we tolerate screamers but not criers, and maybe it would be better if that ratio was flipped. I'm not ready to tell women to go ahead and pull out the tissues, but I admire Bell and others who are trying to change the culture of workplaces.

Too Young and Too Old

It surprised me how often the women I spoke with brought up the issue of age. Many said they were treated like the "digital kid" when they worked in legacy media organizations, and they noted how few older women there are in digital media. These are high-powered women in their thirties and forties, and they already are worried about what will happen to them when they hit fifty or sixty.

"I worry about shelf life for a woman in management, very much so," said Mitra Kalita, senior vice president for news, opinion and programming at CNN Digital. "Every time I walk into any management situation in the industry (and I don't mean CNN), I see a bunch of men who won't let go. They are brought in for summits. They're advisors. They're in academia. They're everywhere. I think about all the women who were there when I was coming up. I don't know where they are."

To stay in the business, you need to stay connected, relevant, energized, and optimistic. Kristin and I are in our sixties and continue to find very meaningful work at the Cronkite School at Arizona State University. Most who know us say we haven't slowed down a bit.

· 9 ·

The Next Generation

What Has Changed and What Has Not

I see more and more young women saying they're not going to put up with this.

—Kate O'Brian

*W*omen who entered the news business in the 1970s and 1980s relished breaking barriers. They called in news stories while in labor and parked their babies under their desks. They had "trailing spouses" who followed them from one end of the country to the other, or they skipped marriage and children altogether, unable or unwilling to sandwich in a personal life against the press of the news. They learned to navigate a world that was male to its core—and they were called pushy broads and worse for their efforts.

These women accepted and even welcomed the challenges they faced, partly for personal reasons and partly because they felt that history was on their side. They chased exciting careers doing important work, and they believed that in doing so they would clear the way for generations of female journalists after them. What they never imagined was that decades later, women would be facing many of the same barriers.

In 2018, women in media held fewer positions of power, were promoted more slowly, and made less money than their male counterparts.[1] And, as the #MeToo movement has so vividly illustrated, women still contend with sexual predators as well as a range of lesser but no less toxic behaviors that former television executive Kate O'Brian describes as "plain old disrespect."

"I find it surprising we haven't made more progress," said Madhulika Sikka, who entered the business in the 1980s and went on to hold top jobs at NPR and the *Washington Post*. "I don't think we did all this work and tried to be role models and examples to other women just to tell them now, 'Well you've just got to keep sucking it up.'"

Susan Goldberg remembers the disbelief she encountered in 1987 when she became the first female managing editor of the *San Jose Mercury News*. When she was introduced to people more often than not the response was an incredulous, *"You're* the managing editor?" She doesn't think the reaction would be much different today. "I would like to tell you I'm having a totally different conversation than I had thirty years ago, but it's the same conversation, and it's so frustrating," said Goldberg, who now heads *National Geographic*. "There are fewer women running newsrooms now than there were then. It's astounding."

Audrey Cooper, the first female editor in chief in 153 years at the *San Francisco Chronicle*, is an anomaly: Not only is she female, but she was just thirty-seven years old when she became editor of the *Chronicle* in 2015. She said she often looks around and wonders where the other women leaders are. "There are so few of us that we know each other," she said.

Cooper joined the *Chronicle* in 2006 as an assistant metro editor. Six years later, while eight months pregnant with her son, she interviewed to be managing editor and got the job. But just a few weeks after returning from maternity leave and assuming her new duties, a new publisher came on board and, shortly after that, the top editor left. Cooper, a first-time mother with a six-month-old baby at home, took over, running the newsroom for the next year before officially winning the title of editor in chief. "I think they thought I was young to be an ME, and then to just hopscotch that level and become editor took some convincing," she said. "It took a year of convincing, actually."

During the year in which she was both acting editor in chief and managing editor, the newspaper's publisher suggested that Cooper might want to think about an executive coach to help her hone her management skills. Cooper readily agreed. "These jobs are really lonely, especially when there are not very many female editors or a lot of contemporaries," she said. "So when you're trying to figure out how to do something, it can be isolating."

Almost every woman she worked with during the first decade of her career has left journalism, Cooper said. Some were laid off, some married other journalists and followed them to their jobs, and others decided the long hours and low pay weren't worth it, especially as they began to have children.

Aminda Marqués Gonzalez, executive editor of the *Miami Herald*, has observed the same thing. After getting her journalism degree from the University of Florida in 1986, Marqués landed her dream job reporting for the *Herald* and, with the exception of four years as the Miami bureau chief for *People* magazine, she has spent her entire career at the paper. Almost none of Marqués's peers—the women she went to college with or started out working with—is still in the business, she said. They all quit. "Women of our generation were sort of sold on this idea that we could do it all," she said. "We could be supermom and Barbie wife and . . . it's really just a big lie."

Beginning in the 1980s, women like Marqués poured into journalism schools. Ever since, they have equaled or exceeded the number of male students enrolled, and they now make up between two-thirds and three-quarters of the student enrollment at most journalism schools. Yet they still account for only about a third of those employed in the news media. Some of the discrepancy results from women going into public relations or other fields, but it's also clear that, while women enter newsrooms at about the same rate as men, their numbers begin dropping after a few years, and that means fewer women in the pipeline for leadership positions.

An Indiana University study published in 2014 found that, on average, women leave the profession much earlier than do men. Among U.S. journalists with fewer than five years of work experience, there were about as many women as men in print, broadcast, and digital newsrooms. Among those with twenty or more years of experience, only about a third were women.[2] Another national survey of people working in the media, conducted in 2018, confirmed the trend, finding that 10 percent of men in media had worked twenty-six or more years in their current positions compared to just 4 percent of women.[3]

As Cooper noted, women leave the business for many reasons, including overload, exhaustion, family obligations, and the chance to make more money doing something else. But Gail Evans thinks there is something else at work.

Evans was the highest-ranking woman at CNN before leaving to write books about gender in the workplace. She believes the playing field is pretty even for women during their first decade of work. "In terms of how they're treated, acknowledgement and assignments, it's fairly level," she said, and that leads women to believe "the system is egalitarian; it's a merit-based system, and so they stop watching. If somebody makes a comment about a gender issue, she gets pooh-poohed. [She's told,] 'Oh, that's not what's happening here; you're just looking for something.' So their antennae totally go down."

Then the women begin to notice things. They get passed over for a promotion or an assignment or discover they're being paid less than male colleagues. They don't feel like they're getting the recognition they deserve, and the subtle and not-so-subtle comments and behavior of the men around them that once seemed harmless, if irritating, don't seem benign anymore. "And the women think they're crazy, so they don't tell anyone," Evans said. "They make an excuse for what's happening."

At some point, usually ten or fifteen years into their careers, women "all of a sudden begin to wake up and say, 'Hey, wait a minute. The playing field is not level; this is not a merit-based system,'" and that, Evans said, is when the retention issues really begin to surface. Women "get frustrated because they gave it their all but got passed over for many reasons, and they leave. Everyone says they left because they had children, but it's not true," she said. "They left because of unfulfilled expectations."

* * *

Tracy Greer is a thirty-nine-year-old journalism dropout who is studying to be a residential real estate appraiser. She can barely fathom the turn her life has taken.

"I knew from the time I was eleven years old that I was put on this earth to be a journalist," she said. "I joined the school newspaper in the sixth grade and never looked back." After getting her undergraduate degree in journalism from New Mexico State University, Greer went to Northwestern University for a master's degree. She paid her way by waiting tables and working in the athletic department's media relations office.

Besides journalism, Greer's other passion is sports. She grew up playing soccer, basketball, and baseball—not softball, baseball. "I was the girl in the Little League with all the boys," she said. As an adult, she fell in love with roller derby. She describes it as "a full-contact sport on roller skates, which makes my inner eight-year-old very happy." And, she said, "It's great for getting out aggression." It also appeals to her that roller derby is "a women's sport run by women for women."

Greer skates under the name "PulHitzHer Prize," a twist on the name of journalism's top prize. Her jersey number is "-30-," a reference to the number journalists in pre-computer days placed at the end of their stories as an alert to their editors that they had reached the story's conclusion.

For nearly five years, roller derby was the antidote to the stresses and pressures of Greer's job at KJZZ, the Phoenix-based National Public Radio affiliate. Playing for the Arizona Roller Derby league was, she said, her sacred time. "You literally have to put the phone away and concentrate because here's a woman on eight wheels ready to tackle you. It forced me to do something that was not work."

Greer joined KJZZ in 2011 as digital editor, managing the station's website. Three years later, she was named managing editor. As the highest-ranking woman in the newsroom and, at times, the station's only female editor, she was typically the sole woman in news meetings and on search committees formed to screen new hires. Search committee meetings were revealing. Greer said some male managers made inappropriate comments about job candidates or applied different standards to male and female applicants. And if a woman did get the job, there was a good chance she would be paid less than a man in the same position.

Greer and several other women went to the human resources department to complain about the pay gaps. "They looked at everything and said, 'You've got a problem; fix it,'" she said. She was assigned the task of coming up with a matrix to match pay with skills and experience, and then she ran the names of the station's news reporters through the matrix. "To a person, the female employees were underpaid," she said. The station raised wages for most of the women, but, still, new hires were brought in at salary levels that made no sense to Greer. While digging into payroll data, she also learned that she was making significantly less than a man on staff who did not supervise anyone.

In addition, Greer became concerned about what she felt was a toxic environment in the newsroom. She said she complained to Rio Salado College, which holds the station's license, about several instances of what she called "bad behavior" on the part of men at the station, but nothing happened. Finally, in March 2017, she quit. "I had done everything I thought I could do, to no avail," she said. "I didn't think anything would be done. I didn't think anything would change."

A few months later, film producer Harvey Weinstein was publicly accused of sexual misconduct and the #MeToo movement erupted. A few months after that, Rio Salado College launched investigations into the behavior of two senior executives at KJZZ. In 2018, the general manager retired after the college issued a report concluding that he had behaved inappropriately with four young men at the station,[4] and the station's associate general manager of news was moved out of the newsroom and demoted for "thoughtless, sexist" behavior, among other infractions.[5]

For the first time, Greer feels like women are being listened to, and while she is buoyed by that fact, she also is angry about what happened to her. "It was hard to navigate the bad behavior on top of what was already a very demanding job," she said. "While I chose to leave that job on my own, they are the ones who made the situation untenable. They are the ones who I feel cost me my career in journalism."

Greer is taking classes to learn how to appraise property, and she is doing her best to disconnect from her former life. She has "unfollowed" some journalism accounts on social media, and she's trying to read something other than news. "I don't know if I'm there yet," she said. "It's like being a smoker and quitting and telling everyone how good it is to quit. But kind of like a smoker, journalism cost me a lot."

* * *

Julie Zeilinger was sixteen years old when she founded the FBomb, a website for teen feminists, in 2009. A high school history teacher turned her onto books like *The Feminine Mystique* and *Sisterhood Is Powerful*, and Zeilinger decided to embrace feminism and try to convince others to embrace it, too. She set up a website and invited other teenaged girls to join her in writing about their gender-related experiences and observations.

Zeilinger and the FBomb got a lot of attention. "Teen feminists weren't really a thing," she said. "It was sort of an anomaly, this teen girl writing about feminism." By the time she graduated from Barnard College in 2015, Zeilinger had written two books, one of them a guidebook to being a young feminist, and was considered something of an expert on the topic.

She went to work for a news website and then moved to an entertainment website, writing about gender and feminism. But she grew more and more disillusioned with what she calls a "gendered" work environment, one in which women are paid less and treated as less than their male counterparts.

Zeilinger compared notes with friends working for other media companies and discovered many were experiencing the same frustrations. They felt overlooked, underpaid, and underappreciated. "There was just this feeling that they weren't prepared to succeed in the workforce, especially newsrooms," she said, while men seemed better primed for success.

It also bothered her that media outlets seemed interested in covering gender issues like pay inequalities yet failed to reflect equality in their own practices.

Zeilinger decided it wasn't worth it. She left to work for a media consulting company that specializes in women's issues.

Like Zeilinger, Samantha Felix and Lily Altavena are millennials who, by their own admission, were almost completely unprepared for what they encountered in the workplace. Unlike Zeilinger, they refused to be forced out of the business.

Since graduating from Chapman University in Orange, California, in 2012, Felix has worked for eight different companies, including several digital start-ups. In 2017, she joined the *New York Times*, where she works on the digital side, managing audience development and platforms.

She isn't sure exactly what she expected when she entered the workforce, but she's sure she wasn't remotely prepared for what she encountered. "I was extremely naïve," she said.

Felix was working at one company when she got pregnant and discovered she wasn't eligible for maternity leave because she had not been an employee long enough. She returned to work three weeks after the baby was born only to find "there was a man in my job. They said, 'Well, we didn't know what was going to happen.'" She worked in another, lesser position for a few months and then left for another company.

At her next job, Felix said she worked for a man "who decided I was a threat." The two of them had similar skills sets, and she ended up getting demoted. She found another job. But her new company quickly made it clear that young women, especially if they might become pregnant young women, weren't exactly welcome, and she moved on to yet another company.

When she landed at the *Times*, it seemed to Felix that she had finally found the right place, and then it happened again: She began feeling undercut by a man who appeared to be threatened by her. "There was a lot of aggressively controlling behavior—things like telling me there were certain people I couldn't speak to," she said. "It was clear that it was a bad situation from the start, but I didn't say anything for a long time. Then, finally, I said to myself, 'No, this has to stop. This is the *Times*. I'm not going to leave this time.'"

Felix took her complaint to her "bosses and her bosses' bosses," and when nothing happened, she kept going back. "I tried to be very clear and unemotional about what was happening, but I didn't stop talking, I had to keep saying the same things over and over and over," she said. Eventually, she moved to another position in the company and, not long after that, the man with whom she had clashed left the *Times*. For the first time, she wasn't the one to head for the door.

Felix thinks many young women respond to difficult situations in the workplace, especially when they feel like sexism is at work, in the same way she did. "My reaction was just to leave," she said. She now tells other women that's not the answer. She tells them, "If we don't talk, things don't change."

Altavena entered the workforce just a few years behind Felix, convinced that the problems her mother's generation had encountered had long since disappeared. Armed with a degree in journalism from New York University and an internship with Ann Curry at NBC News and convinced that she wanted to be a broadcast producer, she took a job at MSNBC and then at a television station in Dallas, Texas.

Altavena soon grew disillusioned with a power structure that skewed heavily male. There were the all-male morning news meetings; the "naked chef" segment featuring a half-naked man making a salad; the male consultant who "had all these ideas about how women should dress and how their hair should be," Altavena said. "I thought, I'm not OK with a man telling me what my hair should look like."

She quit and went home to Phoenix, Arizona, where she moved in with her parents and took a job delivering fast food to make a few bucks while she thought about what to do next. Just before the start of the fall 2015 semester, she made her decision: She would go to graduate school for the time being and figure out the rest of her life later. Over the next two years in graduate school at Arizona State University, she discovered a passion for investigative reporting and a talent for data analysis. She covered local and state elections and was the senior producer and lead reporter on a thirty-minute documentary on prescription opioid abuse. Before graduating, she landed a job at the *Arizona Republic* newspaper doing environmental and watchdog reporting.

Altavena said she feels welcome at the newspaper, where there are a number of female editors and a lot of other young reporters. Sexism isn't overt like it was in her previous jobs, but it still exists. "When I see sexism here, I think it's an undertone," she said. "That almost makes it harder because when you call it out, people just think you're crazy."

There are the occasional "darling" comments and the readers who tell her she doesn't know what she's talking about or say, "You only wrote this story about sexism because you are a woman or you only wrote this story about sexual assault because you are a woman." She sometimes feels like her data skills are overlooked because data is "traditionally male."

She questions herself all the time. Maybe she's not speaking up loudly enough; maybe it isn't enough to let her work speak for itself. Not long ago, she steeled herself to ask for a raise for the first time in her life.

"It was very nerve-racking. I practiced what I was going to say. It was months of me telling myself, 'I'm going to do this. I'm going to do it.' And then it would be, 'Now is not the right time; they're busy.' But I finally did it, and it felt great." She got the raise.

"Sometimes I get really afraid," Altavena added. "I wonder if I talk about my experience, the things I've done that I'm proud of, people will think I'm egotistical. Would I be asking that if I were a guy? I don't know. Men brag about things unabashedly. It's everywhere. It's what they say; it's how they handle situations. I'm experimenting with that now."

*   *   *

The last two decades have seen an explosion of digital-native news outlets such as the HuffPost (news and opinion), Vox (explanatory journalism), BuzzFeed (news and entertainment), Mashable (news about social networks and technology), Vice (news and culture), Blavity (by and for black millennials), and Bleacher Report (sports and culture). In 2017, the Pew Research Center counted thirty-five different digital-only news sites averaging at least ten million unique visitors a month.[6]

These companies are popular destinations for young people coming out of journalism schools, in part because they have been expanding their staffs while legacy news organizations have been downsizing. According to Pew, approximately 13,000 people worked as reporters, editors, photographers, or videographers in the newsrooms of digital-native outlets in 2017, up from about 7,400 in 2008.[7] In addition to the jobs, these sites are appealing to freshly minted graduates who are looking for an alternative news ethos and the opportunity to move up fast.

Maycie Timpone and Jessica Testa were both in their early twenties when they arrived at BuzzFeed, which manages one of the country's most popular online news and entertainment sites. Timpone, just two years out of journalism school, was hired to curate video in 2013. Two and a half years later, she was responsible for all of BuzzFeed's video content on multiple platforms, including YouTube, Facebook, Instagram, Twitter, Pinterest, and Snapchat. At age twenty-nine, Timpone was supervising nearly sixty people: forty-seven in Los Angeles, where she works, and another eleven in New York.

Testa headed to New York for a BuzzFeed internship immediately after getting her undergraduate degree in journalism in 2012. For the first couple of months, she focused on stories related to gender, but Editor in Chief Ben Smith, whom BuzzFeed had plucked from *Politico* a year earlier, wanted to experiment with breaking news, and he knew Testa had some experience covering breaking news during a college internship. He asked her to experiment to see how much audience interest there would be. A week later, when people at a movie theater in Aurora, Colorado, were attacked by a lone gunman armed with hand grenades, Testa hopped on her computer and started sharing reports of what was happening. "I didn't even leave my apartment that morning," she said. "And by the time I came into the office that afternoon, they said, 'So, OK, we want to do this breaking news thing full time.'" She became BuzzFeed's first, dedicated breaking news reporter.

The two women, both graduates of the Walter Cronkite School of Journalism and Mass Communication at Arizona State University, have experienced opposite poles of the BuzzFeed universe. Timpone said what she does is "sillier"—distributing videos about precocious cats and adorable puppies, for example. Her job is all about finding the video that will go viral, and she seems to have a knack for it. She has made personal appearances in several of the company's most popular videos, including "Women Get Lip Injections for the First Time" and "What Do Boyfriends Want Their Girlfriends' Makeup to Be?" which earned more than ten million views in less than a year.

The news side, where Testa worked, is more serious, according to Timpone. "It's almost like they are the grownups in the room and the rest of us are kids and [they're saying,] 'Would you please quiet down a little?'" she said.

BuzzFeed has not escaped the avalanche of sexual abuse complaints about men in the workplace. The company investigated allegations against several employees in 2017, after their names appeared on an anonymous list of male harassers in media, and ended up firing its White House correspondent. Male employees also were fired at Vox and Vice.[8]

Timpone and Testa said they weren't that surprised that problems cropped up at BuzzFeed—hardly any workplace has been exempt—but they think it's unlikely to happen again. If anything, they said, the company leans female.

Testa said when she started at BuzzFeed, she felt a little intimidated because she was the youngest person in the newsroom, but she noticed that women outnumbered men at almost every level. "It's very clear to me who the women leaders are, and it's very important to me that I see women leaders," she said.

Timpone has had a similar experience on the other side of the country. She said there are so many women working in the Los Angeles office that some meetings consist only of women. She is sometimes startled when she meets with her counterparts at other social media outlets and sees a preponderance of men. "I look around and think, 'Well, this must be what it's like in other companies!'"

The Los Angeles office has a distinctly feminine vibe, Timpone said. "There are a lot of crop tops and mesh see-through tops with sports bras underneath, and tight, glittery pants. The women go around saying, 'You look good today, girl,'" she said. "I rarely wear makeup to work, which I think is cool because I don't feel some sort of pressure to do that."

A women's group offers a mentorship program and brings in speakers to talk about gender issues, and staffers have running conversations on Slack, an internal messaging system, about everything from the latest sexual abuse scandal to the best gynecologists in the area.

Timpone has even cried at work a few times without worrying too much about whether it made her look weak. "I think things must have been different for my mom and grandmas," she said. "I imagine they had to be more aggressive or act like one of the guys. I would hope that women my age can be more themselves and not worry so much."

* * *

Arlene Morgan, assistant dean for external affairs at Temple University's Klein College of Media and Communication, worries that young women today don't understand or appreciate the battles her generation faced—not because she's looking for thanks but because she wants them to be vigilant.

Morgan had a thirty-one-year career at the *Philadelphia Inquirer*, beginning as a reporter and ending as assistant managing editor. Sometime in the late 1980s, she was working as deputy metro editor when she discovered that some men in the newsroom were making more money than women in the same jobs.

She announced that she was forming a women's caucus and holding a meeting for anyone interested in parity for women. Ninety women showed up.

Their next step was to ask for a sit-down with the paper's editor, Gene Roberts, a legendary figure in the news industry. "We adored him, but we were serious about this," Morgan said. Roberts, always the Southern gentleman, invited the women to his house to talk. On the appointed evening, half a dozen women carrying sandwiches knocked on his door. "We weren't about to eat his food," Morgan said.

Roberts laughed and invited them in. For the next seven hours, they talked, until, at almost two in the morning, Morgan finally said, "Gene, can we go home now? I think we've made our point.'"

At the time, Roberts was reluctant to send married women on reporting trips abroad or promote them to top newsroom jobs, reasoning that their families came first, Morgan said. There were no such rules for married men and, with a few exceptions, women were confined to writing feature stories. When one female reporter who covered health asked for a raise, the metro editor replied, "Your husband is a dentist. What are you worried about?"

Morgan remembers showing up at city hall to attend a meeting she thought would be of interest to residents of Northeast Philadelphia, an area she covered for the paper as a young reporter. The chief city hall reporter, a man, refused to let her sit at the reporters' table, and she was sent to the gallery, where members of the public sat. "We had to put up with a lot of that kind of crap," she said.

Young women coming into the workplace today need to understand what it was like for women of her generation, Morgan said. "I have to say, I do worry about today's up-and-coming women—that they may not feel or understand that the stigma was there and that they have to constantly fight against it."

Madhulika Sikka, who became executive editor of the *Washington Post* audio team in 2018, thinks there have been three waves of women in modern-day newsrooms. First came the pioneers of the 1960s and 1970s—women like Morgan, who knocked down barriers the hard way. Then there was her generation, the "sandwich generation," she calls it, that came into the business in the 1980s and 1990s and thought the battles had been won, only to discover that wasn't the case. They mostly "sucked it up," she said. Finally, there are young women like Zeilinger and Altavena, who are just beginning their careers and are a different breed entirely. They are much less willing to go along and get along, and if they don't like what they see in a workplace, they will leave and go do something else.

Mitra Kalita, senior vice president at CNN Digital, is part of the "sandwich generation." She started out as a business reporter for the *Washington Post* believing that being a woman and a minority was not going to be an issue. Her generation thought, "Oh, everything is fine," she said, and when they did run into issues, they tried to fix things from within. That, she said, has changed. Her daughter's generation is much more likely to say, "Burn it down!"

Janet Coats, the former editor of both the *Sarasota Herald-Tribune* and the *Tampa Tribune* in Florida, has a nineteen-year-old daughter and step-daughters who are twenty-one and twenty-two. "They don't put up with shit; they just don't," she said. "That's a great thing that women going into the business today have that we didn't."

Young women today are more likely than previous generations to speak up for themselves, agreed Kate O'Brian, who served as senior vice president for news at ABC and president of Al Jazeera America during her long broadcast career. "They want what they think is right, whether that's better working hours or promotions every year," she said. "But they also understand their importance and their value in a work environment. I see more and more young women saying they're not going to put up with this. And, certainly, my daughter and women of her generation are very open in conversations with their bosses, saying, 'Wow, in that meeting no one allowed me to speak, or people have to listen to what I have to say because I have something to say.' I see this generation understanding their power, which I think is transformative."

Jan Leach, the former editor of the *Akron Beacon Journal*, thinks it might actually be harder for young women entering journalism today. They still face many of the same challenges she encountered three decades ago when she was starting her career, only in even more challenging economic times and with higher expectations for their performance.

She tells the young women who crowd her journalism classes at Kent State University in Ohio that there is still much that needs to change in the news business. As women, they will have to work harder than men to prove themselves. They'll have to be more inventive and more innovative than previous generations, and they will never find it easy to balance work and family. But she also tells them, "We belong in newsrooms. We have a place here."

* * *

ADVICE FOR WOMEN LEADERS

Kristin Gilger

As Julia and I interviewed women for this book, we kept thinking about our daughters. My youngest daughter, Lauren, co-hosts a morning news program for the local NPR affiliate in Phoenix. One of the great pleasures of my life is listening to her on the radio each morning as I drive to work. She had not planned to become a journalist. In fact, she resisted, I think because she didn't want to be a junior version of her mom. I'll always remember the day she called from college and said, "OK, Mom. I want to be a journalist. You win!"

The truth is I never pushed her into the profession (although I did secretly think she would be very good at it). Like all mothers, I wanted her to find work that was personally fulfilling, contributed something to the world, and possibly paid the bills. When I asked Lauren why she had changed her mind about journalism, she told me she realized that of all the part-time jobs and internships she had held, the only ones that were truly fun were in newsrooms. "Fun," I thought. "Yes, that's a very good reason to become a journalist."

Journalism is fun. And meaningful. And fulfilling. Like anything that's worth doing, it's also hard, as the stories of many of the women in this book illustrate.

Each fall at the Cronkite School, I teach 250-plus bright-eyed and hopeful freshmen who think journalism might be right for them. We spend the semester talking about journalism greats from Benjamin Franklin to Ida B. Wells and Bob Woodward. We debate the role of journalism in a society that has lost faith in many of its key institutions. We consider how people might get their news ten, twenty, and a hundred years from now. I'm always amazed at how quick they are and how thoughtful. They never fail to make me optimistic about the future of this profession I love so much.

I see in them what Mitra Kalita, Janet Coats, and Kate O'Brian all observed—that the women and men coming into the workplace today are an impatient bunch with little tolerance for the old ways of doing things if those ways make no sense.

Julia's youngest, Eden, thinks there is far too much talking about equality in the workplace and not enough doing. "My generation is at a point where we're done with that," she told me. "If something is wrong, it should change; you shouldn't go along with it. There will be a lot of people who tell you it's not the time, it's not the place, that you're not the right person to do it. That's a cop-out. You need to stand up."

I want Eden and Lauren and all the young women like them to know something about what it was like for earlier generations of women in the workplace, not only because I don't want them to make the same mistakes but because I want them to make it better. That is also the hope of the dozens of women who spoke to us for this book. For the next generation, then, here is their best advice.

Christiane Amanpour
Chief international correspondent, CNN
"Be persistent. Don't give up. Be confident. And don't let people shut [you] up. I won't be talked over at a meeting. Politely and not aggressively, I make sure that the points are made. . . . It's really easy to shut the women up."

Susan Goldberg
Editor in chief, National Geographic *magazine*
"Resilient is my favorite word. You don't have to be the smartest person, and you don't have to have all the answers, but the thing you really need to have is that you keep going back at it—every single day, every single, damn day. . . . And then there's the dirty *a*-word. You're allowed to have it, and you should push to get as far as you can. It's harder for women to express ambition because we're all taught to be nice girls, and we're taught not to be bossy and to take turns. And while it's really nice to take turns, sometimes it doesn't work out."

Jennifer Brandel
CEO and co-founder of Hearken
"Just because it's scary doesn't mean you shouldn't do it. (I have) this great poster at my desk that says, 'I can't do this, but I'm doing it anyway.' I look at it every day. . . . And you don't have to stay somewhere even if it's got a great brand or you think it's going to look good on your resume. Life is too short to be treated shoddily, so find somewhere else."

Nicole Carroll
Editor in chief, USA Today
"I think hard work gets you a lot of places, but I tell everyone that if you can't get that name right or you don't do the math right or you left out an important part of that story, then it doesn't matter. So being above reproach is first and foremost. And then I think having that sense of adventure and trying new things. Why not? What would happen if . . . ? How could we . . . ? Those are great questions to ask."

Arianna Huffington
Co-founder, Huffington Post
"[Don't] buy into the idea that burnout is the price you have to pay for success. It's not. . . . Right now women pay the highest price for our culture of stress and burnout, in which long hours and sleep deprivation are taken as proxies for seriousness and dedication. Given that even when working women are doing the lion's share of the work of keeping up the household, this becomes a backdoor way of excluding women or at least making it harder for them to advance. That's one of the important reasons why it's so urgent that we change the way we work and live.

And if we're going to do that—and I believe we will—it's going to be this next generation that transforms our culture for the better."

Rosemary Armao
Regional editor, Middle East, Organized Crime and Corruption Reporting Project
"Life goes on for a really long time and, when you're in your twenties, you don't think about that. You need to plan for the long haul. . . . And you can't have it all at the same time. You have to sit down and ask yourself, 'What would I like as far as a career and as far as a family? What will happen when the kids grow up and have their own lives?' Where are you then and what will you do then? Women need to plan for themselves."

Margaret Low
Vice president, the Atlantic
"Worry less about the next promotion and more about the work you do and how good you're getting at it. Being a good colleague is important. If people like working with you and trust and respect you, even if gets hard, that's huge. And if you're kind, people will be kind back. People are a little afraid of that. You can be kind and commanding."

Diane McFarlin
Dean, College of Journalism and Communications, University of Florida
"Leadership is a confidence game, and the key is calibrating your confidence. Research demonstrates that women don't rise through the ranks because of a lack of confidence, but there's also the danger of becoming overconfident and losing your humility. Don't allow yourself to be harassed, but don't allow yourself to see any slight as discrimination against you as a female, because that weakens you and makes you more vulnerable. . . . If someone is having a bad day and snaps at you, don't assume it's because you're a woman. Maybe it's just a bad day. We bear this burden that being a woman is going to be a disadvantage."

Anna Holmes
Founder, Jezebel
"The advice would be to not take anyone else's advice—to listen to yourself more. Don't believe anybody who says they have the answers because they do not have the answers."

Rashida Jones
Senior vice president, specials, NBC News
"Do the work; prove them wrong. On my worst days, where people will question or challenge or try to undercut what I'm doing, my strategy has been to do the work and prove them wrong. In the time that I've been in this industry, that's worked for me, and it's a great mantra."

List of Interviews

$\mathcal{W}$e interviewed more than one hundred people, most of them women, in person and by phone in 2017 and 2018 (with one exception for an email interview), for this book. The following is a list of interviews conducted:

Jill Abramson (March 9, 10, and 11, 2017)
Lily Altavena (August 15, 2018)
Christiane Amanpour (June 26, 2018)
Becca Andrews (June 4, 2018)
Rosemary Armao (May 21, 2018)
Meredith Artley (April 25, 2017)
Jim Axelrod (June 19, 2018)
Jim Bankoff (August 17, 2018)
Monika Bauerlein (June 4 and 5, 2018)
Melissa Bell (June 11 and August 8, 2018)
Cathie Black (May 29, 2018)
Meredith Bodgas (July 11, 2018)
Therese Bottomly (July 12, 2018)
Jennifer Brandel (December 7, 2017)
Madeleine Buckingham (June 5, 2018)
Samuel Burke (June 29, 2018)
Gretchen Carlson (September 21, 2018)
Nicole Carroll (February 26, 2018)
Judith Clabes (February 7, 2017)
Janet Coats (June 1, 2018)
Barbara Cochran (May 22, 2018)
Marcia Cohen (June 19, 2018)
Audrey Cooper (June 18, 2018)

Mims Rowe Copeland (June 26, 2018)
Gaby Darbyshire (December 5, 2017)
Patti Dennis (July 21, 2017)
Paula Ellis (May 3, 2017)
Gail Evans (March 14, 2017)
Samantha Felix (October 13, 2018)
Pat Fili-Krushel (May 25, 2018)
Susan Goldberg (October 2, 2017)
Elizabeth Green (August 9, 2018)
Tracy Greer (May 30, 2018)
Kim Guthrie (March 17, 2017)
Tran Ha (June 13, 2018)
Cory Haik (June 6, 2018)
Charlotte Hall (June 19, 2018)
Jay Harris (June 20, 2018)
Meg Heckman (August 3, 2018)
Andrew Heyward (June 5, 2018)
Carrie Hofmann (May 25, 2018)
Anna Holmes (June 14, 2018)
Cynthia Hudson (June 13, 2018)
Arianna Huffington (email interview, July 28, 2018)
Clara Jeffery (June 4 and 5, 2018)
Mandy Jenkins (December 6, 2017)
Madelyn Jennings (February 7, 2017)
Pam McAllister Johnson (June 12, 2018)
Rashida Jones (April 2, 2017)
Karen Jurgensen (May 23, 2018)
Sara Just (March 17, 2017)
Mitra Kalita (June 13, 2018)
Bill Keller (March 24, 2017)
Ezra Klein (July 31, 2018)
Glenn Kramon (October 28, 2018)
Jan Leach (March 22, 2017)
Jessica Lessin (May 30, 2018)
Ann Marie Lipinski (April 4, 2017)
Wanda Lloyd (May 31 and June 1, 2018)
Margaret Low (June 15, 2018)
Susan Lyne (May 21, 2018)
Aminda Marqués Gonzalez (May 8, 2017)
Gracia Martore (June 4, 2018)
Linda Mason (March 21 and 28, 2017)
Dave Mazzarella (September 25, 2018)

Q McElroy (August 2, 2018)
Diane McFarlin (June 6, 2018)
Dyllan McGee (June 13, 2018)
Marcy McGinnis (June 14, 2018)
Carolyn McGourty Supple (May 11, 2018)
Jennifer Mizgata (May 1, 2017)
Nancy Monaghan (February 7, 2017)
Ann Moore (June 8, 2018)
Arlene Morgan (May 31, 2018)
Kenneth Mullinax (June 12, 2018)
Raju Narisetti (August 16, 2018)
Libby Nelson (July 31, 2018)
Jan Neuharth (May 10, 2018)
Kate O'Brian (May 21, 2018)
Charles Overby (May 21, 2018)
Mi-Ai Parrish (July 24 and August 20, 2018)
Kendra Penningroth (February 9, 2018)
Karen Pensiero (May 22, 2018)
Aron Pilhofer (October 25, 2018)
John Reade (June 18, 2018)
Margery Baker Riker (March 23, 2017)
Craig Robinson (June 4, 2018)
Sharon Rosenhause (April 8, 2017)
Shelley Ross (June 1, 2018)
Gerard Rowe (June 26, 2018)
Sandy Rowe (June 25 and 26, 2018)
Sarah Rowe (June 26, 2018)
Carolyn Ryan (October 30, 2018)
Vivian Schiller (May 21, 2018)
Madhulika Sikka (May 24, 2018)
Lauren Smith Brody (July 12, 2018)
Terri Stewart (June 18, 2018)
Kara Swisher (April 5, 2017)
Jessica Testa (May 30, 2018)
Julie Thompson (June 1, 2018)
Maycie Timpone (May 25, 2018)
Nina Totenberg (September 11, 2018)
AJ Vicens (May 29, 2018)
Irving Washington (April 28, 2017)
Dolores Wharton (June 4, 2018)
Judy Woodruff (March 12, 2017)
Julie Zeilinger (June 4, 2018)

Notes

INTRODUCTION: FINISHING THE JOB WE STARTED

1. Valentina Zarya, "The Share of Female CEOs in the Fortune 500 Dropped by 25% in 2018," *Fortune*, May 21, 2018, http://fortune.com/2018/05/21/women-fortune-500-2018.

2. Anna Griffin, "Where are the Women? Why We Need More Female Newsroom Leaders," *Nieman Reports*, September 11, 2014, http://niemanreports.org/articles/where-are-the-women.

3. Alliance for Audited Media (AAM) average Monday-Friday circulation, 2017.

4. "ASNE, Google News Lab Release 2017 Diversity Survey Results," American Society of News Editors, 2017, https://www.asne.org/diversity-survey-2017.

5. "Table of Employment of Men and Women by Job Category," American Society of News Editors, 2016, https://www.asne.org/content.asp?contentid=144.

6. Bob Papper, "2018 Research: Women and People of Color in Local TV and Radio News," RTDNA, June 27, 2018, https://rtdna.org/article/2018_research_women_and_people_of_color_in_local_tv_and_radio_news.

7. Gwyneth Mellinger, *Chasing Newsroom Diversity: From Jim Crow to Affirmative Action* (Urbana: University of Illinois Press, 2013), 73.

8. Proceedings of the 1973 convention of the American Society of Newspaper Editors, May 2–4, 1973.

9. "Thomas Eastham Retires from the Hearst Foundations," Hearst, May 3, 2005, http://www.hearst.com/newsroom/thomas-eastham-retires-from-the-hearst-foundations-paul-dino-dinovitz-succeeds-eastham-as-vice-president-western-director.

10. Lynn Povich, "Women in the Workplace, How 'Good Girls' Fight Back," *Los Angeles Times*, October 7, 2012, http://articles.latimes.com/2012/oct/07/opinion/la-oe-povich-newsweek-discrimination-gender-20121007.

11. Jessica Bennett and Jesse Ellison, "Young Women, Newsweek and Sexism," *Newsweek*, March 18, 2010, https://www.newsweek.com/young-women-newsweek-and-sexism-69339.

12. Bennett and Ellison, "Young Women, Newsweek and Sexism."

13. Stav Ziv, "How 'Good Girls Revolt' Got Shot Down by Amazon—Again," *Newsweek*, January 8, 2018, https://www.newsweek.com/how-good-girls-revolt-got -shot-down-amazon-again-773327.

CHAPTER 1. TOO WIMPY OR TOO BITCHY?
FINDING AN EFFECTIVE WAY TO LEAD

1. Rich Barlow, "BU Research: A Riddle Reveals Depth of Gender Bias," BU Today, January 16, 2014, http://www.bu.edu/today/2014/bu-research-riddle-reveals -the-depth-of-gender-bias.

2. Heather Murphy, "Picture a Leader: Is She a Woman?" *New York Times*, March 16, 2018, https://www.nytimes.com/2018/03/16/health/women-leadership -workplace.html.

3. David G. Smith, Judith E. Rosenstein, and Margaret C. Nikolov, "The Different Words We Use to Describe Male and Female Leaders," *Harvard Business Review*, May 25, 2018, https://hbr.org/2018/05/the-different-words-we-use-to-describe -male-and-female-leaders.

4. Madeline E. Heilman, "Description and Prescription: How Gender Stereotypes Prevent Women's Ascent Up the Organizational Ladder," *Journal of Social Issues* 57, no. 4 (2001): 657–74.

5. Heilman, "Description and Prescription," 667.

6. Shifra Bronznick and Didi Goldenhar, *21st Century Women's Leadership* (Research Center for Leadership in Action, 2018), 5, https://wagner.nyu.edu/files/leader ship/21stCenturyWomensLeadership1108.pdf.

7. "When the Boss Is a Woman," American Psychological Association Research in Action, 2006, http://www.apa.org/research/action/boss.aspx.

8. Kay Mills, *A Place in the News: From the Women's Pages to the Front Pages* (New York: Columbia University Press, 1988), 67–71.

9. Susan Goldberg, "For Decades, Our Coverage Was Racist. To Rise above Our Past, We Must Acknowledge It," *National Geographic*, April 2018, https://www .nationalgeographic.com/magazine/2018/04/from-the-editor-race-racism-history.

10. Leslie Pratch, "Why Women Leaders Need Self-Confidence," *Harvard Business Review*, November 28, 2011, https://hbr.org/2011/11/women-leaders-need-self -confidence.

11. Laura Guillén, Margarita Mayo, and Natalia Karelaia, "Appearing Self-Confident and Getting Credit for It: Why It May Be Easier for Men than Women to Gain Influence at Work," *Human Resource Management* 57, no. 4 (2018), https:// onlinelibrary.wiley.com/doi/abs/10.1002/hrm.21857.

12. Katty Kay and Claire Shipman, "The Confidence Gap," *Atlantic*, May 2014, https://www.theatlantic.com/magazine/archive/2014/05/the-confidence -gap/359815.

13. Just says she can't be sure it was knitting that Roberts brought to the meeting. It may have been needlepoint.

CHAPTER 2. FROM GETTING COFFEE
TO RUNNING THE PLACE

1. Ben Kelly, "Breaking News: Princess Diana's Death in the Pre-Social Media World," *Independent*, August 30, 2017, https://www.independent.co.uk/news/uk/home-news/news-princess-diana-death-pre-social-media-world-a7917366.html.

2. "The Pregnancy Discrimination Law of 1978," U.S. Equal Employment Opportunity Commission, 1978, https://www.eeoc.gov/laws/statutes/pregnancy.cfm.

3. Lynn Povich, "Women in the Workplace, How 'Good Girls' Fight Back," *Los Angeles Times*, October 7, 2012, http://articles.latimes.com/2012/oct/07/opinion/la-oe-povich-newsweek-discrimination-gender-20121007.

4. "Newshens Sue Newsweek for 'Equal Rights,'" *New York Daily News*, March 17, 1970.

5. "ACLU Says A.B.C. News Shows Bias Against Women," *New York Times*, August 13 1970, https://www.nytimes.com/1970/08/13/archives/aclu-says-abc-news-shows-bias-against-women.html.

6. "The Associated Press Agreed Wednesday to Pay $2 Million . . . ," United Press International, June 15, 1983, https://www.upi.com/Archives/1983/06/15/The-Associated-Press-agreed-Wednesday-to-pay-2-million/2645424497600.

7. Kay Mills, *A Place in the News* (New York: Dodd, Mead, 1988), 308–9.

8. David Hosley and Gayle K. Yamada, *Hard News: Women in Broadcast Journalism* (New York: Greenwood Press, 1987), 133.

9. Vaughn Ververs, "CBS' Number Two Steps Down," CBS News, November 15, 2005, https://www.cbsnews.com/news/cbs-news-number-two-steps-down.

CHAPTER 3. DEALING WITH THE LECHERS AMONG US

1. Todd Spangler, "Media Industry Has Highest Incidence of Sexual Harassment among White-Collar Workers, Survey Finds," *Variety*, July 25, 2018, https://variety.com/2018/biz/news/media-industry-sexual-harassment-survey-1202884052.

2. Constance Grady, "The 'Shitty Media Men' List, Explained," Vox, January 11, 2018, https://www.vox.com/culture/2018/1/11/16877966/shitty-media-men-list-explained.

3. Amy Brittain and Irin Carmon, "Charlie Rose's Misconduct Was Widespread at CBS and Three Managers Were Warned, Investigation Finds," *Washington Post*, May 3, 2018, https://www.washingtonpost.com/charlie-roses-misconduct-was-widespread-at-cbs-and-three-managers-were-warned-investigation-finds/2018/05/02/80613d24-3228-11e8-94fa-32d48460b955_story.html?utm_term=.3faab49130db.

4. Ramin Setoodeh and Elizabeth Wagmeister, "Matt Lauer Accused of Sexual Harassment by Multiple Women (EXCLUSIVE)," *Variety*, November 29, 2017, https://variety.com/2017/biz/news/matt-lauer-accused-sexual-harassment-multiple-women-1202625959.

5. Amanda Holpuch, "Fox News Commentator Is Latest to Accuse Roger Ailes of Sexual Harassment," *Guardian*, April 3, 2017, https://www.theguardian.com/media/2017/apr/03/fox-news-roger-ailes-sexual-harassment-lawsuit-julie-roginsky.

6. Sydney Ember, "Michael Oreskes Quits NPR amid Sexual Harassment Accusations," *New York Times*, November 1, 2017, https://www.nytimes.com/2017/11/01/business/media/mike-oreskes-npr-sexual-harassment.html.

7. Steven Zeitchik, Alex Horton, and Sarah Ellison, "CBS Chief Executive Les Moonves Is Departing amid Probe into Allegations of Sexual Misconduct," *Washington Post*, September 10, 2018, https://www.washingtonpost.com/business/2018/09/09/cbs-head-les-moonves-faces-new-sexual-assault-accusations-six-more-women-report-says/?utm_term=.59f69686b7c5.

8. David Folkenflik, "New York 'Daily News' Exec Investigated after Harassment Complaint," NPR, January 22, 2018, https://www.npr.org/sections/thetwo-way/2018/01/22/579840869/new-york-daily-news-exec-investigated-after-harassment-complaint.

9. Judith Levine, "#ThemToo," *Boston Review*, November 2, 2017, http://bostonreview.net/gender-sexuality/judith-levine-themtoo.

10. Brooke Gladstone, "Sexual Harassment, Revisited," *On the Media*, New York Public Radio, October 27, 2017, https://www.wnyc.org/story/sexual-harassment-revisited/?tab=transcript.

11. Stuart Taylor Jr., "Sexual Harassment on Job Is Illegal," *New York Times*, June 26, 1986, https://timesmachine.nytimes.com/timesmachine/1986/06/20/579286.html?action=click&contentCollection=Archives&module=LedeAsset&region=ArchiveBody&pgtype=article&pageNumber=1.

12. Dylan Matthews, "Exclusive: We Re-Ran Polls from 1991 about Anita Hill, This Time about Christine Blasey Ford," Vox, October 4, 2018, https://www.vox.com/policy-and-politics/2018/10/4/17924900/poll-anita-hill-clarence-thomas-christine-blasey-ford-brett-kavanaugh.

13. Mi-Ai Parrish, "Arizona Republic Publisher: Rep. Don Shooter Made a Sexual Comment to Me, and That's Not OK," *Arizona Republic*, November 10, 2017, https://www.azcentral.com/story/opinion/op-ed/2017/11/10/arizona-republic-publisher-mi-ai-parrish-don-shooter-made-sexual-comment/850769001.

14. Dennis Welch, "Powerful Lawmaker Accused of Sexual Harassment at AZ State Capitol," azfamily.com, November 7, 2017, http://www.azfamily.com/story/36788791/powerful-lawmaker-accused-of-sexual-harassment-at-az-state-capitol.

15. Rachel Leingang and Katie Campbell, "Rep. Shooter Accused of Repeated Sexual Harassment of Capitol Women," *Arizona Capitol Times*, November 8, 2017, https://azcapitoltimes.com/news/2017/11/08/arizona-don-shooter-sexual-harassment-capitol-michellle-ugenti-rita-athena-salman.

16. Parrish, "Arizona Republic Publisher: Rep. Don Shooter Made a Sexual Comment to Me, and That's Not OK."

17. Veronica Stracqualursi, "GOP Lawmaker Expelled from Arizona House after Report Finds Pattern of Sexual Harassment," CNN, February 2, 2018, https://www.cnn.com/2018/02/02/politics/arizona-state-lawmaker-expelled-harassment-report/index.html.

18. Elizabeth Jensen, "NPR's Staff Diversity, Numbers, 2017," NPR, January 23, 2018, https://www.npr.org/sections/ombudsman/2018/01/23/570204215/nprs-staff-diversity-numbers-2017.

19. Grace E. Speights, Margaret E. Rogers Schmidt, and Jocelyn R. Cuttino, *Report of Independent Investigation into Allegations of Sexual Harassment at NPR* (Washington, DC: Morgan, Lewis & Bockius, LLP, February 19, 2018).

20. Paul Farhi, "NPR's Top Editor Placed on Leave after Accusations of Sexual Harassment," *Washington Post*, October 31, 2017, https://www.washingtonpost.com/lifestyle/style/nprs-top-editor-accused-of-sexual-harassment-by-two-women/2017/10/31/a2078bea-bdf7-11e7-959c-fe2b598d8c00_story.html?utm_term=.8cc564559a50.

21. Merrit Kennedy, "NPR Board Faces Tough Questions over Sexual Harassment Handling," NPR, February 22, 2018, https://www.npr.org/sections/thetwo-way/2018/02/22/588093337/npr-board-faces-tough-questions-over-sexual-harassment-handling.

22. Farhi, "NPR's Top Editor Placed on Leave after Accusations of Sexual Harassment."

23. Jon Stewart, "Gretchen Carlson Dumbs Down," *The Daily Show with Jon Stewart*, Comedy Central, December 8, 2009, http://www.cc.com/video-clips/ahba3f/the-daily-show-with-jon-stewart-gretchen-carlson-dumbs-down.

24. Gabriel Sherman, "The Revenge of Roger's Angels: How Fox News Women Took Down the Most Powerful, and Predatory, Man in Media," *New York* Intelligencer, September 2, 2016, http://nymag.com/daily/intelligencer/2016/09/how-fox-news-women-took-down-roger-ailes.html.

25. Sherman, "The Revenge of Roger's Angels."

26. Sarah Ellison, "Inside the Final Days of Roger Ailes's Reign at Fox News," *Vanity Fair*, November 2016, https://www.vanityfair.com/news/2016/09/roger-ailes-fox-news-final-days.

27. Sherman, "The Revenge of Roger's Angels."

28. Gretchen Carlson v. Roger Ailes, Smith Mullin, July 16, 2016, https://www.smithmullin.com/wp-content/uploads/2016/07/Carlson-Complaint.pdf.

29. David Bauder, "Carlson Settles Lawsuit against Ailes for $20 Million," AP News, September 6, 2016, https://www.apnews.com/be1a1e0edf754f48bd852982da790ed3.

30. Jodi Kantor and Megan Twohey, "Harvey Weinstein Paid Off Sexual Harassment Accusers for Decades," *New York Times*, October 5, 2017, https://www.nytimes.com/2017/10/05/us/harvey-weinstein-harassment-allegations.html.

31. "Statement from Harvey Weinstein," *New York Times*, October 5, 2017, https://www.nytimes.com/interactive/2017/10/05/us/statement-from-harvey-weinstein.html.

32. Michelle Ferrier, "Attacks and Harassment: The Impact on Female Journalists and Their Reporting," International Women's Media Foundation and Trollbusters, 2018, https://www.iwmf.org/wp-content/uploads/2018/09/Attacks-and-Harassment.pdf.

33. "Women Abused on Twitter Every 30 Seconds—New Study," Amnesty International, UK, December 18, 2018, https://www.amnesty.org.uk/press-releases/women-abused-twitter-every-30-seconds-new-study.

34. Niraj Chokshi, "John Hockenberry, Former WNYC Radio Host, Is Accused of Sexual Harassment," *New York Times*, December 4, 2017, https://www.nytimes.com/2017/12/04/business/media/john-hockenberry-sexual-harassment.html.

35. John Hockenberry, "Exile: And a Year of Trying to Find a Road Back from Personal and Public Shame," *Harper's Magazine*, October 2018, https://harpers.org/archive/2018/10/exile-4.

36. Ronan Farrow, "As Leslie Moonves Negotiates His Exit from CBS, Six Women Raise New Assault and Harassment Claims," *New Yorker*, September 9, 2018, https://www.newyorker.com/news/news-desk/as-leslie-moonves-negotiates-his-exit-from-cbs-women-raise-new-assault-and-harassment-claims.

37. John Koblin and Michael M. Grynbaum, "*60 Minutes* Chief Ousted for a Threatening Text as Upheaval at CBS Continues," *New York Times*, September 12, 2018, https://www.nytimes.com/2018/09/12/business/media/jeff-fager-60-minutes-cbs.html.

38. Koblin and Grynbaum, "*60 Minutes* Chief Ousted for a Threatening Text as Upheaval at CBS Continues."

CHAPTER 4. THE DOLLARS AND SENSE OF DIVERSITY

1. "Table A: Minority Employment in Newspapers," ASNE, 2015, https://www.asne.org/content.asp?contentid=129.

2. J. Donald Brandt, *A History of Gannett* (Arlington, VA: Gannett, 1993), 338.

3. David Colton and Rick Hampson, "*USA Today* Founder Dies at 89," *USA Today*, April 19, 2013, https://www.usatoday.com/story/news/nation/2013/04/19/al-neuharth-newspaper-founder-dies-at-89/2097995.

4. Al Neuharth, *Confessions of an S.O.B.* (New York: Doubleday Business, 1989), 239–40.

5. Kay Mills, *A Place in the News* (New York: Dodd, Mead, 1988), 303.

6. Neuharth, *Confessions of an S.O.B.*, 242.

7. Herbert Buchsbaum, "Al Neuharth, News Executive Who Built Gannett and USA Today Is Dead at 89," *New York Times*, April 19, 2013, https://www.nytimes.com/2013/04/20/business/media/al-neuharth-executive-who-built-gannett-and-usa-today-is-dead-at-89.html.

8. Mills, *A Place in the News*, 300–301.

9. "Sex and Wage Report, Detroit Free Press," Newspaper Guild of Detroit, 2016, https://detroitguild22.files.wordpress.com/2017/06/sex-and-wage-report_free-press_-final-draft.pdf.

10. Lars Willnat and David H. Weaver, *The American Journalist in the Digital Age: Key Findings* (Bloomington: School of Journalism, Indiana University, 2014),

http://archive.news.indiana.edu/releases/iu/2014/05/2013-american-journalist-key
-findings.pdf.

11. "Table L, Employment of Men and Women by Job Category," ASNE, 2015,
https://www.asne.org/content.asp?contentid=144.

12. "The ASNE Newsroom Diversity Survey," ASNE, 2017, https://www.asne
.org/diversity-survey-2017.

13. "2017 ASNE Diversity Survey, Methodology and Tables," ASNE, 2017,
https://www.asne.org//Files/census/2017%20ASNE%20diversity%20survey%20
tables.pdf.

14. Bill Carter, "NBC News President Rouses the Network," *New York Times*,
August 24, 2014, https://www.nytimes.com/2014/08/25/business/media/nbc-news
-president-rouses-the-network.html.

15. *Montgomery Advertiser* Editorial Board, "Our Shame: The Sins of Our Past
Laid Bare for All to See," *Montgomery Advertiser*, April 26, 2018, https://www
.montgomeryadvertiser.com/story/opinion/editorials/2018/04/26/shame-us-sins-our
-past-equal-justice-initiative-peace-memorial-lynching-montgomery-bryan-steven
son/551402002.

CHAPTER 5. A SHORT HISTORY OF THE FIRST
FEMALE EDITOR OF THE *NEW YORK TIMES*

1. Peter Preston, "Jill Abramson's Achievement Is Historic, but Times Can't
Stay Stuck in the Past," *Guardian*, June 4, 2011, https://www.theguardian.com/me
dia/2011/jun/05/jill-abramson-new-york-times-comment.

2. Anna Griffin, "Where are the Women?" *Nieman Reports*, September 11, 2014,
http://niemanreports.org/articles/where-are-the-women.

3. Ken Auletta, "Changing Times, Jill Abramson Takes Charge of the Grey Lady,"
New Yorker, October 24, 2011, https://www.newyorker.com/magazine/2011/10/24/
changing-times-ken-auletta.

4. Dylan Byers, "Jill Abramson Loses the Newsroom," *Politico*, April 23,
2013, https://www.politico.com/blogs/media/2013/04/jill-abramson-loses-the-news
room-162480.

5. McKinsey & Company and LeanIn, "Getting to Gender Equality Starts with
Realizing How Far We Have to Go," *Women in the Workplace 2017*, 2017, https://
womenintheworkplace.com/2017.

6. Alice Eagly and Linda Carli, "Women and the Labyrinth of Leadership,"
Harvard Business Review, September 2007, https://hbr.org/2007/09/women-and
-the-labyrinth-of-leadership.

7. Beth Rothstein, "Lena Dunham Majorly Sucks Up to Ex-NYT Editor Jill
Abramson," *Daily Caller*, April 3, 2017, http://dailycaller.com/2017/04/03/lena
-dunham-majorly-sucks-up-to-ex-nyt-editor-jill-abramson.

8. Auletta, "Changing Times, Jill Abramson Takes Charge of the Grey Lady."

9. Susan B. Glasser, "Editing While Female," *Politico*, May 16, 2014, https://www.politico.com/magazine/story/2014/05/editing-while-female-jill-abramson-106782.

10. Liz Spayd, "The Declining Fortune of Women at the *Times*," *New York Times*, March 4, 2017, https://www.nytimes.com/2017/03/04/public-editor/the-declining-fortunes-of-women-at-the-times.html.

11. "252 Celebrities, Politicians, CEOs and Others Who Have Been Accused of Sexual Misconduct," Vox, October 8, 2018, https://www.vox.com/a/sexual-harassment-assault-allegations-list.

12. "Highlights of Women's Earnings," U.S. Bureau of Labor Statistics, August 2017, https://www.bls.gov/opub/reports/womens-earnings/2017/home.htm.

13. Elisa Boxer, "Home Depot CEO Said He Did This 25,000 Times. Science Says You Should Do It Too," *Inc.*, November 10, 2017, https://www.inc.com/elisa-boxer/home-depots-ceo-did-this-25000-times-science-says-you-should-do-it-too.html.

CHAPTER 6. CHANGING THE NEWS:
HOW WOMEN SHAPE CULTURE AND COVERAGE

1. "Breaking: Mother Jones Editor Russ Rymer Fired," Huffington Post, April 3, 2006, https://www.huffingtonpost.com/eat-the-press/2006/08/03/breaking-mother-jone_e_26459.html.

2. Alex S. Jones, "Radical Magazine Removed Editor, Setting Off a Widening Political Debate," *New York Times*, September 27, 1986, https://www.nytimes.com/1986/09/27/us/radical-magazine-removes-editor-setting-off-a-widening-political-debate.html.

3. J. Trout Lowen, "Power-Sharing Women Take Over Mother Jones," Women's eNews, October 2, 2006, https://womensenews.org/2006/10/power-sharing-women-take-over-mother-jones.

4. "Sarah Josepha Hale," *Encyclopedia Britannica*, accessed April 23, 2018, https://www.britannica.com/biography/Sarah-Josepha-Hale.

5. "Deirdre English," UC Berkeley Graduate School of Journalism, Spring 2018, https://journalism.berkeley.edu/person/deirdre_english.

6. Elliot J. Gorn, "Mother Jones: The Woman," *Mother Jones*, May/June 2001, https://www.motherjones.com/about/history.

7. Randall Rothenberg, "Junk Mail's Top Dogs," *New York Times*, August 5, 1990, https://www.nytimes.com/1990/08/05/magazine/junk-mail-s-top-dogs.html.

8. Jack Hitt, "Harpy, Hero, Heretic: Hillary," *Mother Jones*, January/February 2007, https://www.motherjones.com/politics/2007/01/harpy-hero-heretic-hillary.

9. Dana Goldstein, "Mother Tongue: Mother Jones's New Female Co-Editors on Men, Women and Journalism," *Nation*, February 26, 2007, https://www.the

nation.com/article/mother-tongue-mother-joness-new-female-co-editors-men
-women-and-journalism.

10. Kevin Drum, "The Great Speed-Up," *Mother Jones*, June 20, 2011, https://
www.motherjones.com/kevin-drum/2011/06/great-speedup.

11. "Women Journalists Report Less News than Men: TV Gender Gap Most
Stark," Women's Media Center, March 22, 2017, https://www.womensmediacenter.
com/about/press/press-releases/womens-media-center-report-women-journalists-
report-less-news-than-men-tv-g.

12. Teresa Correa and Dustin Harp, "Women Matter in Newsrooms: How
Power and Critical Mass Relate to the Coverage of the HPV Vaccine," *Journalism and Mass Communication Quarterly* 88, no. 2 (June 1, 2011), https://doi.
org/10.1177/107769901108800205.

13. Jason Turcotte and Newly Paul, "The Role of Gender in U.S. Presidential
Debates," *Political Research Quarterly* 68, no. 4 (September 15, 2018), https://doi.
org/10.1177/1065912915605581; Lindsey Meeks, "Journalist Gender, Political Office and Campaign News," *Journalism and Mass Communication Quarterly* 90, no. 1
(January 10, 2013), https://doi.org/10.1177/1077699012468695.

14. Randal A. Beam and Damon T. Di Cicco, "When Women Run the Newsroom:
Management Change, Gender and the News," *Journalism and Mass Communication
Quarterly* 87, no. 2 (June 1, 2010), https://doi.org/10.1177/107769901008700211.

15. Tracy Everbach, "The Culture of a Women-Led Newspaper: An Ethnographic
Study of the Sarasota Herald-Tribune," *Journalism and Mass Communication Quarterly*
83, no. 3 (September 1, 2006), https://doi.org/10.1177/107769900608300301.

16. "The Power to Grow Readership," Media Management Center at Northwestern University, 2001, https://web.archive.org/web/20150906234217/http://www.
readership.org/impact/impact.asp.

17. Dominic Fracassa, "Mother Jones Magazine Sees a Surge in Reader Support," *San Francisco Chronicle*, March 5, 2017, https://www.sfchronicle.com/business/
article/Mother-Jones-magazine-sees-a-surge-in-reader-10979054.php.

18. Naomi LaChance, "Mother Jones' Legacy Is Haunting Mother Jones as the
Magazine Embraces Neoliberalism," Paste, December 21, 2016, https://www.pastemag
azine.com/articles/2016/12/the-legacy-of-mother-jones-is-haunting-mother-jone.html.

19. Alexander Abad-Santos, "Mother Jones Reportedly Told Its Interns to Go on
Food Stamps Because It Pays So Little," *Atlantic*, December 2, 2013, https://www
.theatlantic.com/entertainment/archive/2013/12/mother-jones-told-its-interns-go
-food-stamps-because-it-didnt-pay-them-enough/355654.

20. Michael Calderone, "David Corn Investigated for Inappropriate Workplace
Behavior," *Politico*, November 2, 2017, https://www.politico.com/story/2017/11/02/
david-corn-mother-jones-workplace-behavior-probe-244482 and http://www
.foxnews.com/entertainment/2017/11/03/mother-jones-journalist-david-corn-joked
-about-rape-gave-unwelcome-shoulder-rubs-emails.html.

CHAPTER 7. WHAT COULD POSSIBLY GO WRONG?
BALANCING WORK AND FAMILY

1. Serena Williams (@serenawilliams), "She took her first steps . . . I was training, and I missed it. I cried." Twitter, July 7, 2018, https://twitter.com/serenawilliams/status/1015514300490960896.

2. Robin J. Ely, Pamela Stone, and Colleen Ammerman, "Rethink What You Know about High-Achieving Women," *Harvard Business Review*, December 2014, https://hbr.org/2014/12/rethink-what-you-know-about-high-achieving-women.

3. Judy Woodruff, *This Is Judy Woodruff at the White House* (Reading, MA: Addison-Wesley, 1982), 178.

4. Kim Parker and Gretchen Livingston, "7 Facts about American Dads," Pew Research Center, June 13, 2018, http://www.pewresearch.org/fact-tank/2018/06/13/fathers-day-facts.

5. Susan Reimer, "Having It All, The Truth and Myth Don't Match," *Baltimore Sun*, May 31, 1998, http://articles.baltimoresun.com/1998-05-31/features/1998151051_1_joyce-purnick-childless-women-working-mother.

6. Cokie Roberts and Steven B. Roberts, "Mom's the Word, Even at Times," *New York Daily News*, May 28, 1998, http://www.nydailynews.com/archives/opinions/mom-word-times-article-1.802184.

7. Felice N. Schwartz, "Management Women and the New Facts of Life," *Harvard Business Review*, January-February 1989, https://hbr.org/1989/01/management-women-and-the-new-facts-of-life.

8. Tamar Lewin, "'Mommy Career Track' Sets Off a Furor," *New York Times*, March 8, 1989, https://www.nytimes.com/1989/03/08/us/mommy-career-track-sets-off-a-furor.html.

9. Lola Akinmade Åkerström, "10 Things That Make Sweden Family Friendly," Official Site of Sweden, 2018, https://sweden.se/society/10-things-that-make-sweden-family-friendly.

10. Rasheed Malik and Katie Hamm, "Mapping America's Child Care Deserts," Center for American Progress, August 30, 2017, https://www.americanprogress.org/issues/early-childhood/reports/2017/08/30/437988/mapping-americas-child-care-deserts.

CHAPTER 8. THE UNFULFILLED PROMISE
OF DIGITAL MEDIA

1. Leslie Kaufman, "Vox Takes Melding of Journalism and Technology to a New High," *New York Times*, April 6, 2014, https://www.nytimes.com/2014/04/07/business/media/voxcom-takes-melding-of-journalism-and-technology-to-next-level.html.

2. Margaret Hartmann, "Ezra Klein's Vox.com Aims to Make Readers Like the 'Vegetables' of Journalism," *New York*, March 9, 2014, http://nymag.com/daily/intel ligencer/2014/03/ezra-klein-vox-com.html.

3. Tim Peterson, "Vox Media CEO Jim Bankoff on Ezra Klein's Plan to Reimagine the News," *AdAge*, January 27, 2014, http://adage.com/article/digital/vox -media-ceo-jim-bankoff-ezra-klein-s-newsier-wikipedia/291315.

4. Greg Marx, "Vox.com Is Going to Be a Great Test of Ezra Klein's Critique of Journalism," *Columbia Journalism Review*, April 7, 2014, https://archives.cjr.org/behind_ the_news/voxcom_is_going_to_be_a_great_test_ezra_klein_critique_journalism.php.

5. Roger Yu, "Ezra Klein Launches News Site Vox.com," *USA Today*, April 7, 2014, https://www.usatoday.com/story/money/business/2014/04/07/klein-launches -vox/7420053.

6. Emily Bell, "Journalism Startups Aren't a Revolution If They're Filled with All These White Men," *Guardian*, March 12, 2014, https://www.theguardian.com/com mentisfree/2014/mar/12/journalism-startups-diversity-ezra-klein-nate-silver.

7. "The Status of Women in the U.S. Media 2017," Women's Media Center, March 21, 2017, https://www.womensmediacenter.com/reports/the-status-of -women-in-u.s.-media-2017.

8. Meg Heckman, "Where the Women Are: Measuring Female Leadership in the New Journalism Ecology," Northeastern University, December 2013, https:// megheckman.files.wordpress.com/2014/04/heckman_thesis.pdf.

9. Meg Heckman, "Women Were Digital Media Pioneers but There's Still a Gender Gap There," March 24, 2014, https://archives.cjr.org/minority_reports/ early_digital_women.php.

10. Guy Raz, "Live Episode! Buzzfeed: Jonah Peretti," NPR, July 26, 2017, https://one.npr.org/?sharedMediaId=539523369:555388442.

11. Daniel McGinn, "How I Did: Arianna Huffington," *Inc.*, February 4, 2010, https://www.inc.com/magazine/20100201/how-i-did-it-arianna-huffington.html.

12. Arianna Huffington, "Celebrating HuffPost's First Ten Years by Looking to the Next 10," Huffington Post, May 6, 2015, https://www.huffingtonpost.com/ arianna-huffington/huffpost-10-years_b_7225620.html.

13. William D. Cohan, "How Arianna Huffington Lost Her Newsroom," *Vanity Fair*, September 7, 2016, https://www.vanityfair.com/news/2016/09/how-arianna -huffington-lost-her-newsroom.

14. Peter Baker, "Alice Marie Johnson Is Granted Clemency by Trump after Push by Kim Kardashian West," *New York Times*, June 6, 2018, https://www.ny times.com/2018/06/06/us/politics/trump-alice-johnson-sentence-commuted-kim -kardashian-west.html.

15. Laura Hazard Owen, "Mic Lays Off Almost Everyone and Goes for a Last-Ditch Sale to Bustle," Nieman Lab, November 29, 2018, http://www.niemanlab .org/2018/11/mic-lays-off-almost-everyone-and-aims-for-a-last-ditch-sale-to-bustle.

16. Lucia Moses, "The Rapid Rise of Vox's Melissa Bell, an Explainer," Digiday, July 6, 2015, https://digiday.com/media/unusual-talents-vox-medias-melissa-bell.

17. Valentina Zarya, "Female Founders Got 2% of Venture Capital Dollars in 2017," *Fortune*, January 31, 2018, http://fortune.com/2018/01/31/female-founders -venture-capital-2017.

18. Gene Teare, "Announcing the 2017 Update to the Crunchbase Women in Venture Report," Techcrunch.com, October 4, 2017, https://techcrunch.com/2017/10/04/ announcing-the-2017-update-to-the-crunchbase-women-in-venture-report.

19. "Our Story," Makers.com, https://www.makers.com/about.

20. Zoe Henry, "She Sold LearnVest for a Reported $250 million," *Inc.*, May 26, 2017, https://www.inc.com/zoe-henry/alexa-von-tobel-learnvest-chief-digital -officer.html.

21. "Diversity and Inclusion at Vox.com," Vox, https://www.voxmedia.com/ pages/careers-diversity.

CHAPTER 9. THE NEXT GENERATION:
WHAT HAS CHANGED AND WHAT HAS NOT

1. Lillian Lodge Kopenhaver and Lillian Anne Abreu, "Women Earn Less, Experience Negative Company Cultures and Still Face a Glass Ceiling in the Communications Industries," *Kopenhaver Center Report*, 2018, http://carta.fiu.edu/kopen havercenter/wp-content/uploads/sites/17/2018/06/Kopenhaver-Center-Report -2018-ver-1.pdf.

2. Lars Willnat and David H. Weaver, *The American Journalist in the Digital Age* (Bloomington: School of Journalism, Indiana University, 2014), http://archive.news .indiana.edu/releases/iu/2014/05/2013-american-journalist-key-findings.pdf.

3. Kopenhaver and Abreu, "Women Earn Less, Experience Negative Company Cultures and Still Face a Glass Ceiling in the Communications Industries."

4. Jeff Tyler, "Reaction to KJZZ Sexual Harassment Report," KJZZ, July 26, 2018, http://kjzz.org/content/676548/reaction-kjzz-sexual-harassment-report.

5. Anne Ryman, "KJZZ Executive Demoted after Workplace Investigation Finds 'Thoughtless, Sexist' Behavior," azcentral, September 13, 2018, https://www.azcen tral.com/story/news/local/arizona-investigations/2018/09/13/maricopa-community -colleges-releases-investigative-report-kjzz-executive-mark-moran/1261607002.

6. "Digital News Fact Sheet," Pew Research Center, June 6, 2018, http://www .journalism.org/fact-sheet/digital-news.

7. "Digital News Fact Sheet."

8. Carlos Ballesteros, "BuzzFeed Fires White House Correspondent," *Newsweek*, December 27, 2017, http://www.newsweek.com/buzzfeed-correspondent-fired-over -inappropriate-behavior-761057.

Index

ABC, 7, 24, 150
ABC News, 26, 43, 112
ABC Sports, 25
ABC Television Network, 17, 25
Abramson, Jill, 1, 47–48, 71–86, photo 15
Abramson, Norman, 72–73
Access Hollywood (television show), 84
AdAge (newspaper), 123
age, of men and women in management, 138
Ailes, Roger, 4, 38, 44, 48–50
Akron Beacon Journal (newspaper), 16, 106, 150
Al Jazeera America, 34, 43, 112, 150
All Things Considered (radio program), 45
Altavena, Lily, 144, 145–46
Amanpour, Christiane, 1, 11–12, 19, 20, 152, photo 2
Amazon Studios, 4
American Civil Liberties Union, 26
American Lawyer (magazine), 83
American Society of Magazine Editors, 98
American Society of News Editors (ASNE), 2, 3, 56, 63, 115
American Society of Newspaper Editors, 3, 21, 56

Amoss, Jim, 68, 138
anchors. *See* news anchors
Andrews, Becca, 89, 94, 104
AOL, 129, 133, 134
Apollo 14, 27
Arizona Capitol Times (newspaper), 44–45
Arizona Republic (newspaper), 42, 43, 86, 146
Arizona State University Walter Cronkite School of Journalism and Mass Communication, 102, 138, 146, 147
Armao, Rosemary, 96–97, 153
Armstrong, Nancy, 133
Armstrong, Tim, 133
ASNE. *See* American Society of News Editors
Associated Press, 4, 26, 47
Atlanta Journal (newspaper), 58
Atlanta Journal-Constitution (newspaper), 69, 86, 87, 125, 129, 138
Atlantic (magazine), 16, 17, 45, 91, 153
Auletta, Ken, 73
Axelrod, Jim, 33

Bankoff, Jim, 123, 132, 135
Baquet, Dean, 75, 77, 80–83

Barnes & Noble, 37
Bauerlein, Monika, 89–94, 98–100, 102–3, photo 16
BBG Ventures, 134
Bell, Emily, 124, 126
Bell, Melissa, 1, 123–24, 126–28, 131, 134–38, photo 23
Bentley, Sara, 101
Berentson, Jane, 83
Bezos, Jeff, 130
Bhatia, Peter, photo 18
Biggs, Gloria, 59
bitch/b-word, 11, 15, 16, 33, 43, 81, 86
Black, Cathie, 61
Blair, Jayson, 81
Blake, Frank, 87
Blavity (website), 146
Bleacher Report (website), 146
Bloomberg Businessweek (magazine), 83
Boas, Phil, 44
Bodgas, Meredith, 117–18, 121
Boeing, 37
Bonner, Alice, 59
Boston.com, 126
Bottomly, Therese, 115
Bradlee, Ben, 58–59, 67
Brandel, Jennifer, 133, 152
Bridgewater Courier-News (newspaper), 60
Brill, Steven, 83
Brown, Helen Gurley, 91
Brown, Tina, 91
Brzezinski, Zbigniew, 121
Buckingham, Madeleine, 90, 100
Bulkeley, Christy, 60
Burke, Samuel, 11–12
Bush, George W., ix–x, 34
business and finances, 76
Bustle Digital Group, 131
BuzzFeed (website), 146–48
Byrd, Harry, Jr., 108

Callahan, Christopher, 138
career paths, 36
Carli, Linda, 78

Carlson, Gretchen, 44, 48–52, photo 10
Carr, David, 81
Carroll, Nicole, 2, 44, 152
Castro, Fidel, photo 7
CBS, 23–24, 26–36, 38, 40, 50–51
CBS Evening News (television show), 28, 98
CBS News, 23, 28–30, 34, 36, 40, 48, 63
CBS This Morning (television show), 38
Center for Public Integrity, 99
Chalkbeat, 126
Chancellor, John, 111
Chicago Sun-Times (newspaper), 41, 119
Chicago Tribune (newspaper), 20
childcare, 62, 109, 113, 118, 120–21
Chira, Susan, 82
Cichowski, Lorraine, 126
Cincinnati Enquirer (newspaper), 16
City Pages (Minneapolis newspaper), 92–93
Civil Rights Act (1964), 25, 39, 57
Cleveland Plain Dealer (newspaper), 14
Clinton, Bill, 47
Clinton, Hillary, x, 43, 93, 99
clothing. *See* personal appearance
CNN, 1, 11–12, 45, 78, 98, 141, 152
CNN Digital, 69
CNN en Español, 7, 16, 53
Coats, Janet, 10–11, 13, 18, 19, 96–97, 102–4, 113, 150, 151
Cochran, Barbara, 40, 45
co-editorship, 89–91, 93–94, 98–100, 102–3
Cohen, Marcia, 90, 100
collaboration, 102–3, 137
Collins, Tom, 3
Columbia Journalism Review (journal), 123
confidence, 15–19
Cooper, Audrey, 18, 20, 140, photo 3
Copeland, Mims Rowe, 105, photo 19
Corn, David, 99
Cosmopolitan (magazine), 91
Cox Media Group, 8, 125

Cronkite, Walter, 27, 28, photo 5
crying, 18, 135, 138, 148
Curry, Ann, 145

Daily Beast (website), 81
Dallas Times Herald (newspaper), 67
Darbyshire, Gaby, 42–43
day care. *See* childcare
Dennis, Patti, 25
Detroit Free Press (newspaper), 14, 62
Detroit News (newspaper), 4, 26
The Devil Wears Prada (magazine), 118
Diana, Princess of Wales, 23, 97
digital publishing, 76, 77, 80, 81, 99,
    123–38, 146–48
Discovery Channel, 98
discrimination, 25–26, 39, 57, 71, 79,
    141–44, 148–49. *See also* gender gap
diversity, 55–69, 124–25
Donegan, Moira, 38
Dowd, Maureen, 73, 83
Dow Jones Newspaper Fund, 57
Drudge Report (website), 128
Dunham, Lena, 81

Eagly, Alice, 78
The Early Show (television show), 48
Eastham, Tom, 3
Economist (magazine), 91
Ellis, Paula, 18, 19, 40, 116–17
English, Deirdre, 91
Ephron, Nora, 4
Epstein, Barbara, 91
Equal Rights Amendment, 59
Evans, Gail, 20, 77–78, 141–42
Everbach, Tracy, 95–96

Facebook, 36, 47
Fager, Jeff, 33, 50–51
failure, learning from, 137
Faludi, Susan, 89
family. *See* marriage; work-family
    balance
Farley, Lin, 39
FBomb (website), 143–44

Federal Communications Commission,
    26
Feinstein, Dianne, 3
Felix, Samantha, 144–45
Fili-Krushel, Pat, 17, 25, 78
Ford, Christine Blasey, 39, 52
Fortune (magazine), 2, 36
Fox & Friends (television show), 48
Fox News, 38, 44, 48–50
Frederick, Pauline, 24
Freedom Forum, 65
fundraising, 132–34

Galant, Richard, photo 26
Gannett, 26, 56, 59–65, 68
Gawker Media, 42
Gelb, Arthur, 74
gender gap: in digital media, 125–26; in
    fundraising, 132–34; in journalism,
    2–4, 10, 24–26, 56–69, 139–44; in
    leadership, 8–9; in pay, 62, 79–80,
    86–87, 142–44, 148–49. *See also*
    discrimination
Gibson, Janine, 80
Gift of Courage, 49
Gilt.com, 7, 134
Gilt Group, 134
Ginsberg, Ruth Bader, 133
Gizmodo Media, 138
Glamour (magazine), 120
Glasser, Susan, 82–83
Godey's Lady Book, 90
Goldberg, Susan, 13–15, 19, 20, 140,
    152
Golden, Michael, 79
Gomez, Selena, 106
Gone with the Wind (film), 10–11
Good Girls Revolt (television series), 4
Goodman, Ellen, 3–4
Gore, Al, ix
Gould, Bruce and Beatrice, 91
GQ (magazine), 98
Green, Elizabeth, 123, 126
Greenville (South Carolina) *News*
    (newspaper), 55, 64–65

Greer, Tracy, 142–43, photo 27
Guardian (newspaper), 80, 124, 126
Guthrie, Kim, 8, 19

Haaga, Paul, 46
Haik, Cory, 130–31, 136, 137, photo 25
Hale, Sarah Josepha, 90
Hall, Charlotte, 10
Hall, Grover, 65
Halperin, Mark, 4
Hanks, Tom, 17
Harper's Magazine, 50, 93
Harris, Jay, 89–90, 91, 99
Harvard University, 84–85
Hearken, 152
Hearst Magazines, 61
Heckman, Meg, 125, 126
Heilman, Madeline, 9
Henley, Deborah, 2
Heyward, Andrew, 23, 28–29, 31–32, 34, 36
Hill, Anita, 39–40, 52
Hill, Retha, 126
Hindustan Times (newspaper), 128
Hirsch, Rick, photo 22
Hochschild, Adam, 92
Hockenberry, John, 50
Hofmann, Carrie, 106–7, 113, photo 27
Holmes, Anna, 153
Horner, Bob, 30
Hudson, Cynthia, 7, 16, 20, 53, photo 4
Huffington, Arianna, 1, 16, 126, 128–29, 152–53
Huffington Post (website) [now HuffPost], 126, 128–29, 146, 152
Hunt, Al, 111
Hussein, Saddam, 11

Idaho Statesman (newspaper), 42
Iger, Bob, 25
Inc. (magazine), 83
The Information, 7
Intel, 37

International Women's Media Foundation, 50
Ithaca Journal (newspaper), 60

Jacobs, Paul, 92
Jayme, Bill, 92
Jeffery, Clara, 89–94, 98–100, 102–3, photo 17
Jenkins, Mandy, 125
Jennings, Madelyn, 60–61, photo 13
Jezebel, 153
Johnson, Alice, 130–31
Johnson, Lyndon, 57
Johnson, Michelle, 126
Johnson, Pam McAllister, 60, photo 14
Johnson, Tom, 61–62
Jones, Mary Harris, 91–92
Jones, Rashida, 153
Jossip (blog), 90
Jurgensen, Karen, 20–21, 59, 62–63
Just, Sara, 18, 19–20

Kalita, Mitra, 69, 138, 149–50, 151, photo 26
Kansas City Star (newspaper), 42
Kantor, Jodi, 84
Kardashian West, Kim, 131
Kavanaugh, Brett, 39
Kay, Katty, 16
Keller, Bill, 73–74, 80
Kerner Commission, 57
King, Martin Luther, Jr., 65–66
KJZZ, 142–43
Klein, Ezra, 123–24, 132, 134–35, 137
KMGH-TV, 106
Knight Ridder, 18, 40, 116–17
KOCO-TV, 25
Kournikova, Anna, 97
Kramon, Glenn, 74, 76, 82
KSHB-TV, 106
Ku Klux Klan, 65

Ladies' Home Journal (magazine), 91
Lake Wales Daily Highlander (newspaper), 12

Lauer, Matt, 4, 38
lawsuits: on employment discrimination, 4, 26, 35, 71; on sexual harassment, 49; on wage discrimination, 26, 62
Leach, Jan, 16, 106, 150
leaders and leadership, 7–21; advice for, 19–21, 35–36, 52–53, 68–69, 86–87, 102–4, 119–22, 136–38, 152–53; characteristics of, 15–17, 33, 78, 95–96, 137; dilemmas of, 9–11; gender gap in, 8–9; obstacles for, 77–79; styles of, 9, 10, 14–15, 19, 79, 86, 93, 95–96; team building by, 75, 78, 87. *See also* management, women in
Leadership in Action, 9
A League of Their Own (film), 17–18
LearnVest, 134
Lee, Robert E., 66
Legal Times (journal), 74
Lenny's Letter (online newsletter), 81
Lerer, Ken, 128
Lessin, Jessica, 7–8
Levine, Judith, 38–39
Lifetime Channel, 78
Lipinski, Ann Marie, 20
Lloyd, Wanda, 55–68, photo 12
Lloyd, Willie, 58
Los Angeles Herald-Express (newspaper), 9
Los Angeles Times (newspaper), 61, 63
Los Angeles Times-Washington Post New Service, 58
Low, Margaret, 7, 17, 19, 45–46, 153
Lyne, Susan, 7, 133–34

MacKinnon, Catharine, 39
magazine industry, 90–91
Makers.com, 133, 136
Mallory, James, 87
management, women in, 23–36, 51, 61–63, 71–86, 89–95, 112–13, 137, 140. *See also* leaders and leadership
Marqués Gonzalez, Aminda, 113, 121–22, 140–41, photo 22

marriage, 29–30, 42, 117. *See also* work-family balance
Martha Stewart Living Omnimedia, 7, 134
Martin, Ron, 59, 68–69, 138
Martore, Gracia, 56, 62
Mashable (website), 146
Mason, Linda, 28, 98, photo 7
maternity leave, 26, 68, 109, 112, 118, 144
Mayer, Marissa, 2
Maynard, Bob, 59
Mazzarella, Dave, 63
McElroy, Q, 125–26, 129–30, photo 24
McFarlin, Diane, 12–13, 19, 20, 96, 102, 104, 117, 153, photo 1
McGee, Dyllan, 133, 136–37
McGinnis, Marcy, 23–36, photo 5, photo 6
McKinsey & Company, 78
McManus, Sean, 34
Melbourne (Florida) *Times* (newspaper), 59
Mencken, H. L., 91
#MeToo movement, 4, 37, 44, 45, 48, 50, 53, 99, 137–38, 139, 143
Metz, Jennifer Musser, 126
Miami Herald (newspaper), 58, 113, 121, 140
Mic, 130–31
Mills, Kay, 9, 26, 60
Mims, Lathan, 107–9
Minneapolis Star Tribune (newspaper), 42
minorities, in journalism, 55–69, 129
Monaghan, Nancy, 137
Le Monde (newspaper), 72
Montgomery (Alabama) *Advertiser* (newspaper), 55, 65–67
Moonves, Leslie, 4, 33, 38, 50
Moore, Ann, 97–98
Moore, Michael, 89
Moore, Robert, 38

Morgan, Arlene, 98, 119–20, 148–49
Morrison, Denise, 2
Mother Jones (magazine), 89–94, 98–
    100, 102–4
MSNBC, 145
Mullinax, Kenneth, 65–66

Narisetti, Raju, 128, 131–32, 137–38
Nathan, George Jean, 91
Nation (magazine), 91, 93
National Association of Black
    Journalists, 121
National Geographic (magazine), 4,
    14–15, 98, 140, 152
National Organization for Women, 26
National Review (magazine), 91
National Rifle Association, 50, 128
National Security Agency, 80
NBC, ix–x, 24, 38, 106–7
NBC News, 10, 64, 111, 145, 153
NBCUniversal News Group, 17, 25,
    64, 78
Nelson, Libby, 123, 135
Neuharth, Allen, 26, 56, 58–62, 65, 68,
    69, photo 13
Neuharth, Jan, 69
New Orleans Times-Picayune
    (newspaper), 68, 130, 138
New Republic (magazine), 38
news anchors, women as, 3, 24–25, 45
news coverage, women's effect on,
    93–104
Newsday (newspaper), 2, 3, 10
NewsNet, 31
Newsweek (magazine), 3–4, 25–26
New York Daily News (newspaper), 26,
    38, 116
New Yorker (magazine), 49, 50–51, 73,
    81, 91, 98
New York Magazine, 48, 123
New York Post (newspaper), 71
New York Review of Books (magazine), 91
New York Times (newspaper), 1, 4, 10,
    26, 38, 44, 46, 47, 49, 64, 71–85,
    116, 123, 144–45

Nieman Reports (journal), 72
Nixon, Richard, 58
NOLA.com, 130
No Passport Required (radio program),
    135
Norfolk Ledger-Star (newspaper), 109–
    10, 114
Norfolk Virginian-Pilot (newspaper), 114
Northwestern Mutual, 134
Nougayrède, Natalie, 72
NPR, 10, 17, 18, 38, 45–47, 51, 98,
    116, 139, 151

Obama, Barack, x, 82, 121
O'Brian, Kate, 1, 43, 112–13, 121, 139,
    150, 151, photo 11
O'Connor, Sandra Day, 43
Online News Association, 125
O'Reilly, Bill, 38
Oreskes, Michael, 4, 38, 46–48
Organized Crime and Corruption
    Reporting Project, 153
Overby, Charles, 65
Owens, Arrie Mae, 109–10, 113–14

Parks, Rosa, 65–66
Parrish, Dave, 42
Parrish, Mi-Ai, 37, 41–45, 52, 53,
    photo 8, photo 9
PBS, 3, 38, 133, 135
PBS NewsHour (television show), 18,
    24, 110
Pensiero, Karen, 111–12, 121
People (magazine), 97, 140
Peretti, Jonah, 128
personal appearance, 13, 20, 41, 67, 73,
    145, 148
Philadelphia Inquirer (newspaper), 98,
    119–20, 148
Philly.com, 126
Pilhofer, Aron, 81
policies, women- and family-oriented,
    26, 68–69, 94, 96, 105–22
Politico (news outlet), 76, 77, 82, 99,
    147

Pollock, Ellen, 83
Portland Oregonian (newspaper),
    114–15
Povich, Lynn, 25
power, 2, 102
Pratch, Leslie, 15
Preston, Peter, 71
Price, Roy, 4
producers, 27–31
professionalism, 20, 135
Providence Evening Bulletin (newspaper),
    57–58
Public Radio International, 50
Pulitzer Prize, 3, 42, 65, 77, 114, 115,
    130, 142
Purnick, Joyce, 116

Quill (magazine), 55
Quinn, Jane Bryant, 4

Radio Television Digital News
    Association, 2
Raines, Howell, 76, 81, 82
Rather, Dan, 32, 34, photo 6, photo 7
Read, Richard, photo 18
Reade, John, 29, 33
Readership Institute, 95
Reasoner, Harry, 24
Recode (website), 136
relationship skills, in business and
    management, 77–78, 87
Rent the Runway, 134
Richard Clurman Award, 116
Richman, Joan, 28–29, 36
Riker, Margery Baker, 40
Rio Salado College, 143
Roberts, Cokie, 18, 45, 116
Roberts, Gene, 149
Robinson, Craig, 64
Rockey, Allison, 135, photo 23
Rock Island Argus (newspaper), 35
Rose, Charlie, 4, 12, 38
Rosenhause, Sharon, 83
Rowe, Gerard, 105, 108–9, 113–15,
    118, photo 19

Rowe, Sandy, 105, 107–10, 113–16,
    118–20, 122, photo 18, photo 19
Rowe, Sarah, 100, 114–115, 118, photo
    19
Ryan, Carolyn, 84
Rymer, Russ, 89

salary and wage gap, 62, 79–80, 86–87,
    142–44, 148–49
Salem (Oregon) *Stateman Journal*
    (newspaper), 100–101
Sandberg, Sheryl, 36
Sanders, Bernie, 99
San Francisco Chronicle (newspaper), 18,
    42, 140
San Francisco Examiner (newspaper), 3,
    83
San Jose Mercury News (newspaper), 14,
    140
Sarasota Herald-Tribune (newspaper),
    10, 13, 95–97, 102–3, 113, 117, 150
Sarasota Journal (newspaper), 13
Saratoga Springs Saratogian (newspaper),
    60
Savannah State University, 67
SB Nation (website), 132
Schiller, Vivian, 10, 17, 46, 51, 98
Schroeder, Patricia, 116
Schwartz, Felice, 116
Seattle Post-Intelligencer (newspaper), 13
Seattle Times (newspaper), 130
self-doubt, 16–17, 146
Sellers, Patricia, 36
September 11, 2001 terrorist attacks,
    106, 119, 127
sexual abuse, 97
sexual harassment, 4, 12, 33, 37–53,
    84, 99–100, 137–38, 139, 143, 146,
    147–48
Shipman, Claire, 16
Shitty Media Men list, 38, 99
Shooter, Don, 44–45
Sikka, Madhulika, 139, 149
Silvers, Robert, 91
60 Minutes (television show), 50

Slate.com, 132
Smart Set (magazine), 91
Smith, Ben, 147
Smith Brody, Lauren, 120, 121
Snowden, Edward, 80
Society of Professional Journalists, 55
South Florida Sun-Sentinel (newspaper),
     83
Spayd, Liz, 83
Spitzer, Eliot, 77
Sports Illustrated Kids (magazine), 98
Stamberg, Susan, 45
Stewart, Jon, 48
Stewart, Martha, 7, 134
Stewart, Potter, 52
Stewart, Terri, 33
Stony Brook University, 34
Streep, Meryl, 118, 133
Sulzberger, Arthur, Jr., 75–77, 79–82
Sweeney, David, 46
Swisher, Kara, 136
syndication, 30–31

The Takeaway (radio program), 50
Tampa Tribune (newspaper), 10, 97,
     113, 150
Target, 66
Taylor, Arthur, 26
TEGNA, 25
Temple University Klein College of
     Media and Communication, 148
Testa, Jessica, 147–48
Thomas, Clarence, 39–40
Thompson, Mark, 76, 80
Time Inc., 97
Time Warner Inc., 17
Timpone, Maycie, 147–48, photo 28,
Title IX, Education Amendments Act
     (1972), 25
Today (television show), x, 38, 111
Today, Explained (podcast), 135
Totenberg, Nina, 37, 45, 47
TrollBusters, 50
Trump, Donald, 50, 84, 93, 99, 131
Turness, Deborah, 25, 63–64

Ugenti-Rita, Michelle, 44
Underwood, Agnes, 9–10
University of Florida College of
     Journalism and Communications,
     102, 117, 153
USA Today (newspaper), 2, 14, 20, 35,
     58–59, 61–65, 67–68, 123, 126, 136,
     138, 152
U.S. News & World Report (magazine),
     91
U.S. Supreme Court, 39, 43

Vanity Fair (magazine), 81, 91, 129
Variety (magazine), 91
venture capital, 132–34
Verizon Media, 133
Vice (website), 146, 148
Vinson, Mechelle, 39
Virginian-Pilot (newspaper), 41
Vogue (magazine), 91
Vox (website), 1, 4, 123–24, 132, 134–
     35, 137, 146, 148
Vox Media, 132, 135

wages. *See* salary and wage gap
Wall Street Journal (newspaper), 7, 63,
     74, 111–12, 128
Walt Disney Company, 25, 133–34
Walters, Barbara, 24
Washington City Paper (newspaper), 93
Washington Post (newspaper), 26, 46,
     47, 55, 58–59, 62, 63, 130, 131–32,
     139, 149
Washingtonpost.com, 126
Washington Star (newspaper), 40
WBEZ, 133
Weinstein, Harvey, 44, 49–50, 84, 143
Weiss, Ellen, 46
Wertheimer, Linda, 45
Wharton, Dolores, 61
White House Project, 9
Whitman, Meg, 2
Williams, Lauren, 135, photo 23
Williams, Serena, 105
Wilson, Dave, photo 22

Wilson, Lori, 59
Winfrey, Oprah, 133
Wintour, Anna, 91
WNYC, 50
women: exhibiting behaviors deemed
    masculine, 9–11, 13, 18, 28–29,
    87, 98, 110; judgments of behavior
    of, 9, 15, 73–74, 76–77, 79, 86,
    90, 129; mutual supportiveness
    of, 20–21, 30, 47, 53; policies and
    practices concerning, 26, 68–69, 94,
    96, 105–22; stereotypes of, 9. *See
    also* management, women in; news
    anchors, women as
Women's Media Center, 95, 125

Woodhull, Nancy, 67–68
Woodruff, Judy, 3, 24–25, 110–11,
    photo 20
work-family balance, 105–22. *See also*
    marriage
Working Mother (magazine), 117
Wussler, Bob, 24

Yglesias, Matt, 132
Young, Coleman, 14

Zeilinger, Julie, 143–44, 149
Zirinsky, Susan, 63
Zuckerberg, Mark, 133
Zwerdling, Daniel, 46